SO-ABA-647

A BASIC GUIDE TO
EXPORTING

THE OFFICIAL GOVERNMENT RESOURCE FOR SMALL AND MEDIUM-SIZED BUSINESSES

10TH EDITION REVISED

U.S. Department of Commerce, International Trade Administration

Washington, D.C.

LIBRARY OF CONGRESS CATALOGING-IN-PUBLICATION DATA
A basic guide to exporting : the official government resource for small and medium-sized businesses / U.S. Department of Commerce, International Trade Administration.—10th ed., rev.
    p. cm.
  ISBN 978-0-16-086953-2 (alk. paper)
  1. Export marketing—United States—Handbooks, manuals, etc. 2. Exports—United States—Handbooks, manuals, etc.
  3. Export sales contracts—United States—Handbooks, manuals, etc. I. United States. International Trade Administration.
  HF1416.5.B37 2011b
  658.8'40973—dc22

                                                                    2011015795

Certain materials included in this book are reprinted with the kind permission of their copyright holders. A full list of permissions appears on page 254.

Published 2011 by the U.S. Department of Commerce, International Trade Administration.

Federal Recycling Program
Printed on recycled paper
Printed in the United States of America

A MESSAGE FROM THE SECRETARY OF COMMERCE

American companies produce goods and services that are desired all over the world. Today, approximately 95 percent of the world's consumers exist outside the borders of the United States and yet only 1 percent of America's 30 million companies export. The global economy has created a global marketplace and an opportunity to grow your business.

In March 2010, President Barack Obama signed an executive order launching the National Export Initiative and instructing the federal government to use every available resource to help double American exports over the next five years to support 2 million jobs.

Through the National Export Initiative, American businesses that want to export—especially small and medium-sized enterprises—are going to have a much stronger partner in the Department of Commerce and the International Trade Administration (ITA). ITA has a global network of trade specialists who are posted in 109 U.S. cities and at 128 U.S. embassies and consulates in 77 countries and are ready to assist you. Last year, ITA helped nearly 5,600 companies increase their exports—85 percent of which were small and medium-sized businesses.

Let us help your company. We have updated *A Basic Guide to Exporting* to provide you expert advice and detailed information on resources that can help you get started. The National Export Initiative is the Obama Administration's commitment to helping you find new opportunities for your business.

Learn more about ITA's programs by visiting us at *www.export.gov* or by calling (800) USA-TRADE (800-872-8723).

We look forward to working with you.

Best regards,

Gary Locke
Secretary of Commerce
Washington, DC

ACKNOWLEDGMENTS

Publishing a book is a journey that requires endurance, persistence, and, above all, dedication. Many people contributed to this one, and prime among them was Doug Barry of the U.S. Commercial Service, who guided its updating and production. He brought together the knowledge and skills of many individuals in the world of international trade and lent a fresh voice to this venerable text. It is due to his efforts that this book appears again, 70 years after the publication of its first edition in 1938.

Colleagues at the International Trade Administration (ITA) who contributed to this new edition include Jennifer Kirsch, who looked after all the details and kept the project moving forward. There would be no book without her skill.

John Ward, the publications director in the ITA's Office of Public Affairs, has encyclopedic knowledge of how books come together and much of what he knows is applied in the pages that follow. A book should be a pleasure to pick up. Because of John, this one is.

The work of updating this new edition began several years ago at the U.S. Export Assistance Center in Atlanta, Georgia. Tom Strauss heard from clients that a new book was needed, and he started compiling information with the help of an international trade specialist, Bob Abrahams. Others throughout the International Trade Administration made considerable subsequent contributions. Trade specialists Keith Hwang and Bob Deane read the manuscript and provided useful comments and clarifications. Curt Cultice, senior media specialist at the U.S. Commercial Service, assisted in writing of some of the case studies. Michele Robinson of the ITA's Office of Public Affairs and Philip Kolb of the U.S. Commercial Service provided production assistance. Interns Robert Herren and Courtney Trumpler also assisted production by researching the book's photos and publishing history.

On the production side, many thanks are due to Linda Stringer of Publications Professionals LLC for her careful editing of the text, to Kia Penso and Ashley Young for additional editorial assistance, and to the book's design team, led by Amanda Drake of the Creative Services division of the U.S. Government Printing Office and Anne Masters of Anne Masters Design Inc.

Contents

CONTENTS

A BASIC GUIDE TO
EXPORTING

chapter 1

INTRODUCTION:
THE WORLD IS OPEN FOR BUSINESS

In This Chapter

- **Selling globally is easier than ever.**

- **More help is available than ever.**

- **Your assumptions may not be accurate.**

- **You can transform your business—and yourself.**

The world is open for business: your business. Today it's easier than ever for a company like yours, regardless of size, to sell goods and services across the globe. Depending on what you're selling, with the right kind of phone directory for Toronto or Vancouver you can make sales calls and ship product to Canada tomorrow. In fact, more small U.S. companies sell to Canadian buyers than to buyers in any other country.

More U.S. small and medium-sized companies are exporting than ever before. In 2005, 232,600 small and medium-sized companies exported to a least one international market, a nearly 3 percent increase over 2004. The value of total goods and services exports grew almost 17 percent from 2009 to 2010, to more than $1.8 trillion. Your company may be included in these numbers but could sell even more. Or if your company hasn't made an international sale yet, yours could be the next one to sell globally.

If you have a Web presence, you have a global marketing and order-taking platform. For a few more dollars, you can process credit card payments for buyers in Australia or translate key pages into Spanish and other languages to further your reach. Easy.

Want more sales channels? Online marketplaces offer virtual storefronts and a ready-made global army of shoppers. They also offer payment solutions, and you can choose a shipper that will take care of the required documentation for you. The shippers want to help make things easier too, and many offer free international business advice, customer broker services, cost calculators, and financing. Plus, they'll pick up goods and documents from your back door and deliver them to almost any address in the world. And you can track everything on their Web site. Easy.

Want even more sales channels? If Web-based marketing and sales are insufficient to meet your sales growth appetite, you can attend trade shows in the United States where buyers from around the world come to purchase U.S. goods and services. Show organizers will facilitate introductions to the buyers, working with agencies of the U.S. government to provide matchmaking services on the show floor. These same government agencies can arrange for you to attend shows in other countries, where the connections and influence of your embassy network can save you time and money generating new business. Government agencies can find buyers for you and arrange introductions in more than 100 countries. Call this service "customized business matchmaking." Easy. (See Figure 1.1.)

Today's global trading system is ideal for the smaller company employing more than one marketing and sales channel to sell into multiple overseas markets. But most U.S. exporters currently sell to one country market—Canada, for example (see Figure 1.2). And the smaller the company, the less likely it is to export to more than one country. For example, 60 percent of all exporters with fewer than 19 employees sold to one country market in 2005. Imagine the boost in the bottom line if they could double the number of countries they sell to.

The opportunity for selling into a single region, such as Central America, and taking advantage of free trade agreements, such as the Central America Free Trade Agreement (CAFTA), is substantial. The help available and discussed in this book can quickly expand your thinking—and your sales—from one market to many.

In choosing from among these channels, markets, and countries, what's the best strategy for your business? There's help for that too—from private consultants, from your home state and local U.S. government sources, from the Web, and from this book. And much of the help is free or costs very little. It is easy to access, easy to use.

If what you read so far comes as a surprise—particularly that exporting is relatively easy, even for very small businesses, and that there are scores of local yet worldly folks ready to help you succeed—then you are not alone. The people whom we interviewed for the case studies in this book—like many potential exporters—say that their number one need is for more basic information on how to export.

FIGURE 1.1 FOUR GLOBAL CHANNELS

SMALL BUSINESS SALES

FIGURE 1.2 FOREIGN MARKETS

**NUMBER OF FOREIGN MARKETS SOLD TO
BY U.S. EXPORTERS, 2005**

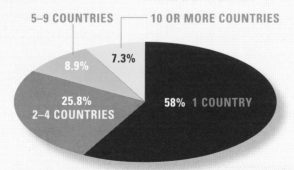

5–9 COUNTRIES   10 OR MORE COUNTRIES

8.9%   7.3%

25.8%   58% 1 COUNTRY
2–4 COUNTRIES

Source: U.S. Department of Commerce, Bureau of the Census.

Most U.S.
exporters
sell to one
country market
(Canada)

Surprised? Then you also might be surprised by the old global business assumptions and the new ones replacing them (Table 1.1).

This book is mainly written for you, the millions of business owners or their business development gurus who could export or export more. You've asked to have spelled out in plain language how people busy running their businesses can learn what they need to know to grow their sales globally. And here it is: *A Basic Guide to Exporting.*

If you purchased this book or received it from one of our corporate partners, chances are you have already answered for yourself this fundamental question: Why bother?

Exporting can be one of the best ways to grow your business:

• Grow your bottom line.

• Smooth your business cycles.

• Use production capabilities fully.

• Defend your domestic market.

• Increase your competitiveness in all markets.

Exporting is strategic in another way. With the volume of trade growing exponentially and barriers to trade falling, competition in a company's domestic market is intensifying, particularly from foreign competitors. We need to compete in our own backyard while we simultaneously open markets for our products and services in other markets:

• Ninety-five percent of the world's consumers live outside the United States. That is a lot of potential customers to just ignore.

• Foreign competition is increasing domestically. To be truly competitive, companies must consider opening markets abroad.

• Exporting is profitable. In fact, 60 percent of small companies that engage in exporting derive 20 percent of their annual earnings from exports.

• Exporting helps businesses learn how to compete more successfully.

According to a World Bank report, *Global Economic Prospects,* trade in goods and services is likely to more than triple by 2030. Over the same period, the global economy will probably expand from $35 trillion in 2005 to $72 trillion. The number of people considered "middle-class" will triple to 1.2 billion, enabling them to afford international travel, better education, and imported goods from the United States. Exports from the United States, according to the same report, are expected to grow by nearly 10 percent per year for the next several years. Your product or service could be among them.

With this significant projected growth in global trade, fueled in large part by newly affluent consumers in China, India, and other developing economies, the challenge for businesses of all sizes in the United States is how to dip into this incredible revenue torrent. *A Basic Guide to Exporting* aims to help prime your pump.

TABLE 1.1 GLOBAL BUSINESS ASSUMPTIONS

OLD ASSUMPTION	NEW ASSUMPTION
Exporting is too risky.	Exporting to some markets, such as Canada, is no more risky than selling in the United States. Different international markets have different levels of risks. Almost any perceived risk can be identified and reduced by using the affordable export assistance now available.
Getting paid is cumbersome, and I'll lose my shirt.	Trade finance and global banking have evolved to the point where buying and selling things internationally is routine, safe, and efficient. Reliable payment collection methods are numerous and include letters of credit through banks, credit cards, and online payments. Some delivery firms will even collect payment at the buyer's backdoor. Commercial payments between countries are predicted to grow by more than 10 percent per year through 2010.
Exporting is too complicated.	Most exporting requires minimal paperwork. Researching markets and finding buyers can, in many instances, be done from your computer using free or low-cost information.
My domestic market is secure. I don't need to export.	Globalization has made it easier to buy and sell goods in multiple markets. Few markets remain static, and new markets are constantly opening to competition. Most U.S. businesses are involved in or affected by international business, whether they realize it or not. More small and medium-sized U.S. firms need an international strategy that includes diversifying markets.
I'm too small to go global.	No company is too small to go global. In fact, nearly 42 percent of all U.S. exporters in 2005 had fewer than 19 employees.
My product or service probably won't sell outside the United States.	If your product or service sells well in the United States, there's a good chance an overseas market can be found for it. What's more, help is available to test acceptance of your service or product in more than 100 countries around the globe. In some markets, you may have to make some modifications because of cultural or regulatory differences. But by learning how to sell into another market, you will become a better marketer, and your company will be more successful in all markets in which it competes.
I won't be successful because I don't speak another language and have never been abroad.	Cultural knowledge and business etiquette are always helpful, but you can pick these things up as you go. The English language will take you a very long way, and help is readily available for situations in which interpreters and translators are necessary. We Americans regularly lampoon ourselves for being "ugly." A level of introspection and culturally specific knowledge can help prevent potentially deal-breaking faux pas, but a friendly disposition and willingness to learn can make up for a multitude of unintended mistakes.

FACT:

Some small business owners
think that exporting is too risky.

INSIGHT:

Exporting to some markets,
such as Canada, is no more
risky than selling in the United
States. Different international
markets have different levels of
risks. Almost any perceived risk
can be identified and reduced
by using the affordable export
assistance now available.

As global trade grows, companies that engage in it report a shift in income derived from their export sales compared with sales in their domestic markets. A 2002 study of U.S. exporters found that 60 percent of small companies in the survey derived 20 percent of annual earnings from exports, while 44 percent of medium-sized companies did. When asked whether export sales would grow at least 5 percent per year for the next three years, 77 percent of the small firms and 83 percent of the medium-sized firms said they would.

You might reasonably respond by saying, "That's all well and good, but do I have what a person in another country will buy?" As you delve further into this book, you'll read about companies of all sorts that produce an amazing array of products and services and have grown their businesses through exports. Waterless urinals to Japan? Flooded with new orders. Chocolates to the Middle East? No problem. Fiberglass dome houses to India? Business is booming. Pollution-eating microbes to Argentina? Can't keep the little critters in stock. Industrial lubricants to Vietnam? The skids are being greased for other markets in Southeast Asia. Franchise concepts in Europe? Everything from furniture moving to senior citizens' companion services.

Even companies that don't make anything are flourishing abroad. These companies make money by providing wholesale and distribution services. And there are thousands of them—all small.

Another answer to "Why bother?" is that exporting adds to the knowledge and skills of everyone in a company who does it. Doing business in a market that's beyond one's borders can have a transformational effect on its practitioners. The experience of forming new relationships, getting up close and personal with another culture, figuring out how to meet the needs of others, and learning how to be inventive in addressing new business challenges not only is personally rewarding; it also leads to improvements in products and makes companies stronger in whatever market they compete.

As one small exporter interviewed for this book put it, "Exporting is easier than we imagined. Exporting opens your horizons to what's going on in the world economy. We need to take that step outside ourselves and develop relationships and open doors. It may start out small. It did for us. But it's growing. We are a better company and better managers. Maybe even better persons. And to me that's what success is all about."

CASE STUDY:
Domes International

"There's no doubt that Domes International is a better company as a result of our experience in India."

—Steve Pope, director of international business development and marketing, Domes International Inc.

THE COMPANY

For developing countries in need of efficient, inexpensive housing, a Mississippi-based company with its International Sales Office in Memphis, Tennessee, has just the thing: domes. Domes International Inc. manufactures its bulbous structures out of molded fiberglass. Some look like igloos, others like marshmallows. Among the most attractive benefits of fiberglass domes is their low maintenance. Termite resistant and energy efficient, they also protect against dangerous weather conditions, including severe monsoons that cause horrific damage and loss of life in certain areas of the world.

THE CHALLENGE

When Domes International decided to expand internationally, it was already selling houses to the U.S. military for faraway bases on tropical islands. Director of International Business Development and Marketing Steve Pope was assigned the job. He is also president of World Discoveries Inc., an export–import and international manufacturing and marketing consulting company based in Memphis. The company is contracted with Domes for its global manufacturing operations.

THE SOLUTION

Pope contacted his local Export Assistance Centers in Memphis, Tennessee, and Jackson, Mississippi. After talking with trade specialists at the centers, Pope and his company decided to focus on India. The combined forces of the U.S. Commercial Service in Mumbai, Delhi, and the United States provided Pope with market research and help on doing business with the Indian government, including contacts within the government who might be interested in purchasing domes. Those contacts included officials from Gujarat state who needed to house thousands of homeless families. The state placed an order, and later the Indian military did as well.

Pope and his partners soon realized they needed a facility in India to assemble components shipped from the United States. Having a local facility is a "win–win," Pope says, because the "jobs created help the local economy, while we benefit stateside by providing the higher-end components." The Commercial Service then helped Domes International apply for a $1.2 million U.S. government–backed loan from the Overseas Private Investment Corporation (OPIC). Then, when the first shipment of the fiberglass molds and machinery got hung up in customs, Commercial Service officials helped retrieve them and arranged for operating permits and inspection protocols. Additionally, the U.S. Commercial Service offices in Mumbai, New Delhi, and Ahmedabad, India, helped obtain some necessary product registration certificates from the Indian Ministry of Commerce.

These early experiences led to more sales as Domes International began to adapt the product to fit local needs. Domes can be used as offices, schools, military barracks, and warehouses. A religious group is interested in replacing more expensive marble temples with fiberglass domes. You never know what new opportunities might arise when you're on the ground observing what people need.

In another case, a government client for a school building pointed out that people in one part of the state considered round structures with a hole in them as kind of a temple of doom and gloom. "Local folks wouldn't go near them. So we developed flat fiberglass panels and added ribs and steel struts for strength." It became a more acceptable box, not a dome, Pope explains.

"We couldn't have done any of this without the U.S. Commercial Service," says Pope, who also called on the organization to make inroads into Afghanistan, Niger, Nigeria, and other countries in the Middle East and Africa. "Thanks to the Commercial Service, we have opened our factory in Ahmedabad and are selling houses, schoolrooms, and warehouses in the surrounding area."

LESSONS LEARNED

One lesson Pope has learned is to be flexible. "Our initial business plan was based on the then current oil prices." The company's raw materials are 70 percent petroleum based. "We went [to India] expecting to sell lots of single-family homes, and by the time we finally opened our factory, oil prices had doubled, and hence our raw materials as well. We discovered the better market was local governments and the military. We had to go there, make this discovery, then adjust on the fly."

"There's no doubt that Domes International is a better company as a result of our experience in India," Pope says. "We are much more flexible and also innovative. The client wanted a less expensive structure, so we went back to our labs and came up with an insulation solution that met their needs. Now we use these discoveries to improve core products and to offer more variations. We are much more confident going into new situations—listening, adapting, and finding the best solution. That we've been able to transform through our experiences overseas in just a few years is amazing."

ACTION

Is your company considering entering an emerging market? If so, here are some things you can do:

- **Conduct market research.** Big emerging markets such as India have a lot of potential for U.S. exporters. A good place to start your research of this market of more than 1 billion people is to visit *www.buyusa.gov/india/en.* Operated by the Commercial Service India, the site includes current market research, information about trade shows, and updates about changing customs laws. The site also offers Featured U.S. Exporters, where U.S. businesses can present product information, including photos and company contact information.

- **Visit the market.** One way to find out if a market is right for your product is to visit it. Luckily, it's easier today than ever to make the most out of your travel dollars. Consider the Commercial Service's AsiaNow program. With it, you can attend a trade show in Singapore, meet with prospective buyers in Malaysia, and then fly north several hours to the booming Indian city of Bangalore for more buyer meetings and product demonstrations. The Commercial Service arranges everything, including hotels. Visit *www.buyusa.gov/ asianow/.*

- **Secure funding.** OPIC, established as a development agency of the U.S. government in 1971, helps U.S. businesses invest overseas and fosters economic development in new and emerging markets. OPIC evaluates all project applications on the basis of their contribution to economic development. OPIC projects also support American jobs and exports. For more information, visit *www.opic.gov.*

- **Get help with your shipping needs.** If you have found a buyer but have questions about shipping or customs clearance issues, visit the National Customs Brokers & Forwarders Association of America at *www. ncbfaa.org.*

Through a joint venture with an Indian partner, Mississippi-based Domes International is supplying its structures throughout India. Buyers in India find the domes attractive because of their easy maintenance, energy efficiency, and durability.

chapter 2

DEVELOPING AN EXPORT STRATEGY

In This Chapter

- **Is your company ready to export?**

- **How will exporting affect your company?**

- **How do you create an export plan?**

DETERMINING YOUR PRODUCTS' EXPORT POTENTIAL

There are several ways to evaluate the export potential of your products and services in overseas markets. The most common approach is to examine the domestic sales of your products. If your company is successful in the U.S. market, there is a good chance that it will also sell in markets abroad, at least in those markets where similar needs and conditions exist.

Another way to assess your company's potential in exporting is by examining the unique or important features of your product. If those features are hard to duplicate abroad, then it's likely that your product will be successful overseas. A unique product may have little competition; thus, demand for it may be quite high.

Finally, your product may have export potential even if sales are declining in the U.S. market. Sizable export markets may still exist, especially if the product once did well here but is now losing market share to more technically advanced products. Other countries may not need state-of-the-art technology and may be unable to afford the most sophisticated and expensive products.

ASSESSING YOUR COMPANY'S EXPORT READINESS

As Box 2.1 suggests, export-ready companies possess certain qualities that increase the likelihood that their exporting efforts will be successful. Answering these important questions about how exporting will enhance your company's goals will help determine your company's readiness to export:

① How do you understand if your company is ready to export?

- What does your company want to gain from exporting?

- Is exporting consistent with other company goals?

- What demands will exporting place on your company's key resources, management and personnel, production capacity, and financing, and how will these demands be met?

- Are the expected benefits worth the costs, or would company resources be better used for developing new domestic business?

For a more in-depth assessment of whether your company is ready to export, it's a good idea to take the export readiness assessment. Your company can use an interactive version, which can be found at *www.citd.org/startupkit/eras/index.cfm*. Among the issues you'll be asked to consider are your company's current operations, attitudes, and products.

For a more theoretical assessment, it is helpful to examine some of the motivational and organizational factors behind your company's decision to export. Thinking about these factors will help you decide if your company and your product are ready to export.

Motivational factors include the following:

- **Long-term expansion.** Building an exporting plan takes time, so it is important to focus on expanding your business over the long term and not to look for immediate returns.

- **Increased competitiveness.** By selling internationally, your company can gain insights into different ways of doing business.

- **Exploitation of unique technology and expertise.** If your product quality or expertise is superior, you'll have a competitive edge in the international marketplace.

- **Improved return on investment.** Your company should seek multiple benefits from exporting, such as expanded customer networks and exposure to new ideas and technology.

- **Increased capabilities.** You'll develop better products and services, acquire better leadership abilities, and collaborate better with customers and suppliers.

BOX 2.1 QUALITIES OF AN EXPORT-READY COMPANY

EXPORT-READY COMPANIES

- Have commitment from management and are prepared to fund exporting activities.

- Understand the added demands international business can place on key resources.

- Have realistic expectations regarding return on investment from international activities.

- Are prepared to modify products and services by market as well as provide training and after-sales service.

Organizational factors include the following:

- **Management commitment.** Total backing from management is the number one determining factor of export success.

- **Funding support.** Management must be willing to allocate sufficient time, enough resources, and an adequate budget for export activities.

- **Personal expertise and commitment.** Having staff members with international experience or having employees learn about your target market's language and culture will help you enter the international marketplace.

- **Product capabilities.** Your company must possess the space and equipment needed to manufacture for the specific countries you are selling to (each of which will have its own product standards and regulations).

- **Company's exporting goals.** Whatever your goal, consider whether the expected benefits outweigh the costs.

Is your product ready to export? To determine export readiness, consider these additional factors:

- **Selling points.** If your product is a success domestically, the next step is to identify why it sells or has sold so well here, keeping in mind that conditions abroad may be somewhere between slightly and significantly different (socially, culturally, economically, politically, and environmentally).

- **Modifications.** You may sell your product without modifications to international markets, as long as it meets the standards and regulations set by the respective countries. Some countries have strict governmental regulations that require special testing, safety, quality, and technical conformity measures.

- **Product licensing.** Some classifications of products require special approval from the U.S. Department of Commerce before you export, and some of those products require export licenses.

- **Required training.** Products that require training to operate place a greater responsibility on your company and distributor or agent, and you must decide how to support that training.

- **After-sales service.** Products that require considerable after-sales support must be handled by a distributor or agent who is well positioned to provide such a service.

- **Product distinctiveness.** Products that have unique features enjoy a competitive advantage and better reception in foreign markets. Such unique features include patents, superior quality, cutting-edge technology, and adaptability.

FACT:
Many companies never explore the possibility of exporting because they think that they are too small.

INSIGHT:
Nearly 97 percent of U.S. exporters are small and medium-sized companies.

BOX 2.2 MANAGEMENT ISSUES INVOLVED IN THE EXPORT DECISION

MANAGEMENT OBJECTIVES

• What are the company's reasons for pursuing export markets? Are they solid objectives (such as increasing sales volume or developing a broader, more stable customer base) or are they frivolous (for example, the owner wants an excuse to travel)?

• How committed is top management to an export effort? Is exporting viewed as a quick fix for a slump in domestic sales? Will the company neglect its export customers if domestic sales pick up?

• What are management's expectations for the export effort? How quickly does management expect export operations to become self-sustaining? What level of return on investment is expected from the export program?

EXPERIENCE

• With what countries has business already been conducted, or from what countries have inquiries already been received?

• Which product lines are mentioned most often?

• Are any domestic customers buying the product for sale or shipment overseas? If so, to which countries?

• Is the trend of sales and inquiries up or down?

• Who are the main domestic and foreign competitors?

• What general and specific lessons have been learned from past export attempts or experiences?

MANAGEMENT AND PERSONNEL

• What in-house international expertise does the firm have (for example, international sales experience and language capabilities)?

• Who will be responsible for the export department's organization and staff?

• How much senior management time (a) should be allocated and (b) could be allocated?

• What organizational structure is required to ensure that export sales are adequately serviced?

• Who will follow through after the planning has been done?

PRODUCTION CAPACITY

• How is the present capacity being used?

• Will filling export orders hurt domestic sales?

• What will be the cost of additional production?

- Are there fluctuations in the annual workload? When? Why?

- What minimum-order quantity is required?

- What would be required to design and package products specifically for export?

FINANCIAL CAPACITY

- What amount of capital can be committed to export production and marketing?

- What level of operating costs can be supported by the export department?

- How are the initial expenses of export efforts to be allocated?

- What other new development plans are in the works that may compete with export plans?

- By what date must an export effort pay for itself?

FACT:
Depending on the target market, it can take months, sometimes even several years, before an exporting company begins to see a return on investment of time and money.

INSIGHT:
Written plans provide a clear understanding of your long-term exporting objectives and ensure that management is committed to achieving them.

For a more complete list of factors and questions your company should consider, visit California's trade portal at *www.tradeport.org/tutorial/starting/* or refer to Box 2.2.

If you're still unsure of your company's readiness to export, you may find it useful to take the U.S. Department of Agriculture's Export Questionnaire. It consists of only nine questions and will give you an assessment of how export ready your company is and what you need to work on. This Export Questionnaire can be found on the U.S. Department of Agriculture's Web site at *www.fas.usda.gov/agx/buying_us/export_questionnaire.asp.*

DEVELOPING AN EXPORT PLAN

Once you've decided to sell your products abroad, you'll need to develop an export plan. A crucial first step in planning is to develop broad consensus among key management personnel on the company's goals, objectives, capabilities, and constraints. (Answering the questions listed in Box 2.2 is one way to start.) In addition, because they will ultimately be responsible for its successful implementation and execution, the personnel involved in the exporting process should agree on all aspects of an export plan.

The purposes of the export plan are (a) to assemble facts, constraints, and goals and (b) to create an action statement that takes all of those elements into account. The plan includes specific objectives, sets forth time schedules for implementation, and marks milestones so that the degree of success can be measured and motivate personnel.

The following 10 questions should ultimately be addressed:

1. Which products are selected for export development, and what modifications, if any, must be made to adapt them for overseas markets?

2. Which countries are targeted for sales development?

3. In each country, what is the basic customer profile, and what marketing and distribution channels should be used to reach customers?

4. What special challenges pertain to each market (for example, competition, cultural differences, and import controls), and what strategy will be used to address them?

5. How will your product's export sales price be determined?

6. What specific operational steps must be taken and when?

7. What will be the time frame for implementing each element of the plan?

8. What personnel and company resources will be dedicated to exporting?

9. What will be the cost in time and money for each element?

10. How will results be evaluated and used to modify the plan?

The first time an export plan is developed, it should be kept simple. It need be only a few pages long because important market data and planning elements may not yet be available. The initial planning effort itself gradually generates more information and insight. As you learn more about exporting and your company's competitive position, the export plan will become more detailed and complete. An outline of an export plan is presented in Box 2.3.

From the start, your plan should be written and viewed as a flexible management tool, not as a static document. Objectives in the plan should be compared with actual results to measure the success of different strategies. Your company should not hesitate to modify the plan and make it more specific as new information and experience are gained.

FACT:
Many companies begin export activities haphazardly and are unsuccessful in their early efforts because of poor or no planning, which often leads them to abandon exporting altogether.

INSIGHT:
Formulating an export strategy that is based on good information and proper assessment increases the chances that the best options will be chosen, that resources will be used effectively, and that efforts will be carried through to success.

BOX 2.3 SAMPLE OUTLINE FOR AN EXPORT PLAN

Table of Contents

Executive Summary
(one or two pages maximum)

**Introduction: Why This Company
Should Export**

Part I: Export Policy Commitment Statement

Part II: Situation or Background Analysis

- Product or Service for Export
- Operations
- Personnel and Export Organization
- Resources of the Firm
- Resources Outside the Firm
- Industry Structure, Competition, and Demand

Part III: Marketing Component

- Identifying, Evaluating, and Selecting Target Markets
- Product Selection and Pricing
- Distribution Methods
- Terms and Conditions

- Internal Organization and Procedures
- Sales Goals: Profit and Loss Forecasts

Part IV: Tactics—Action Steps

- Primary Target Countries
- Secondary Target Countries
- Indirect Marketing Efforts

Part V: Export Budget

- Pro-forma Financial Statements

Part VI: Implementation Schedule

- Follow-up
- Periodic Operational and Management Review (Measuring Results against the Plan)

**Addenda: Background Data on Target
Countries and Market**

- Basic Market Statistics: Historical and Projected
- Background Facts
- Competitive Environment

A detailed plan is recommended for companies that intend to export directly. Companies that choose indirect export methods may use much simpler plans. For more information on different approaches to exporting and their advantages and disadvantages, see Chapter 5.

CASE STUDY:
Mykytyn Enterprises Inc.

"After I was on the Oprah show, I received hundreds of e-mails from women wanting to start or expand their own businesses. I told them to think globally and contact the U.S. Commercial Service for help getting there."
—Rosie Herman, founder, Mykytyn Enterprises Inc.

THE COMPANY

The tabloid headline, "Penniless Mom Strikes It Rich," summed up the story of Rosie Herman of Houston, Texas, and the million-dollar nail and hand care business she created from everyday ingredients in her kitchen.

Herman had been a salon owner and manicurist for 15 years when expensive fertility treatments put her into debt. She gave birth to twin girls, and at that point her goal was to be a stay-at-home mom. That phase didn't last long, and Herman was soon in her kitchen mixing natural ingredients into lotions to fix what she calls "lizard skin"—hands cracked and bleeding from too much cooking, cleaning, and care giving. She calls the recipe "a little bit of this and a little bit of that." But would the potion stop the bleeding from the family balance sheet?

Herman sold the mixture, which includes grapefruit, peppermint, spearmint, avocado, rosemary, and apricot, to some local salons, and soon they were clamoring for more. Her husband renamed the product the One Minute Manicure, which made marketing easier.

Business took a leap when Herman gave a manicure to Oprah Winfrey on *The Oprah Winfrey Show* and was featured in *People Magazine* and a tabloid as the former "penniless mom." *The Oprah Winfrey Show* is syndicated worldwide, and Herman is now getting e-mail inquiries and orders from Australia and the Netherlands. Celebrities Billy Joel and Jenna Elfman also provided endorsements.

THE CHALLENGE

Herman realized she had a product for which there was interest beyond the United States. But her company, Mykytyn Enterprises Inc. (named for her husband), was a small family startup business. She wondered how she would navigate the world of commerce. The world is awash in beauty products. How would Herman's stand out?

THE SOLUTION

With the help of her sister-in-law, who engaged in international marketing, and the U.S. Commercial Service, Herman lined up distributors outside the country. International sales were a priority from the start because they offered faster growth and greater efficiencies. In just a few years, Herman has formed an international network of 200 distributors and has plans to supply some retailers with product directly.

International sales for the company, with its 12 full-time employees plus production staff, are about 20 percent of total earnings, and Herman wants them to account for 40 percent in two years. "I've developed a product that does not require a lot of modification because of consumer or cultural differences," she says. "Looking and feeling good is a universal desire."

Herman holds up an e-mail from her distributor in France, who tells her, "You are seducing the French, which is not an easy task." Herman and her products are apparently seducing more than the French; sales are also good in Belgium, Mexico, the Netherlands, and the United Kingdom. A distributor in Peru has just placed an order for $10,000, and South Korea has welcomed the product. According to Herman's international sales manager, sister-in-law Margie Mykytyn, China will be next.

Hasn't all this success created envy and knockoffs around the world? "Yes," says Herman. At one point, there were 50 different variations of the One

Minute Manicure, some with remarkably similar packaging and branding. But none provided much competition for Herman's product. Certainly none were as good, Herman explains. Only a handful remain—and they probably won't survive.

Herman continues to work with the U.S. Commercial Service and its Export Assistance Center in Houston. In addition to finding distributors, the Commercial Service trade specialists provide background checks on prospective buyers, many of whom are coming to Herman's company through her Web site. A buyer in India ordered $400,000 worth of product. But a Commercial Service trade specialist ran a background check and discovered that all the information provided, including the bank account numbers, was phony.

Does this mean exporting is too risky? "Not at all," explains Herman. "You just have to do your homework and make use of the government export assistance programs that are available."

"After I was on the Oprah show," she recalls, "I received hundreds of e-mails from women wanting to start or expand their own businesses. I told them to think globally and contact the U.S. Commercial Service for help getting there."

LESSONS LEARNED

Herman follows the Three P's: passion, perseverance, and patience. In other words,

- Follow your dream.
- Don't accept "no" for an answer.
- Be patient and tackle one problem at a time.

She adds that you should always ask for assistance and advice when engaging in international business.

ACTION

How can you take your small business global? Here are some tips:

- **Conduct market research.** Good market research can help you determine which markets are right for your product. For a complete listing of the market research that the Commercial Service offers, visit *www.export.gov/mrktresearch*. The Commercial Service can also help you find international buyers with the International Partner Search and the Gold Key Service. See Chapter 6 for a description.

- **Know your customer.** Perhaps you have already started receiving orders on your Web site. The Commercial Service can conduct background checks to make sure that buyers are reputable. For a description of the International Company Profile, see Chapter 6. Herman's Web site allows her to receive international orders and to collect payment for them. See Chapter 11 for tips on creating an effective Web site with an overseas audience in mind.

- **Get counseling.** Small companies may find it daunting to enter the international marketplace. In addition to the U.S. Commercial Service, the Small Business Administration (SBA) provides a range of export assistance to small businesses, particularly those new to exporting. Counseling is provided at no cost. To learn more about the SBA, visit *www.sba.gov*.

Rosie Herman used her background as a salon owner and manicurist to develop her own company. "One Minute Manicure" is now sold in dozens of countries, with help from an international network of 200 distributors.

DEVELOPING A MARKETING PLAN

In This Chapter

- **Writing a marketing strategy**
- **Researching foreign markets**
- **Researching the market**

Many foreign markets differ greatly from markets in the United States. Some differences include climatic and environmental factors, social and cultural factors, local availability of raw materials or product alternatives, lower wage costs, varying amounts of purchasing power, availability of foreign exchange, and government import controls. Once you've decided that your company is able to export and is committed to it, the next step is to develop a marketing plan.

A clear marketing strategy offers six immediate benefits:

1. Written plans readily display strengths and weaknesses.

2. Written plans are not easily forgotten, overlooked, or ignored by those charged with executing them. If deviation from the original plan occurs, it is likely to be the result of a deliberate and thoughtful choice.

3. Written plans are easier to communicate to others and are less likely to be misunderstood.

4. Written plans allocate responsibilities and provide for an evaluation of results.

5. Written plans are helpful when you are seeking financial assistance. They indicate to lenders that you have a serious approach to the export venture.

6. Written plans give management personnel a clear understanding of what will be required of them and help ensure a commitment to exporting.

This last advantage is especially important. Building an international business takes time. It often takes months, sometimes even several years, before an exporting company begins to see a return on its investment of time and money. By committing to

BOX 3.1 THE BENEFITS OF MARKET RESEARCH

Solid up-to-date market research will help you determine the following:

- Which countries are currently buying products similar to yours and the size of the potential market
- Who your competitors are
- The specific standards your products must meet in markets
- Whether your products have to be modified, such as labeling and packaging
- Pricing strategies
- Optimal distribution channels
- Duties, taxes, and other costs or restrictions
- Additional testing or certifications required

the specifics of a written plan, you can make sure that your company will finish what it begins and that the hopes that prompted your export efforts will be fulfilled.

MARKET RESEARCH

To successfully export your product, you should research foreign markets. The purpose is to identify marketing opportunities and constraints abroad, as well as to identify prospective buyers and customers (Box 3.1). Market research encompasses all methods that your company may use to determine which foreign markets have the best potential for your products. Results of this research tell you the following:

- The largest markets for your product and the fastest-growing markets
- Market trends and outlook
- Market conditions and practices
- Competing firms and products

Your firm may begin to export without conducting any market research if it receives unsolicited orders from abroad. A good first step is to review your current customer list; if you are engaged in e-commerce, you probably already have customers in foreign countries or have received queries from foreign buyers. These current and prospective foreign customers can be a good barometer for developing an export marketing plan. Although this type of research is valuable, your company may discover even more promising markets by conducting a systematic search.

Primary Market Research

You may research a market by using either primary or secondary data resources. When conducting primary market research, you collect data directly from the foreign marketplace through interviews, surveys, and other direct contact with representatives and potential buyers. Primary market research has the advantage of being tailored to your company's needs and provides answers to specific questions, but the collection of such data on your own is time consuming and expensive and may not be comprehensive. The U.S. Commercial Service can collect primary data for you and help you analyze it. This service costs, on average, several hundred dollars for each market analyzed and does not require you to travel there. The U.S. Commercial Service can also help you find intermediaries with specific market expertise.

Secondary Market Research

When conducting secondary market research, your company collects data from various sources, such as trade statistics for a country or a product. Working with secondary sources is less expensive and helps your company focus its marketing efforts. Although secondary data sources are critical to market research, they do have limitations. The most recent statistics for some countries may be more than a few years old, or the data may be too broad to be of much value to your company.

METHODS OF MARKET RESEARCH

Because of the expense of primary market research, most firms rely on secondary data sources. These three recommendations will help you obtain useful secondary information:

1. Keep abreast of world events that influence the international marketplace, watch for announcements of specific projects, or simply visit likely markets. For example, a thawing of political hostilities often leads to the opening of economic channels between countries. A steep depreciation in the value of the dollar can make your product considerably more competitive.

2. Analyze trade and economic statistics. Trade statistics are generally compiled by product category and by country. Such statistics provide your firm with information concerning shipments of products over specified periods of time. Demographic and general economic statistics, such as population size and makeup, per capita income, and production levels by industry, can be important indicators of the market potential for your company's products.

FACT:
Many firms export indirectly, through intermediaries such as export management companies, export trading companies, or other kinds of trading firms.

INSIGHT:
If your company does so, it may wish to select markets and conduct market research before selecting the intermediary.

3. Obtain advice from experts. There are several ways of gathering this advice:

   • Contact experts at the U.S. Department of Commerce and other government agencies.

   • Attend seminars, workshops, and international trade shows in your industry.

   • Hire an international trade and marketing consultant.

   • Talk with successful exporters of similar products, including members of District Export Councils in your local area.

   • Contact trade and industry associations.

Gathering and evaluating secondary market research may be complex and tedious. However, several publications are available that may simplify the process. The following approach to market research refers to the publications and resources that are described later in this chapter.

A STEP-BY-STEP APPROACH TO MARKET RESEARCH

Your company may find the following approach useful. It involves screening potential markets, assessing the targeted markets, and drawing conclusions (see Box 3.2).

Screening Potential Markets

STEP 1: OBTAIN EXPORT STATISTICS

Published statistics that indicate product exports to various countries provide a reliable indicator of where U.S. exports are currently being shipped. The U.S. Census Bureau provides these statistics in a published format at *www.census.gov/foreign-trade/www/*.

STEP 2: IDENTIFY POTENTIAL MARKETS

First, you should identify 5 to10 large and fast-growing markets for your firm's product. Look at trends over the past three to five years. Has market growth been consistent year to year? Did import growth occur even during periods of economic recession? If not, did growth resume with economic recovery?

Then, take a look at some smaller, fast-emerging markets that may provide ground-floor opportunities. If the market is just beginning to open up, there may be fewer competitors than in established markets. To qualify as up-and-coming markets, these countries should have substantially higher growth rates. Libya (which recently opened its economy after years of economic sanctions) and Morocco (which entered into a free trade agreement with the United States in 2005) are good examples of such markets.

Look also at groupings of countries such as those the United States has free trade agreements with in Latin America. Or look at regions within large countries such as western Canada or far eastern Russia. The U.S. Commercial Service has regional services that

BOX 3.2 THE ELEMENTS OF MARKET RESEARCH

SCREEN POTENTIAL MARKETS

- Step 1: Obtain export statistics
- Step 2: Identify potential markets
- Step 3: Tarket the most promising markets

ASSESS THE TARGETED MARKETS

- Step 1: Examine product trends
- Step 2: Research the competition
- Step 3: Analyze marketing factors
- Step 4: Identify barriers
- Step 5: Identify any incentives

DRAW CONCLUSIONS

will help you find buyers in multiple countries in, for example, East Asia. If you're targeting Hong Kong and the Pearl River Delta area, why not stop in nearby Thailand or Singapore?

STEP 3: TARGET THE MOST PROMISING MARKETS

Of the markets you have identified, select three to five of the most statistically promising for further assessment. Consult with a U.S. Commercial Service Export Assistance Center (see Appendix B or *www.export.gov/eac/*), business associates, freight forwarders, and others to further evaluate targeted markets.

Assessing Targeted Markets

STEP 1: EXAMINE PRODUCT TRENDS

Look not only at company products but also at related products that could influence demand. Calculate overall consumption of the product and the amount accounted for by imports. The U.S. Commercial Service (at *www.export.gov/mrktresearch/*) offers market research reports that provide economic background and market trends by country and industry. Demographic information (such as population and age) can be obtained from the Census Bureau at *www. census.gov/ipc/www/idb* and from the United Nations Statistics Division at *http://unstats. un.org/unsd/databases.htm.*

STEP 2: RESEARCH THE COMPETITION

Sources of competition include the domestic industry in each targeted market and competitors from other foreign countries. Look at each competitor's U.S. market share as well as its share in the targeted market. U.S. Commercial Service market research reports and other competitive assessments are available at *www.export.gov/mrktresearch/*.

STEP 3: ANALYZE MARKETING FACTORS

Analyze factors affecting the marketing and use of your product in each market, such as end-user sectors; channels of distribution; cultural idiosyncrasies (for example, does your product's name, when translated into the local language, mean something undesirable?); and business practices. Again, the market research reports and customized market research offered by the U.S. Commercial Service are useful.

STEP 4: IDENTIFY ANY BARRIERS

Foreign barriers to imports can be tariff or non-tariff. U.S. barriers could include export controls. If you make a product that may have dual use (civilian and military), you may be required to have an export license. The U.S. Commercial Service can help you determine whether a license is necessary. Most applications are approved. Call (800) USA-TRADE (800-872-8723) for more information.

STEP 5: IDENTIFY ANY INCENTIVES

The U.S. or foreign government may offer incentives that promote exporting of your particular product or service (see Chapter 10).

Drawing Conclusions

After analyzing the data, your company may conclude that your marketing resources would be applied more effectively to a few select countries. In general, if your company is new to exporting, then efforts should be directed to fewer than 10 markets. Exporting to a manageable number of countries allows you to focus your resources without jeopardizing your domestic sales efforts. Your company's internal resources should determine what choices you make. The U.S. government, though, has export promotion programs that can assist you with exporting to multiple markets in the same region. The U.S. Commercial Service, for example, has regional export promotion programs in Asia, Europe, the Middle East, and the Americas in addition to country- and industry-specific resources.

SOURCES OF MARKET RESEARCH

There are many domestic and international sources of information concerning international markets. This section describes the market research sources that have been mentioned, as

FACT:

Many small companies could sharply boost exports by entering new markets. In 2005, nearly two-thirds of the small firms that exported posted sales to only one foreign market.

INSIGHT:

The U.S. Commercial Service's standardized and customized market research can help you identify additional markets that are appropriate for your products and services.

well as some additional ones. Because so many research sources exist, your firm may wish to seek advice from your local Export Assistance Center to find the best and most current information (see Chapter 4 or go to *www.export.gov/eac/*).

Research sources range from simple trade statistics, to in-depth market surveys, to firsthand interviews with public- and private-sector experts. Trade statistics indicate total exports or imports by country and by product. They allow you to compare the size of the market for a product in various countries. Some statistics also reflect the U.S. share of the total market in a country in order to gauge the overall competitiveness of U.S. producers. By looking at statistics over several years, you can determine which markets are growing and which are shrinking for your product.

Market surveys provide a narrative description and assessment of particular markets along with relevant statistics. The reports are often based on original research conducted in the countries studied and may include specific information on both buyers and competitors.

One of the best sources of information is personal interviews with private and government officials and experts. A surprisingly large number of people in both the public and private sectors are available to assist you in any aspect of international market research. Either in face-to-face interviews or by telephone, these individuals can provide a wealth of market research information.

Other sources of market research expertise include local chambers of commerce, world trade centers, or clubs and trade associations. Many state governments maintain active export promotion offices. In the federal government, industry and commodity experts are available through the U.S. Departments of Commerce, State, and Agriculture and through the Small Business Administration (SBA).

The following sources are divided into several categories: (a) general information about exporting, (b) statistical and demographic information, (c) export opportunities at development agencies, (d) industry information, and (e) regional and country information.

General Information about Exporting

The following resources are an excellent starting point for obtaining general information.

TRADE INFORMATION CENTER

The Trade Information Center (TIC) of the U.S. Commercial Service is the first stop for companies seeking export assistance from the federal government. TIC trade specialists can

- Give you information about all government export programs
- Direct you to your local Export Assistance Center for face-to-face export counseling
- Guide you through the export process
- Provide business counseling by country and region on standards and trade regulations, distribution channels, opportunities and best prospects for U.S. companies, tariffs and border taxes, customs procedures, and common commercial difficulties
- Direct you to market research and trade leads
- Provide information on overseas and domestic trade events and activities

Extensive market and regulatory information by region and country is available, including assistance with the North American Free Trade Agreement (NAFTA) certificate of origin and other free trade agreement processes. Call (800) USA-TRADE (800-872-8723) to speak to a TIC specialist.

SMALL BUSINESS ADMINISTRATION EXPORTING TOOLS AND RESOURCES

SBA provides tools and resources to assist small businesses that are considering exporting or those looking to expand into foreign markets. Publications, training, podcasts, videos, and success stories are available at *www.sba.gov*.

Statistical and Demographic Information

Current statistical and demographic information is easy to find and available from many sources.

STAT-USA/INTERNET

This service, available at *www.stat-usa.gov,* provides a comprehensive collection of business, economic, and trade information available on the Web. Through this address, you can access daily trade leads and economic news, as well as the latest economic press releases and statistical series from the federal government. For more information on this low-cost service, call (800) STAT-USA (800-782-8872).

USA TRADE ONLINE

This service, offered by STAT-USA in conjunction with the U.S. Census Bureau and available at *www.usatradeonline.gov,* offers specific, up-to-date export information on more than

18,000 commodities worldwide. For a small subscription fee, you can access the latest official statistics on U.S. foreign trade.

EUROTRADE ONLINE
This service, also offered by STAT-USA, provides access to statistics on import and export merchandise trade for each of 25 European countries. Trade data are provided for over 12,000 commodities, using the eight-digit Harmonized System tariff classification structure. These are the official European foreign trade statistics from the European Union's statistical agency, EuroStat. For more information, visit *www.eurotradeonline.gov* or call (800) STAT-USA (800-782-8872).

TRADESTATS EXPRESS
This Web site is a comprehensive source for U.S. export and import data, both current and historical. Maintained by the U.S. Commerce Department's Office of Trade and Industry Information, it contains U.S. trade statistics by country and commodity classifications, state and metropolitan area export data, and trade and industry statistics. Much of the data are downloadable at *http://tse.export.gov*.

STATISTICAL YEARBOOK
Published by the United Nations, this yearbook is one of the most complete statistical reference books available. It provides international trade information on products, including information on importing countries, which can be useful in assessing import competition. The yearbook contains data on more than 550 commodities for more than 200 countries and territories on economic and social subjects, including population, agriculture, manufacturing, commodity, export–import trade, and many other areas. The book is available only in hard copy; however, the data in the book can be found online in the United Nations Common Database. Visit the database at *http://unstats.un.org/unsd/cdb*. You can order the book from United Nations Publications, Room DC2-0853, New York, NY 10017 or by telephone at (212) 963-3489.

WORLD BANK ATLAS AND WORLD DEVELOPMENT INDICATORS
Published every two years, the *World Bank Atlas* provides demographics, gross domestic products, and average growth rates for every country. *World Development Indicators* is an annual publication containing more than 800 economic, social, and other indicators for 159 economies, plus basic indicators for another 55 economies.

You can order World Bank publications by mail from The World Bank, P.O. Box 960, Herndon, VA 20172-0960. Purchase World Bank publications by telephone at (800) 645-7247 or on the Web at *http://publications.worldbank.org/howtoorder*.

WORLD FACTBOOK

Produced annually by the U.S. Central Intelligence Agency (CIA), this publication provides country-by-country data on demographics, the economy, communications, and defense. To purchase the latest print edition, contact the U.S. Government Printing Office Order Desk at *http://bookstore.gpo.gov* or telephone (202) 512-1800. You may also visit the CIA's World Factbook Web site at *www.cia.gov/cia/publications/factbook.*

INTERNATIONAL FINANCIAL STATISTICS

Published by the International Monetary Fund (IMF), *International Financial Statistics* presents statistics on exchange rates, money and banking, production, government finance, interest rates, and other subjects. It is available in hard copy as a monthly subscription, on CD-ROM, or as an online service. Contact the International Monetary Fund, Publication Services, 700 19th St., N.W., Room 12-607, Washington, DC 20431, or telephone (202) 623-7430. Information on *International Financial Statistics* as well as many other IMF resources can be found at *www.imf.org.*

GLOBAL POPULATION PROFILE

This resource is produced by the Census Bureau of the U.S. Department of Commerce. The bureau collects and analyzes worldwide demographic data that can help exporters identify potential markets for their products. Information on each country—total population, fertility, and mortality rates; urban population; growth rate; and life expectancy—is updated every two years. The document also contains detailed demographic profiles of individual countries, including analyses of labor force structure and infant mortality. To purchase the latest print edition, contact the U.S. Government Printing Office Order Desk at *http://bookstore.gpo. gov* or telephone (202) 512-1800. The information is also available on the Census Bureau's Web site at *www.census.gov/ipc/www/idb.*

Export Opportunities at Development Agencies

International development agencies offer many opportunities for exporters. Here are a few sources to explore.

MULTILATERAL DEVELOPMENT BANKS

Multilateral development banks (MDBs) are institutions that provide financial support and professional advice for economic and social development activities in developing countries. The term *multilateral development bank* typically refers to the World Bank Group or four regional development banks: the African Development Bank, the Asian Development Bank, the European Bank for Reconstruction and Development, and the Inter-American Development Bank. Development projects funded by these banks often offer export opportunities. The

U.S. Department of Commerce maintains liaison offices with each of the MDBs in an effort to provide information to U.S. companies on procurements for these projects. To learn more about a particular MDB, visit *www.export.gov/Advocacy/MDBs.html.*

BUDGET JUSTIFICATION TO THE CONGRESS
OF THE U.S. AGENCY FOR INTERNATIONAL DEVELOPMENT

Published by the Office of Small and Disadvantaged Business, U.S. Agency for International Development (USAID), the annual *Budget Justification to the Congress* contains individual reports on countries that USAID will provide funds to in the coming year, as well as detailed information on past funding activities in each country. Because the initiatives require U.S. goods and services, these reports give U.S. exporters an early look at upcoming projects. (See Chapter 6 for more details on USAID's programs.) Budget justifications for the current and previous years are available online at *www.usaid.gov/policy/budget/.*

Industry Information

Industry-specific information is important in any exporting venture. Here are a few research avenues.

U.S. DEPARTMENT OF AGRICULTURE, FOREIGN AGRICULTURAL SERVICE

The Foreign Agricultural Service (FAS) serves as the first point of contact for those needing information on foreign markets for agricultural products. The Office of Outreach and Exporter Assistance of the FAS can provide basic export counseling and direct you to the appropriate Department of Agriculture office to answer specific questions on exporting. The staff can provide country- and commodity-specific foreign market information reports, which focus on the best market prospects and contain contact information on distributors and importers. Extensive information on the FAS is also available through the Web at *www.fas. usda.gov.* For additional information, contact the Office of Outreach and Exporter Assistance by telephone at (202) 720-7420 or by fax at (202) 690-4374.

TEXTILE AND APPAREL DATABASE

Prepared by the U.S. Department of Commerce's Office of Textiles and Apparel, this database provides information on overseas markets and the rules and regulations affecting U.S. exports. The database provides specific country profiles, which include information on marketing and distribution, market-entry requirements, shipment and entry procedures, and trade policy. More general information, such as export procedures, potential buyers and suppliers, current trade issues, and background on textile and apparel trade policy agreements, is also available. The Web site is *www.otexa.ita.doc.gov.*

PRIVATE-SECTOR PRODUCT AND INDUSTRY RESOURCES

The U.S. and foreign private sectors publish numerous guides and directories that provide valuable information for your company. For specific references, consult your local Export Assistance Center at *www.export.gov* or the Trade Information Center at (800) USA-TRADE (800-872-8723).

Regional and Country Information

Information on individual countries and regions is widely available. Here are some places you can explore individual markets.

CHINA BUSINESS INFORMATION CENTER

The China Business Information Center (BIC) is a comprehensive source of information on China published by federal and state government agencies, associations, and private-sector entities. Companies that are new to the market or are current market participants can use the China BIC to

- Identify sources of U.S. and state government assistance
- Learn how to protect their intellectual property rights
- Monitor China's compliance with its World Trade Organization (WTO) obligations
- Obtain industry-specific market research to evaluate export prospects
- Search for trade leads and tender offers
- Participate in trade events in the United States and China
- Identify sources of trade finance
- Monitor changes in Chinese import regulations
- Identify relevant U.S. export regulations
- Quickly find tips on doing business in China
- Learn about economic and political conditions in China

      To access the China BIC, go to *www.export.gov/china.*

FACT: China is our third-largest export market. U.S. exports to China were up more than 30 percent for 2006, compared with 2005.

INSIGHT: Your company can benefit from this growing market. Visit the China Business Information Center at *www.export.gov/china.*

ASIA NOW

This program brings together the resources of U.S. Commercial Service offices in 14 markets in the Asia-Pacific region and Export Assistance Centers throughout the United States, providing your company with a single point of access to regional trade events, extensive services of the Commercial Service, and research covering Asian markets. Asia Now can be found at *www.buyusa.gov/asianow*.

MIDDLE EAST AND NORTH AFRICA BUSINESS INFORMATION CENTER

The Middle East and North Africa Business Information Center (MENABIC) covers information on markets throughout the region: Algeria, Bahrain, Egypt, Iraq, Israel, Jordan, Kuwait, Lebanon, Morocco, Oman, Qatar, Saudi Arabia, Tunisia, the United Arab Emirates, and the West Bank and Gaza. The Web site includes detailed country and industry information, trade leads, lists of trade events both domestically and in MENABIC countries, and information on regulations, licensing, documents, financing, and anything else your company needs to do business in the Middle East and North Africa. To access the MENABIC, go to *www.export.gov/middleeast*.

SHOWCASE EUROPE

This program provides U.S. companies easy access to European export markets. The U.S. Commercial Service at U.S. embassies and consulates works with companies to increase exports of U.S. products and services to Europe. You will find trade opportunities, new business partners, market research, and one-on-one assistance for eight key industry sectors, including medical equipment, information technology, and aerospace equipment. The advantages for your company include the following:

• Services at major European trade shows that enable U.S. exhibitors to leverage the event for maximum success

• A systematic approach to counseling in areas such as developing market entry strategies and replicating best practices throughout Europe

• A coordinated approach to market research in an effort to offer U.S. exporters market intelligence that can be more easily replicated across national borders

• Services such as "Quick Take" that provide a quick assessment of your product or service in specific markets

To learn more about Showcase Europe, visit *www.buyusa.gov/europe/*.

TRADE AMERICAS

The Trade Americas program offers U.S. companies the opportunity to find out more about business opportunities in more than 20 countries throughout the Western Hemisphere.

By combining resources across the region, the U.S. Commercial Service helps exporters find sales opportunities in several countries, saving time and money and generating more profits. Trade Americas has a Web site that provides information on existing and proposed free trade agreements throughout the region, market research, best prospects in the region, trade event lists, industry-specific information, business service providers, useful links, and key contacts. For more information about Trade Americas, visit *www.buyusa.gov/tradeamericas/*.

OECD PUBLICATIONS

The chartered mission of the Organization for Economic Cooperation and Development (OECD) is to promote its member countries' policies. These policies have been designed to support economic growth, employment, and a high standard of living and to contribute to sound economic expansion in development and trade. OECD publications focus on a broad range of social and economic issues, concerns, and developments. Country-by-country reports on international market information contain import data useful in assessing import competition.

The OECD also publishes economic development surveys that cover each of the 30 member countries of the OECD, plus some additional countries. Each survey presents a detailed analysis of recent developments in market demand, production, employment, prices, wages, and more. Short-term forecasts and analyses of medium-term problems relevant to economic policies are also provided.

Print copies of OECD publications are available from the OECD Publications and Information Center, 2001 L St., NW, Suite 650, Washington, DC 20036-4922, or telephone (202) 785-6323. You can also order the books on the Web or purchase an online subscription. Visit the OECD at *www.oecdbookshop.org*.

MARKET RESEARCH LIBRARY

The U.S. Commercial Service's Market Research Library contains more than 100,000 industry- and country-specific market reports, Web sites, events, and trade directory listings, and it covers more than 120 countries and 110 industry sectors. Reports include Country Commercial Guides, Industry Sector Analyses, Marketing Insights, Multilateral Development Bank Reports, Best Markets, other industry or regional reports, and more. Reports are available at *www.export.gov/mrktresearch/*.

CUSTOMIZED MARKET RESEARCH

These reports make use of the worldwide network of the U.S. Commercial Service to help U.S. exporters evaluate their sales potential in a market, choose the best new markets for their products and services, establish effective marketing and distribution strategies in their target markets, identify the competition, determine which factors are most important to overseas buyers, pinpoint impediments to exporting, and understand many other pieces of critical market intelligence. The reports are customized to your specifications. Contact your local Export Assistance Center at *www.export.gov/eac/* for more information.

Vellus Products

"Exporting has made me more broad minded, and I have developed a great appreciation for other cultures and the way others live their lives."

—Sharon Doherty, president, Vellus Products Inc.

THE COMPANY

Is your pet having a bad hair day? Well, Sharon Doherty, president of Vellus Products Inc., can help. Her small Columbus, Ohio–based company makes a line of pet grooming products, including customized shampoos, conditioners, brushing sprays, satin cream, and detanglers.

According to Doherty, shampoos for people don't work well on pets because animal skin is more sensitive than human skin and is more easily irritated. Most available pet shampoos, though sensitive to the skin, tend to leave hair unmanageable and without the glamour needed for the show dog or pampered pet. Dr. David Tanner, Doherty's nephew, used his expertise as a chemist in the personal care industry to develop the salon-type formulas that Doherty thought would be good for animal hair and skin. This family-operated company also involves Doherty's husband, Robert, and daughter, Teryl Hotz.

THE CHALLENGE

Vellus Products' first export sale occurred in 1993, when a Taiwanese businessperson, after trying the Vellus line, bought $25,000 worth of the company's products to sell in Taiwan through dog shows. The word was out. "I started receiving calls from people around the world who would hear of our products at dog shows and ask organizers how they could get in touch with me to buy our products," Doherty recalls. "But I needed a way to find market research and learn more about ways of doing business in these countries."

THE SOLUTION

Doherty soon tapped the services of the U.S. Commercial Service in Columbus. "As business has grown, I have gone from ordering country profiles to requesting customized export and financing strategies tailored to maximize export potential," Doherty says.

The Commercial Service relied on its worldwide network and partners such as the Small Business Administration and the state of Ohio to provide customized market research and information on financing and other programs for Vellus. Today, Vellus sells to more than 28 countries. "I credit the Commercial Service for helping me expand my exports, as it would have been much more difficult to do this on my own," Doherty says.

LESSONS LEARNED

Doherty learned several lessons from her exporting experience:

- **Know whom you are dealing with.** "Developing business relationships is critical to successful exporting," Doherty says. Doherty often gives advice and guidance to her distributors, sharing her knowledge and understanding of importing along with marketing in the dog show network. She says this advice is much appreciated and goes a long way toward building long-term relationships. "Be smart, but humble," she advises. "Whenever there is a problem, I don't e-mail; I pick up the phone."

- **Do a background check on potential business partners.** Doherty was once duped by a businessman from another country who said he knew all about the pet market there. She followed some of his advice, and it caused her to lose customers in that country. The experience was a lesson well learned. "Always do a thorough check on your potential business partners," she says. "Gather as much information as you can. Don't make any assumptions; the wrong choice can cost your business valuable time and money." Doherty also notes that it is her business practice to have orders prepaid by the purchaser, and once the bank receives the money, to ship the orders. This practice helps prevent any problems with delinquent payments.

- **Learn the culture.** Doherty has become familiar with the cultural aspects of pet care. Vellus shampoos and other products can easily be varied for different grooming techniques. In England, dog exhibitors prefer less pouffy topknots than those on show dogs in the United States, where owners tend to be more exotic with topknots. There also can be different preferences for the look of show dogs.

- **Enjoy the ride.** Doherty says that exporting has changed her life. "I love exporting because it has enabled me to meet so many people from other cultures. Exporting has made me more broad minded, and I have developed a great appreciation for other cultures and the way others live their lives," she says. "You are put in contact with real people on the other side."

ACTION

Are you ready to promote your product or service in other cultures? Try this advice:

- **Pay attention to the target market's social customs.** People interested in exporting should look closely at the social customs in the country where they would like to do business. Contacting the U.S. Commercial Service office in that country is an excellent way to learn about cultural issues and ways of doing business, and exporters like Doherty have found the customized market reports to be especially helpful. Simply visit *www.export.gov* or check Appendix B for the nearest U.S. Export Assistance Center, and that office can contact the appropriate Commercial Service post in the country of interest.

- **Use trade shows to promote your products and services.** The Commercial Service sponsors U.S. pavilions in many trade shows. Further information on overseas trade shows is available at *www.export.gov/tradeevents*.

- **Promote your company in target markets.** You might also want to advertise in *Commercial News USA*. The catalog-style magazine is designed to help American companies promote products and services to buyers in more than 145 countries at a fraction of the cost of other advertising options. Each issue reaches an estimated 400,000 readers worldwide. The bimonthly magazine, which is free, is mailed directly to qualified recipients outside the United States and is distributed by Commercial Service personnel at U.S. embassies and consulates throughout the world. See *www.thinkglobal.us/*.

Sharon Doherty, president of Vellus Products Inc., poses with a well-coifed friend. Her Columbus, Ohio, company produces pet shampoos and conditioners. Doherty made her first export sale in 1993 and has since expanded to 28 countries.

chapter 4

EXPORT ADVICE

In This Chapter

- U.S. Commercial Service assistance

- Other government agency assistance

- Assistance from chambers of commerce

FACT:
About 30 percent of non-exporters say they would export if they had information on how to get started, such as best markets, potential buyers, and export procedures.

INSIGHT:
The U.S. government is the leading provider of this kind of essential market information. To figure out where to begin, visit www.export.gov or call an international trade specialist at (800) USA-TRADE (800-872-8723).

MAKING THE GOVERNMENT WORK FOR YOU

Now that you've had an opportunity to examine some of the factors involved in an exporting and marketing plan, let's review some key sources of assistance. Lots of help is available to your company at little or no cost and makes the exporting process much easier. This chapter gives a brief overview of the assistance available through federal, state, and local government agencies, as well as in the private sector. Other chapters in this guide provide more information on the specialized services of these organizations and how to use them.

U.S. COMMERCIAL SERVICE EXPORT ASSISTANCE CENTERS

The U.S. Commercial Service of the U.S. Department of Commerce maintains a network of international trade specialists in the United States to help American companies export their products and conduct business abroad. International trade specialists are employed in offices known as Export Assistance Centers in more than 100 cities in the United States and Puerto Rico to assist U.S. exporters, particularly small and medium-sized companies. Export Assistance Centers are known as "one-stop shops" because they combine the trade and marketing expertise and resources of the Commercial Service along with the financial expertise and resources of the Small Business Administration and the Export–Import Bank.

Export Assistance Centers also maximize resources by working closely with state and local governments as well as private partners to offer companies a full range of expertise in international trade, marketing, and finance. International trade specialists will counsel your company on the steps involved in exporting, help you assess the export potential of your products, identify markets, and locate potential overseas partners. They work with their international colleagues in more than 80 countries to provide American companies with turnkey solutions in foreign markets.

Each Export Assistance Center can offer information about the following:

• Services to locate and evaluate overseas buyers and representatives, distributors, resellers, and partners

• International trade opportunities

• Foreign markets for U.S. products and services

• Foreign economic statistics

• Export documentation requirements

• U.S. export licensing requirements and import requirements of foreign nations

• Export trade finance options

• International trade exhibition participation and certification

• Export seminars and conferences

To find the Export Assistance Centers nearest you, see Appendix B or visit *www.export.gov/eac.*

U.S. COMMERCIAL SERVICE OVERSEAS POSTS

Much of the information about trends and actual trade leads in foreign countries is gathered on site by the officers of the Commercial Service. Those officers have a personal under-standing of local market conditions and business practices in the countries in which they work. The Commercial Service officers work in more than 150 offices located in more than 80 countries. They provide a range of services to help companies sell in foreign markets:

• Background information on foreign companies

• Agent–distributor locator services

• Market research

• Business counseling

• Assistance in making appointments with key buyers and government officials

• Representations on behalf of companies adversely affected by trade barriers

Some of the more important services are described in Chapter 6. You can access those services by contacting your nearest U.S. Export Assistance Center. The centers can also provide assistance with business travel before departure by arranging advance appointments with embassy personnel, market briefings, and other services in the cities you will be visiting.

TRADE INFORMATION CENTER, U.S. COMMERCIAL SERVICE

The Trade Information Center (TIC) is a comprehensive resource for information on all federal government export assistance programs and for information and assistance on exporting to most countries. TIC can be reached at (800) USA-TRADE (800-872-8723) or *www.export.gov*.

U.S. TRADE AND DEVELOPMENT AGENCY

Industry and international trade specialists in the U.S. Trade and Development Agency (TDA) work directly with individual firms and manufacturing and service associations to identify trade opportunities and obstacles by product or service, industry sector, and market. TDA analysts participate in trade policy development and negotiations, identify market barriers, and advocate on behalf of U.S. companies. TDA's statistical data and analyses are useful in export development. The TDA staff also develops export marketing programs and obtains industry advice on trade matters. To assist U.S. businesses in their export efforts, TDA's industry and international experts conduct executive trade missions, trade fairs, marketing seminars, and business counseling and provide product literature centers.

For further information, contact TDA at *www.tda.gov*.

EXPORT–IMPORT BANK OF THE UNITED STATES

The Export–Import Bank is committed to supporting small business exporters. In fact, about 85 percent of its transactions support small businesses. The Ex–Im Bank's products include specialized small business financing tools such as working capital guarantee and export credit insurance.

The working capital guarantee and insurance products enable small businesses to increase sales by entering new markets, to expand their borrowing base, and to offer buyers financing while carrying less risk. The Ex–Im Bank's working capital guarantee assumes up to 90 percent of the lender's risk so exporters can access the necessary funds to purchase or produce U.S.–made goods and services for export.

For more information, contact the Ex–Im Bank at *www.exim.gov*.

ADVOCACY CENTER, U.S. COMMERCIAL SERVICE

For a U.S. company bidding on a foreign government procurement contract, exporting today can mean more than just selling a good product at a competitive price. It can also mean

FACT:
Private consultants are expensive.

INSIGHT:
It pays to take full advantage of publicly funded sources of assistance before hiring a consultant. When you do hire the consultant, you will receive greater value because your requirements will be more focused.

chapter
4

EXPORT ADVICE

dealing with foreign governments and complex rules. If you feel that the bidding process is not open and transparent or that it may be tilted in favor of your foreign competition, then you need to contact the Advocacy Center. This center coordinates the actions of 19 U.S. government agencies involved in international trade. Advocacy assistance may involve a visit to a key foreign official by a high-ranking U.S. government official, direct support from U.S. officials stationed overseas, letters to foreign decision-makers, and coordinated action by U.S. government agencies and businesses of all types and sizes. For more information, call (202) 482-3896 or visit *www.export.gov/advocacy.*

TRADE COMPLIANCE CENTER, U.S. DEPARTMENT OF COMMERCE

The U.S. Department of Commerce's Trade Compliance Center (TCC) is an integral part of efforts by the U.S. government to ensure foreign compliance with trade agreements. Located within the Market Access and Compliance (MAC) unit of the International Trade Administration, TCC systematically monitors, investigates, and evaluates foreign compliance with multilateral, bilateral, and other international trade agreements and standards of conduct to ensure that U.S. firms and workers receive all the benefits that market-opening initiatives provide.

The TCC Web site at *http://tcc.export.gov* provides a one-stop shop for American exporters facing market access and agreements compliance problems. The fully searchable database contains the texts of approximately 270 bilateral, regional, and multilateral trade and trade-related agreements, along with detailed market access information for more than 90 major U.S. markets. The online service enables U.S. exporters to file complaints about market access and agreements.

TCC can be reached by phone at (202) 482-1191 or by mail at the U.S. Department of Commerce, Room 3415, 14th St. and Constitution Ave., NW, Washington, DC 20230.

BUREAU OF INDUSTRY AND SECURITY, U.S. DEPARTMENT OF COMMERCE

The Bureau of Industry and Security (BIS) is responsible for control of exports for reasons of national security, foreign policy, and short supply such as "dual use" items with both military and commercial applications. Assistance with compliance with export controls can be obtained directly from your local BIS district office or from the Outreach and Educational Services Division within the BIS's Office of Exporter Services in Washington, D.C., which you may reach at (202) 482-4811. BIS also has two field offices that specialize in counseling on export controls and regulations; call the Western Regional Office at (949) 660-0144 or the San Jose Office at (408) 291-4212. For more information, visit the BIS Web page at *www.bis.doc.gov.*

MINORITY BUSINESS DEVELOPMENT AGENCY, U.S. DEPARTMENT OF COMMERCE

The Minority Business Development Agency (MBDA) identifies opportunities for U.S. minority business enterprises by promoting their ability to grow and compete in the global economy in selected industries. Through an agreement with the International Trade Administration, MBDA provides information on market and product needs worldwide and identifies ways to access education, finance, and technology to help minority businesses succeed. For example, MBDA and the International Trade Administration coordinate minority business participation in trade events. And the Minority Business Development Center network helps minority businesses to prepare international marketing plans and promotional materials and to identify financial resources.

For general export information, the field organizations of both MBDA and the International Trade Administration provide information kits and details about local seminars. Contact MBDA by phone at (888) 324-1551 or online at *www.mbda.gov/*.

WHERE ELSE TO LOOK FOR ASSISTANCE

Small Business Administration

The U.S. Small Business Administration (SBA) and its nationwide network of resource partners can assist you with export counseling, training, and financing. SBA has trade promotion and finance managers located in the U.S. Export Assistance Centers. In addition, you can find out more about exporting through the following:

• **SBA district offices**. The Small Business Administration has district offices in every state and territory that are staffed by specialists who understand SBA programs. These specialists can help small businesses succeed in exporting and put them in touch with other local resources.

• **Small Business Development Centers (SBDCs)**. SBDCs provide a full range of export assistance services to small businesses, particularly those new to exporting. They also offer counseling, training, managerial support, and trade-finance assistance. Counseling services are provided at no cost to the small business exporter, but fees are generally charged for export training seminars and other SBDC-sponsored export events.

• **SCORE—Counselors to America's Small Businesses**. Many members of SCORE have practical experience in international trade. They can evaluate your company's export potential and strengthen your domestic operations by identifying financial, managerial, or technical problems. SCORE advisers can also help you develop and implement basic export marketing plans that show where and how to sell your goods abroad. You can find more information at *www.score.org/*.

For information on any of the programs funded by SBA, contact your nearest SBA field office by calling (800) 8-ASK-SBA (800-827-5722) or access the SBA home page at *www.sba.gov/*.

U.S. Department of Agriculture

The U.S. Department of Agriculture offers exporting assistance through the Office of Outreach and Exporter Assistance (OOEA). A part of the Foreign Agricultural Service (FAS), OOEA serves as the first point of contact for exporters of U.S. food, farm, and forest products. It provides them guidance, referrals, and access to foreign market information and assistance in getting information about export-related programs managed by the U.S. Department of Agriculture and other federal agencies. It also serves as a contact point for minority-owned and small businesses seeking assistance in these areas. OOEA will provide basic export counseling and connect you to the appropriate export program, such as the Market Access Program. Questions regarding any of the programs offered by the Department of Agriculture should be directed to OOEA at (202) 720-7420. The Web site is *www.fas.usda.gov/*.

National Center for Standards and Certification Information

The National Center for Standards and Certification Information (NCSCI) provides information about foreign standards and certification systems and requirements. In addition to providing comprehensive information on existing standards and certification requirements, NCSCI began a new service in 2005 known as Notify U.S. This free, Web-based e-mail subscription service offers U.S. citizens, industries, and organizations an opportunity to review and comment on proposed foreign technical regulations that can affect their businesses and their access to international markets. By subscribing to the Notify U.S. service, U.S. entities receive, by e-mail, notifications of drafts or changes to domestic and foreign technical regulations for manufactured products. To register, visit the Notify U.S. Web site at *http://tsapps. nist.gov/notifyus/data/index.*

District Export Councils

Besides the immediate services of its Export Assistance Centers, the U.S. Commercial Service has direct contact with seasoned exporters in all aspects of export trade. The U.S. Export Assistance Centers work closely with 58 District Export Councils (including those in Puerto Rico and the U.S. Virgin Islands) made up of nearly 1,500 business and trade experts who volunteer to help U.S. firms develop solid export strategies.

District Export Councils assist in many of the workshops and seminars on exporting that are arranged by the Export Assistance Centers, and they also sponsor their own. District Export Council members may also provide direct, personal counseling to less experienced exporters by suggesting marketing strategies, trade contacts, and ways to maximize success in overseas markets. You can obtain assistance from District Export Councils through the Export Assistance Centers that they are affiliated with.

State and Local Governments

State, county, and city economic development agencies; departments of commerce or development; and other government entities often provide valuable assistance to exporters. The assistance offered by these groups typically includes the following:

- **Export education.** Helping exporters analyze export potential and introducing them to export techniques and strategies, perhaps in the form of group seminars or individual counseling sessions

- **Trade missions.** Organizing trips abroad to enable exporters to call on potential foreign customers (see also Chapter 6)

- **Trade shows.** Organizing and sponsoring exhibitions of state-produced goods and services in overseas markets

Financial Institutions

Many U.S. banks have international departments with specialists who are familiar with specific foreign countries and various types of commodities and transactions. Large banks located in major U.S. cities maintain correspondent relationships with smaller banks throughout the country. And with banks in many foreign countries, they may operate their own overseas branches, providing a direct channel to foreign customers.

International banking specialists are generally well informed about export matters, even in areas that fall outside the usual limits of international banking. Banks frequently provide consultation and guidance free of charge to their clients because they derive income from loans to the exporter and from fees for special services. Many banks also have publications available to help exporters. These materials are often devoted to particular countries and their business practices, and they may be a valuable tool for familiarization with a foreign industry. Finally, large banks frequently conduct seminars and workshops on letters of credit, documentary collections, and other banking subjects of concern to exporters.

Among the many services a commercial bank may perform for its clients are the following:

- Exchange of currencies
- Assistance in financing exports
- Collection of foreign invoices, drafts, letters of credit, and other foreign receivables
- Transfer of funds to other countries
- Letters of introduction and letters of credit for travelers
- Credit information on potential representatives or buyers overseas
- Credit assistance to the exporter's foreign buyers

Export Intermediaries

Export intermediaries range from giant international companies to highly specialized small operations. For a fee, they provide a multitude of services, including performing market research, appointing and managing overseas distributors or commission representatives, exhibiting a client's products at international trade shows, advertising, and shipping and preparing documentation. In short, the intermediary can often take full responsibility for the export end of business, relieving the exporter of all details except filling orders.

Intermediaries may work simultaneously for a number of exporters for a commission, salary, or retainer plus commission. Some intermediaries take title to the goods they handle, buying and selling in their own name. The products of a trading company's various clients are often related, although the items usually are not competitive. One advantage to using an intermediary is that it can immediately make available marketing resources that exporters might take years to develop on their own. Many export intermediaries also finance sales and extend credit, facilitating prompt payment to the exporter. For more information on using export intermediaries, see Chapter 5.

World Trade Centers, International Trade Clubs, and Local Chambers of Commerce

Local or regional World Trade Centers and international trade clubs are composed of area businesspeople who represent firms engaged in international trade and shipping, banks, forwarders, customs brokers, government agencies, and other service organizations involved in world trade. Such organizations conduct educational programs on international business and organize promotional events to stimulate interest in world trade. There are nearly 300 World Trade Centers or affiliated associations in major trading cities in almost 100 countries. By participating in a local association, a company can receive valuable and timely advice on world markets and opportunities from businesspeople who are already knowledgeable in virtually every facet of international business. Among the advantages of membership are the services, discounts, and contacts from affiliated clubs in foreign countries. For more detailed information, visit *http://world.wtca.org/portal/site/wtcaonline.*

Many local chambers of commerce in the United States provide sophisticated and extensive services for members interested in exporting. Among these services are the following:

• Conducting export seminars, workshops, and roundtable discussions

• Providing certificates of origin

• Developing trade promotion programs, including overseas missions, mailings, and event planning

• Organizing U.S. pavilions at foreign trade shows

• Providing contacts with foreign companies and distributors

FACT:

Fifty-eight percent of small business owners belong to one business organization (e.g., an association), and 42 percent belong to more than one.

INSIGHT:

Business and trade associations have these benefits:

- Inform you about government rules and obligations
- Promote your industry or community
- Provide technical information specific to your industry

- Relaying export sales leads and other opportunities to members
- Organizing transportation routings and shipment consolidations
- Hosting visiting trade missions from other countries
- Conducting international activities at domestic trade shows

Industry and Trade Associations

In addition, some industry and trade associations can supply detailed information on market demand for products in selected countries, or they can refer members to export management companies. Industry trade associations typically collect and maintain files on international trade news and trends affecting their industry or line of business. They often publish articles and newsletters that include government research. National and International trade associations often organize large regional, national, and international trade shows themselves. To find a chamber in your area, visit *www.uschamber.com.*

American Chambers of Commerce Abroad

A valuable and reliable source of market information in any foreign country is the local chapter of the American Chamber of Commerce (AMCHAM). These local chapters are knowledgeable about local trade opportunities, actual and potential competition, periods of maximum trade activity, and similar considerations.

AMCHAMs usually handle inquiries from any U.S. business. Detailed services are ordinarily provided free of charge for members of affiliated organizations. Some AMCHAMs have a set schedule of charges for services rendered to non-members. For contact information on AMCHAMs in major foreign markets, call (800) USA-TRADE (800-872-8723).

International Trade Consultants and Other Advisers

International trade consultants can advise and assist a manufacturer on all aspects of foreign marketing. Trade consultants do not normally deal specifically with one product, although they may advise on product adaptation to a foreign market. They research domestic and foreign regulations and also assess commercial and political risk. They conduct foreign-market research and establish contacts with foreign government agencies and other necessary resources, such as advertising companies, product service facilities, and local attorneys.

Consultants in international trade can locate and qualify foreign joint venture partners and can conduct feasibility studies for the sale of manufacturing rights, the location and construction of manufacturing facilities, and the establishment of foreign branches. After sales agreements are completed, trade consultants can also ensure that implementation is smooth and that any problems that arise are dealt with effectively.

Trade consultants usually specialize by subject matter and by global area or country. These consultants can advise on which agents or distributors are likely to be successful, what kinds of promotion are needed, who the competitors are, and how to conduct business with the agents and distributors. They are also knowledgeable about foreign government regulations, contract laws, and taxation. Some firms may be more specialized than others. For example, some may be thoroughly knowledgeable about legal issues and taxation and less knowledgeable about marketing strategies.

Many large accounting firms, law firms, and specialized marketing firms provide international trade consulting services. When selecting a consulting firm, you should pay particular attention to the experience and knowledge of the consultant who is in charge of the project. To find an appropriate firm, seek advice from other exporters and from the other resources listed in this chapter, such as the Export Assistance Centers and local chambers of commerce.

Consultants are of greatest value to a firm that has specific requirements. For that reason, and because private consultants are expensive, it pays to take full advantage of publicly funded sources of assistance before hiring a consultant.

Export Seminars

Besides individual counseling sessions, an effective method of informing local business communities of the various aspects of international trade is through conferences, seminars, and workshops. Each year, Export Assistance Centers participate in approximately 5,000 programs on topics such as export documentation and licensing procedures, country-specific market opportunities, export trading companies, and U.S. trade promotion and trade policy initiatives. The seminars are usually held in conjunction with District Export Councils, local chambers of commerce, state agencies, and other trade organizations. Small Business Administration field offices also co-sponsor export training programs with the Department of Commerce, other federal agencies, and various private-sector international trade organizations. For information on scheduled seminars, contact your nearest Export Assistance Center (see Appendix B) by calling (800) USA-TRADE (800-872-8723) or by going online to *www.export.gov/eac.*

Solatube

"Diversifying economic risks really does work. When it's sunny in some of our markets, it's snowing in others. When business is down in the States, it's up somewhere else."

—Brett Hanley, international sales vice president, Solatube Global Marketing Inc.

THE COMPANY

Solatube is a San Diego–based maker of tubular skylights. But these aren't ordinary skylights. They employ patented technologies that bring more natural light in, and they come with optional kits that convert the skylight into a light fixture as the natural light fades or into a ventilator for kitchen and bathroom use. As the price of electricity increases, skylights for both home and commercial use save money and are good for the environment.

THE CHALLENGE

Solatube was founded in Australia in 1991. Its directors disagreed on whether going international was the best direction for the company, but in the end they elected to give it a try. They then decamped for California to be closer to the U.S. domestic market and to Europe and Latin America. According to Solatube Global Marketing's President Brett Hanley, "A smaller company like ours can't be experts in every market. We're not that naive to think we can do it all."

Solatube also needed a way to insulate itself from the bottom end of the business cycle in its new home market.

"We needed to find entrepreneurial folks overseas who can find the people working on the roofs. We need national distributors with business backgrounds who can set up everything for us," says Hanley.

THE SOLUTION

At first, Solatube was mostly passive in its outreach, meeting potential distributors at trade shows or evaluating prospects who contacted Solatube through the Web or by phone. Results were very mixed, and the company spent more time on unfocused searching than on selling and growing the business.

So Solatube approached the U.S. Commercial Service's Export Assistance Center in San Diego. "We did things the hard way for a number of years until we met the Commercial Service. We wished we had met them before," says Hanley.

Trade Specialist Julia Rauner Guerrero entered the picture as Solatube set its sights on France. With help from her colleague Eva Prevost in Marseille, Guerrero identified a number of master distributor prospects, including one who had seen Solatube promoted on the U.S. Commercial Service Web site in France

(*www.buyusa.gov/france*). In the end, Solatube chose this distributor to represent the product line. Everything was wrapped up in less than six months, and orders were placed for $100,000 worth of product.

Guerrero says, "We encouraged Solatube to develop a regional sales strategy in France and helped develop that strategy. They also followed our advice to engage a French-speaking staff person at their San Diego office, as language was going to be a barrier in developing their business further."

Thanks to the Commercial Service, Solatube is now selling more than 160,000 units per year in 40 different overseas markets. International sales have surpassed 15 percent of total sales with no ceiling in sight for the company's skylights, which are brightening homes and businesses from London to Mexico.

LESSONS LEARNED

Hanley says that Solatube's number one lesson learned was that small companies can expand internationally, gain significant new sales, and add jobs.

Don't try to do it all yourself, says Hanley. It's easy to get overstretched and to waste valuable time. "There is a lot of excellent free and low-cost help out there, including that of the U.S. government and its partners," he advises. "In the case of France, our Commercial Service contact there served as a filter for us. The French distributor would talk to Eva as both our representative there and as a representative of the U.S. government, and she would interpret things for us. There was a French-to-French thing going there that worked out great for us."

The most important thing you can do is to find good distributors in your target markets. You can spend lots of time and money finding them on your own, but Hanley offers this recommendation: "Let the government do it for you. This is their niche, and they're the best at it."

Hanley is a strong advocate of diversification: "Diversifying economic risks really does work. When it's sunny in some of our markets, it's snowing in others. When business is down in the States, it's up somewhere else. Our overseas sales have been growing 25 percent a year for the past six years. We now enjoy a benefit of a strengthening euro against the dollar."

Moreover, Hanley says, "Our international success has improved our acquisition profile. Not that we're looking to sell, but if we ever are in the future we'll be worth a lot more because of the international dimension of our business."

Navigating cultural issues with distributors can be a challenge. Don't be reluctant to ask for help. "In one instance," says Hanley, "After we agreed on a deal, we sent a contract to a distributor unsigned by us. The distributor was very upset, believing we didn't trust him. This would be unthinkable in his culture. There was no legal risk for us to sign it, so the

reason we didn't was probably cultural." Knowing how *not* to unintentionally give offense is an important and easily learnable business skill.

Exporting has made Solatube's domestic business stronger also. Hanley explains, "Experience in Europe and elsewhere in the world has turned us into something of a thought leader in our U.S. business dealings." Environmental practices in commercial buildings are sometimes more advanced in Europe than in the United States. Solatube has brought those ideas back to the United States and had them adopted by its U.S. customers. "It gives us a competitive advantage," Hanley says. "Also the U.S. companies we do work for overseas are eager to use us here in the United States. The international work gives us credibility."

ACTION

- **Use of Web-based channels to reach out to prospective distributors.** Your company's Web site is a good way to troll for new business. Even though English is understood widely in the global business world, it's often helpful to translate your product information into the language of the market you are entering. Contact a professional translation company to help ensure that the translation is accurate.
- **Consider using the Featured U.S. Exporter service.** Solatube used this service to find its French distributor. The service is highly targeted, and U.S. companies pay only for the cost of translating their materials. A link to your e-mail account is included. For more information, visit *www.buyusa.gov*.

- **Learn about the culture of your target markets.** Selling consumer items to Canada may require no more cultural knowledge than how to use a phone book. Selling to Paris or Pakistan, however, may not be the same. There are many good books on doing business in different cultures, and a quick visit to your local public library will be time well spent. Cultural information is also available through consultants and your local Export Assistance Center of the U.S. Commercial Service.

Based in San Diego, California, Solatube builds unique skylights with options that allow them to be transformed into light fixtures. According to Brett Hanley, Solatube's international sales vice president, sales in 2006 exceeded 160,000 units in 40 overseas markets.

METHODS AND CHANNELS

The most common methods of exporting are indirect selling and direct selling. In *indirect selling,* an export intermediary such as an export management company (EMC) or an export trading company (ETC) assumes responsibility for finding overseas buyers, shipping products, and getting paid. In *direct selling,* the U.S. producer deals directly with a foreign buyer. The paramount consideration in determining whether to market indirectly or directly is the level of resources your company is willing to devote to your international marketing effort. Other factors to consider when deciding whether to market indirectly or directly include the following:

- The size of your firm

- Tolerance for risk

- Resources available to develop the market

- The nature of your products or services

- Previous export experience and expertise

- Business conditions in the selected overseas markets

APPROACHES TO EXPORTING

The way you choose to export your products can have a significant effect on your export plan and specific marketing strategies. The various approaches to exporting relate to your company's level of involvement in the export process. There are at least four approaches that may be used alone or in combination:

1. **Passively filling orders from domestic buyers, who then export the product.** These sales are indistinguishable from other domestic sales as far as the original seller is concerned. Another party has decided that the product in question meets foreign demand. That party assumes all the risks and handles all the exporting details, in some cases even without the awareness of the original seller. (Many companies take a stronger interest in exporting when they discover that their product is already being sold overseas.)

2. **Seeking out domestic buyers who represent foreign end users or customers.** Many U.S. and foreign corporations, general contractors, foreign trading companies, foreign government agencies, foreign distributors, retailers, and others in the United States purchase for export. These buyers constitute a large market for a wide variety of goods and services. In this approach, your company may know that its product is being exported, but the domestic buyer still assumes the risks and handles the details of exporting.

3. **Exporting indirectly through intermediaries.** With this approach, your company engages the services of an intermediary firm that is capable of finding foreign markets and buyers for your products. EMCs, ETCs, international trade consultants, and other intermediaries can give you access to well-established expertise and trade contacts, but you retain considerable control over the process and can realize some of the other benefits of exporting, such as learning more about foreign competitors, new technologies, and other market opportunities.

4. **Exporting directly.** This approach is the most ambitious and challenging because your company handles every aspect of the exporting process from market research and planning to foreign distribution and payment collections. A significant commitment of management time and attention is required to achieve good results. However, this approach may also be the best way to achieve maximum profits and long-term growth. With appropriate help and guidance from the U.S. Department of Commerce, state trade offices, freight forwarders, shipping companies, international banks, and others, even small or medium-sized firms can export directly. The exporting process today is easier and has fewer steps than ever before. For those who cannot make that commitment, the services of an EMC, ETC, trade consultant, or other qualified intermediary can be of great value.

The first two approaches represent a substantial proportion of total U.S. exports. They do not, however, involve the firm in the export process. Consequently, this book concentrates on the latter two approaches. If the nature of your company's goals and resources makes an indirect method of exporting the best choice, little further planning may be needed. In such a case, the main task is to find a suitable intermediary firm that can handle most export details. Firms that are new to exporting or are unable to commit staff and funds to more complex export activities may find indirect methods of exporting more appropriate.

However, using an EMC or other intermediary does not exclude the possibility of direct exporting for your firm. For example, your company may try exporting directly to nearby mar-

BOX 5.1 INDIRECT VS. DIRECT EXPORTING

INDIRECT EXPORTING:

The principal advantage of indirect exporting for a smaller U.S. company is that it provides a way to enter foreign markets without the potential complexities and risks of direct exporting.

DIRECT EXPORTING:

The advantages of direct exporting for your company include more control over the export process, potentially higher profits, and a closer relationship to the overseas buyer and marketplace, as well as the opportunity to learn what you can do to boost overall competitiveness.

kets such as the Bahamas, Canada, or Mexico, while letting an EMC handle more challenging sales to Egypt or Japan. You may also choose to gradually increase the level of direct exporting once you have gained enough experience and sales volume to justify added investment.

Before making those kinds of decisions, you may want to consult trade specialists such as those at the U.S. Commercial Service. They can be helpful in determining the best approach or mix of approaches for you and your company.

DISTRIBUTION CONSIDERATIONS

Here are some points to consider when distributing your product:

• Which channels of distribution should your company use to market its products abroad?

• Where should your company produce its products, and how should it distribute them in the foreign market?

• What types of representatives, brokers, wholesalers, dealers, distributors, or end-use customers should you use?

• What are the characteristics and capabilities of the available intermediaries?

• Should you obtain the assistance of an EMC or an ETC?

Your answers from Box 2.2 in Chapter 2 can help you determine whether indirect or direct exporting methods are best for your company. See also Box 5.1.

INDIRECT EXPORTING

The principal advantage of indirect exporting for a smaller U.S. company is that an indirect approach provides a way to enter foreign markets without the potential complexities and risks of direct exporting. Several kinds of intermediary firms provide a range of export services, and each type of firm can offer distinct advantages to your company.

Confirming Houses

Confirming houses or buying agents represent foreign firms that want to purchase your products. They seek to obtain the desired items at the lowest possible price and are paid a commission by their foreign clients. In some cases, they may be foreign government agencies or quasi-governmental firms empowered to locate and purchase desired goods. An example is a foreign government purchasing mission.

A good place to find these agents is through foreign government embassies and embassy Web sites or through the U.S. Commercial Service.

Export Management Companies

An export management company can act as the export department for producers of goods and services. It solicits and transacts business in the names of the producers it represents or in its own name for a commission, salary, or retainer plus commission. Some EMCs provide immediate payment for the producer's products by either arranging financing or directly purchasing products for resale. Typically, only larger EMCs can afford to purchase or finance exports.

EMCs usually specialize by product or by foreign market, or sometimes by both. Because of their specialization, the best EMCs know their products and the markets they serve very well and usually have well-established networks of foreign distributors already in place. This immediate access to foreign markets is one of the principal reasons for using an EMC, because establishing a productive relationship with a foreign representative may be a costly and lengthy process.

One disadvantage of using an EMC is that you may lose control over foreign sales. Most exporters are understandably concerned that their product and company image be well maintained in foreign markets. A way for your company to retain sufficient control in such an arrangement is to carefully select an EMC that can meet your company's needs and maintain close communication with you. For example, your company may ask for regular reports on efforts to market your products and may require approval of certain types of efforts, such as advertising programs or service arrangements. If your company wants to maintain this kind of relationship with an EMC, you should negotiate points of concern before entering an agreement.

Export Trading Companies

An export trading company can facilitate the export of U.S. goods and services. Like an EMC, an ETC can either act as the export department for producers or take title to the product. A special kind of ETC is a group organized and operated by producers. These ETCs can be organized along multiple- or single-industry lines and can also represent producers of competing products.

Exporters may consider applying for an Export Trade Certificate of Review under the Export Trading Company Act of 1982. A certificate of review provides limited antitrust immunity for specified export activities. For more information, see *www. trade.gov/td/oetca* or call (202) 482-5131.

Export Agents, Merchants, or Remarketers

Export agents, merchants, or remarketers purchase products directly from the manufacturer, packing and labeling the products according to their own specifications. They then sell these products overseas through their contacts in their own names and assume all risks.

In transactions with export agents, merchants, or remarketers, your firm relinquishes control over the marketing and promotion of your product. This situation could have an adverse effect on future sales abroad if your product is underpriced or incorrectly positioned in the market or if after-sales service is neglected. However, the effort required by the manufacturer to market the product overseas is very small and may lead to sales that otherwise would take a great deal of effort to obtain.

Piggyback Marketing

Piggyback marketing is an arrangement in which one manufacturer or service firm distributes a second firm's product or service. The most common piggybacking situation occurs when a U.S. company has a contract with an overseas buyer to provide a wide range of products or services.

Often, the first company does not produce all the products that it is under contract to provide, and it turns to other U.S. companies to provide the remaining products. The second U.S. company then piggybacks its products onto the international market, generally without incurring the marketing and distribution costs associated with exporting. Successful arrangements usually require that the product lines be complementary and appeal to the same customers.

DIRECT EXPORTING

The advantages of direct exporting for your company include more control over the export process, potentially higher profits, and a closer relationship to the overseas buyer and marketplace, as well as the opportunity to learn what you can do to boost overall competitiveness. However, those advantages come at a price; your company needs to devote more time, personnel, and resources to direct exporting than it would to indirect exporting.

If your company chooses to export directly to foreign markets, it usually will make internal organizational changes to support more complex functions. As a direct exporter,

FACT:
Many companies that are new to exporting choose to market indirectly through an export intermediary.

INSIGHT:
The most important consideration in determining whether to use an export intermediary is the level of staff time and effort your company is willing to devote to international marketing.

chapter
5

METHODS AND CHANNELS

you'll normally select the markets you wish to penetrate, choose the best channels of distribution for each market, and then make specific connections with overseas buyers in order to sell your product.

GETTING ORGANIZED FOR EXPORTING

A company new to exporting generally treats its export sales no differently from its domestic sales, using existing personnel and organizational structures. As international sales and inquiries increase, your company may choose to separate the management of its exports from that of its domestic sales.

The advantages of separating international from domestic business include the centralization of specialized skills needed to deal with international markets and the benefits of a focused marketing effort that is more likely to increase export sales. A possible disadvantage is that segmentation might be a less efficient use of company resources.

Your company can separate international from domestic business at different levels in the organization. For example, when you first begin to export, you may create an export department with a full- or part-time manager who reports to the head of domestic sales and marketing. At a later stage, your company may choose to increase the autonomy of the export department to the point of creating an international division that reports directly to the president. Many smaller companies absorb export sales into existing functions; such an arrangement works effectively until export sales increase significantly.

Regardless of how your company organizes its exporting efforts, the key is to facilitate the marketer's job. Good marketing skills can help your firm operate in an unfamiliar market. Experience has shown that a company's success in foreign markets depends less on the unique attributes of its products than on its marketing methods.

Once your company is organized to handle exporting, a proper channel of distribution needs to be carefully chosen for each market. These channels include sales representatives, agents, distributors, retailers, and end users.

Sales Representatives

An overseas sales representative is the equivalent of a manufacturer's representative in the United States. The representative uses your company's product literature and samples to present the product to potential buyers. Ordinarily, a representative handles many complementary lines that do not conflict. The sales representative usually works for a commission, assumes no risk or responsibility, and is under contract for a definite period of time (renewable by mutual agreement). The contract defines territory, terms of sale, method of compensation, reasons and procedures for terminating the agreement, and other details. The sales representative may operate on either an exclusive or a non-exclusive basis.

Agents or Representatives

The widely misunderstood term *agent* means a representative who normally has authority—perhaps even a power of attorney—to make commitments on behalf of the firm that he or she represents. Firms in the United States and other developed countries have stopped using that term because *agent* can imply a power of attorney. They rely instead on the term *representative.* It is important that the contract state whether the representative or agent has the legal authority to obligate your firm.

Distributors

The foreign distributor is a merchant who purchases goods from a U.S. exporter (often at a discount) and resells them for a profit. The foreign distributor generally provides support and service for the product, relieving the U.S. exporter of those responsibilities. The distributor usually carries an inventory of products and a sufficient supply of spare parts and also maintains adequate facilities and personnel for normal servicing operations. Distributors typically handle a range of non-competing, complementary products. End users do not usually buy from a distributor; they buy from retailers or dealers.

FACT:
Most companies that are new to exporting do not separate export sales from domestic sales.

INSIGHT:
As your exporting activities increase, you may need to add functions and specialized skills sets to your operation—such as foreign-language speakers.

Regardless of how your company organizes its exporting efforts, the key is to facilitate the marketer's job. Good marketing skills can help your firm operate effectively in unfamiliar markets.

The terms and length of association between your company and the foreign distributor are established by contract. Some U.S. companies prefer to begin with a relatively short trial period and then extend the contract if the relationship proves satisfactory to both parties. The U.S. Commercial Service can help you identify and select distributors and can provide general advice on structuring agreements.

Foreign Retailers

You may also sell directly to foreign retailers, although in such transactions products are generally limited to consumer lines. The growth of major retail chains in markets such as Canada and Japan has created new opportunities for this type of direct sale. The approach relies mainly on traveling sales representatives who directly contact foreign retailers, although results might also be achieved by mailing catalogs, brochures, or other literature.

The direct mail approach has the benefits of eliminating commissions, reducing travel expenses, and reaching a broader audience. For optimal results, a company that uses direct mail to reach foreign retailers should support it with other marketing activities. For more information, contact the Direct Marketing Association at *www.the-dma.org* or the U.S. Postal Service at *www.usps.com.*

American manufacturers with ties to major domestic retailers may also be able to use them to sell abroad. Many large American retailers maintain overseas buying offices and use those offices to sell abroad when practical.

Direct Sales to End Users

You may sell your products or services directly to end users in foreign countries. The buyers may be foreign government institutions or they may be businesses. The buyers can be identified at trade shows, through international publications, or by the overseas posts of the U.S. Commercial Service.

You should be aware that if a product is sold in such a direct fashion, your company is responsible for shipping, payment collection, and product servicing unless other arrangements are made. If the cost of providing these services is not built into the export price, you could have a smaller profit than you had anticipated.

If you choose to use foreign representatives, you can meet them during overseas business trips, at domestic or international trade shows, or through Web sites such as the U.S. Department of Commerce's at *www.buyusa.gov/matchmaking.* A comprehensive list of upcoming trade shows can be found at *www.export.gov/tradeevents.* There are other effective methods that you can use without leaving the United States, including e-commerce platforms. Ultimately, you may need to travel abroad to identify, evaluate, and sign up overseas representatives; however, you can save time by first conducting background research in the country you're targeting. The Commercial Service can provide the market research you need and introduce you to buyers in more than 80 countries.

FACT:
Many distribution channels are open to you, including sales representatives, agents, distributors, retailers, and end users.

INSIGHT:
The one you choose should be based on your evaluation of the following:
- Size of sales force
- Sales record
- Territorial analysis
- Product mix
- Facilities and equipment
- Marketing policies
- Customer profiles
- Principals represented
- Promotional capabilities

Contacting and Evaluating Foreign Representatives

Once your company has identified a number of potential representatives or distributors in the selected market, you should write, e-mail, or fax each one directly. Just as your firm is seeking information on the foreign representative, the representative is interested in corporate and product information on your firm. The prospective representative may want more information than your company normally provides to a casual buyer. Your firm should provide full information on its history, resources, personnel, product line, previous export activity (if any), and all other relevant matters. Your firm may wish to include a photograph or two of plant facilities and products—and even product samples when practical. You may also want to consider inviting the foreign representative to visit your company's operations. Whenever the danger of intellectual property theft is significant, you should guard against sending product samples that could be easily copied. (For more information on correspondence with foreign firms, see Chapter 17.)

Your firm should investigate potential representatives or distributors carefully before entering into an agreement with them. (See Box 5.2 for an extensive checklist of factors to consider in such evaluations.) You also need to know the following information about the representative or distributor:

- Current status and history, including background on principal officers

- Methods of introducing new products into the sales territory

- Trade and bank references

- Data on whether your firm's special requirements can be met

You should also ask for the prospective representative or distributor's assessment of the in-country market potential for your firm's products. Such information is useful in gauging how much the representative knows about your industry; it provides valuable market research as well.

Your company may obtain much of this information from business associates who work with foreign representatives. However, you should not hesitate to ask potential representatives or distributors detailed and specific questions. Suppliers have the right to explore the qualifications of those who propose to represent them overseas. Well-qualified representatives will gladly answer questions that help distinguish them from less qualified competitors. Your company should also consider other private-sector and U.S. government sources for credit checks of potential business partners.

In addition, your company may wish to obtain at least two supporting business and credit reports to ensure that the distributor or representative is reputable. By using a second credit report from a different source, you may gain new or more complete information. Reports from a number of companies are available from commercial firms and from the Commercial Service's International Company Profiles. Commercial firms and banks are also

chapter
5

METHODS AND CHANNELS

BOX 5.2 CHOOSING A FOREIGN REPRESENTATIVE OR DISTRIBUTOR

Each company should tailor the following checklist to its own needs. Key factors vary significantly according to the products and countries involved.

SIZE OF SALES FORCE

• How many field salespeople does the representative or distributor have?

• What are the short- and long-range expansion plans, if any?

• Would the representative company need to expand to accommodate your account properly? Would it be willing to do so?

SALES RECORD

• Has the sales growth of the representative company been consistent? If not, why not? Try to determine its sales volume for the past five years.

• What is the average sales volume per outside salesperson?

• What are the sales objectives of the representative or the distributor for next year? How were they determined?

TERRITORIAL ANALYSIS

• What sales territory does the representative company now cover?

• Is the sales territory consistent with the coverage you desire? If not, is the representative or distributor able and willing to expand the territory?

• Does the representative company have any branch offices in the territory to be covered? If so, are they located where your sales prospects are greatest?

• Does it have any plans to open additional offices?

PRODUCT MIX

• How many product lines does the representative company handle?

• Are these product lines compatible with yours?

• Is there any conflict of interest?

• Does it represent any other U.S. firms? If so, which ones? (names and addresses)

• Would the representative company be willing to alter its present product mix to accommodate yours?

• What is the minimum sales volume that the representative or distributor needs to justify handling your lines? Do its sales projections reflect that minimum figure? From what you know of the territory and the prospective representative or distributor, is the projection realistic?

FACILITIES AND EQUIPMENT

- Does the representative company have adequate warehouse facilities?

- What is the method of stock control?

- Does it use computers? Are they compatible with yours?

- What communications facilities does it have (fax, modem, e-mail)?

- If your product requires servicing, is the representative company equipped and qualified to perform that service? If not, is it willing to acquire the needed equipment and arrange for training? To what extent will you have to share the training cost? Are there alternative ways in the market to service the product?

- If necessary and customary, is the representative or distributor willing to inventory repair parts and replacement items?

MARKETING POLICIES

- How is the sales staff compensated?

- Does the representative company have special incentive or motivation programs?

- Does it use product managers to coordinate sales efforts for specific product lines?

- How does it monitor sales performance?

- How does the representative or distributor train its sales staff?

- Would it pay or share expenses for its sales personnel to attend factory-sponsored seminars?

CUSTOMER PROFILE

- What kinds of customers is the representative company currently contacting?

- Are its interests compatible with your product line?

- What are the key accounts?

- What percentage of the total gross receipts do those key accounts represent?

PRINCIPALS REPRESENTED

- How many principals is the representative or distributor currently representing?

- Would you be its primary supplier?

continued on next page

BOX 5.2 (CONTINUED)

• If not, what percentage of the total business would you represent? How does this percentage compare with other suppliers?

PROMOTIONAL THRUST

• Can the representative company help you compile market research information to be used in making forecasts?

• What media does it use, if any, to promote sales?

• How much of the budget is allocated to advertising? How are those funds distributed among various principals?

• Will you be expected to contribute funds for promotional purposes?

• How will the amount be determined?

• If the representative or distributor uses direct mail, how many prospects are on the mailing list?

• What type of brochure does it use to describe the companies and products that it represents?

• If necessary, can it translate your advertising copy?

• Does the representative have a Web site to promote the product?

• Can it provide product demonstrations and training if needed?

sources of credit information on overseas representatives. They can provide information directly or from their correspondent banks or branches overseas. Directories of international companies may also provide credit information on foreign firms.

Once your company has prequalified some foreign representatives, you may wish to travel to the foreign country to observe the size, condition, and location of their offices and warehouses. In addition, your company should meet each sales force and try to assess its strength in the marketplace. If traveling to each distributor or representative is difficult, you may decide to meet each of them at U.S. or worldwide trade shows. The Commercial Service can arrange the meetings; it also offers videoconferencing, which can, in many instances, replace the need to travel.

Negotiating an Agreement with a Foreign Representative

When your company has found a prospective representative that meets its requirements, the next step is to negotiate a foreign sales agreement. Export Assistance Centers provide advice to firms contemplating that step. The International Chamber of Commerce also provides useful guidelines and can be reached at (212) 703-5065 or *www.iccwbo.org.*

Most representatives are interested in your company's pricing structure and product profit potential. They are also concerned with the terms of payment; product regulation; competitors and their market shares; the amount of support provided by your firm, such as sales aids, promotional material, and advertising; training for the sales and service staff; and your company's ability to deliver on schedule.

The agreement may contain provisions that specify the actions of the foreign representative, including the following:

• Not having business dealings with competing firms (because of antitrust laws, this provision may cause problems in some European countries)

• Not revealing any confidential information in a way that would prove injurious, detrimental, or competitive to your firm

• Not entering into agreements with other parties that would be binding to your firm

• Referring all inquiries received from outside the designated sales territory to your firm for action

To ensure a conscientious sales effort from the foreign representative, the agreement should include a requirement that the representative apply the utmost skill and ability to the sale of the product for the compensation named in the contract. It may be appropriate to include performance requirements, such as a minimum sales volume and an expected rate of increase.

In drafting the agreement, you must pay special attention to safeguarding your company's interests in case the representative proves less than satisfactory. (See Chapter 10 for recommendations on specifying terms of law and arbitration.) It is vital to include an escape clause in the agreement that allows you to end the relationship safely and cleanly if the representative does not fulfill expectations. Some contracts specify that either party may terminate the agreement with written advance notice of 30, 60, or 90 days. The contract may also spell out exactly what constitutes "just cause" for ending the agreement (for example, failure to meet specified performance levels). Other contracts specify a certain term for the agreement (usually one year) but arrange for automatic annual renewal unless either party gives written notice of its intention not to renew.

In all cases, escape clauses and other provisions to safeguard your company may be limited by the laws of the country in which the representative is located. For this reason, you should learn as much as you can about the legal requirements of the representative's coun-

FACT:
Care should be taken in entering into foreign sales agreements.

INSIGHT:
Export Assistance Centers can provide counseling to U.S. companies planning to negotiate foreign sales agreements with representatives and distributors. To find an international trade specialist in your area, visit www.export.gov or call (800) USA-TRADE (800-872-8723).

try and obtain qualified legal counsel in preparing the contract. These are some of the legal questions to consider:

• How far in advance must the representative be notified of your intention to terminate the agreement? Three months satisfy the requirements of many countries, but a registered letter may be needed to establish when the notice was served.

• What is "just cause" for terminating a representative? Specifying causes for termination in the written contract usually strengthens your position.

• Which country's laws (or which international conventions) govern a contract dispute? Laws in the representative's country may forbid the representative company from waiving its nation's legal jurisdiction.

• What compensation is due to the representative on dismissal? Depending on the length of the relationship, the added value of the market that the representative created for you, and whether termination is for just cause as defined by the foreign country, you may be required to compensate the representative for losses.

• What must the representative give up if dismissed? The contract should specify the return of property, including patents, trademarks, name registrations, and customer records.

• Should the representative be referred to as an agent? In some countries, the word *agent* implies power of attorney. The contract needs to specify whether the representative is a legal agent with power of attorney.

• In what language should the contract be drafted? In most cases, the contract should be in both English and the official language of the foreign country.

Foreign representatives often request exclusivity for marketing in a country or region. It is recommended that you not grant exclusivity until the foreign representative has proven his or her capabilities or that it be granted for a limited, defined period of time, such as one year, with the possibility of renewal. The territory covered by exclusivity may also need to be defined, although some countries' laws may prohibit that type of limitation.

The agreement with the foreign representative should define what laws apply to the agreement. Even if you choose U.S. law or that of a third country, the laws of the representative's country may take precedence. Many suppliers define the United Nations Convention on

FACT:
Foreign representatives often request exclusivity for marketing in a country or region.

INSIGHT:
You should not grant exclusivity unless the foreign representative has proven capabilities. It is advisable to put a time limit on such grants.

Contracts for the International Sale of Goods (CISG, or the Vienna Convention) as the source of resolution for contract disputes, or they defer to a ruling by the International Court of Arbitration of the International Chamber of Commerce. For more information, refer to the International Chamber of Commerce arbitration page, which is accessible at *www.iccwbo.org.*

LightStream Technologies

"What would have easily taken a month on our own was accomplished in days through the Commercial Service."

—Josh Lanier, vice chairman, LightStream Technologies

THE COMPANY

Some U.S. companies add exporting as a business strategy after they have been successful domestically. Others, such as Virginia-based LightStream Technologies, which manufactures devices using ultraviolet (UV) light to purify water, build their businesses and products around exporting.

When Vice Chairman Josh Lanier and his cofounders started LightStream in 1998, they knew that water purification was a $6 billion business, largely dominated by the production and sale of chlorine. But dependence on chlorine is changing, Lanier insists, because of health and environmental problems associated with excessive chlorine use and security concerns about transporting the chemical.

Although other UV light disinfection systems exist, LightStream's product is different from conventional systems. It uses pulsed UV light, which disinfects by means of short bursts of UV light that are of much stronger intensity.

THE CHALLENGE

Lanier and his colleagues needed a fast, reliable, cost-effective way of finding distributors in key markets. They assumed their technology would be in demand, especially in developing countries, where pollution management is a primary need. "Water is a necessity of life," notes Lanier. "There are markets around the world that meet our criteria: one, an immediate need, and two, the ability to buy." But how does a startup find buyers without experiencing undue financial risk?

Lanier had a fortuitous background—experience in government relations. "Water is policy and politics," he observes, "and in working with governments and business associations in Washington, D.C., I had honed good instincts for finessing sales once I got in the door." But getting in the door was a challenge for the fledgling business.

THE SOLUTION

It remained a challenge until Lanier met Sandra Collazo, a U.S. Commercial Service trade specialist at the Northern Virginia Export Assistance Center. Collazo, whose specialties include environmental

equipment, told Lanier about a Commercial Service trade mission to India. Numerous trade missions are organized each year, some of which are specific to a country, region, or industry. Participants pay their own travel expenses, plus a fee that covers finding interested, qualified buyers.

Navigating the shoals of India's environmental sector can be tricky. Many firms are eager to partner with U.S. companies, but finding the right one is crucial. Some appear established but are financially shaky. Others present long lists of contacts but lack the network to distribute products. Choosing the right partner can take months.

This is where Collazo and her Commercial Service colleagues in India came in. As Lanier traveled to New Delhi, Mumbai, and Chennai with the trade mission, he met with representatives of companies that Commercial Service officers had prescreened to fit LightStream's needs. The schedule was hectic but worthwhile. Dozens of companies were interested in becoming LightStream Authorized Solution Providers. "We were able to survey and better understand the Indian market by participating in the trade mission," says Lanier. "What would have easily taken a month on our own was accomplished in days through the Commercial Service."

With help from the Commercial Service, Lanier whittled the list of candidates down to Subhash Projects and Marketing Ltd., a leading Indian engineering and construction firm. LightStream formed a strategic alliance with Subhash, and both companies expect sales of $15 million in India over the next five years. The agreement calls for technology transfer and joint marketing throughout India. "Subhash is a good group," says Lanier. "They're solid, they have growth potential, and they are publicly traded."

Lanier accelerated his overseas business development and took advantage of more Commercial Service products. Under the Gold Key program, U.S. businesspeople travel on their own to a market and meet potential buyers selected by Commercial Service officers. Lanier calculates that he has participated in dozens of Gold Keys around the world. Recently, he took a Gold Key trip to Europe. A cheap dollar makes LightStream's products a relative bargain in Europe right now. The Gold Key visit to Ireland concluded with a distribution agreement for the United Kingdom and South Africa, generating sales of $4.2 million, with subsequent purchases of 40 systems worth even more.

Lanier's next project is to conduct 30 Gold Keys in 30 countries. The Commercial Service will find suitable partners in each country; in turn, those companies will be asked to go to a special Web site where they can view information about LightStream. The prospective partners will then complete a questionnaire that Lanier has honed to eliminate all but the most qualified candidates. Then, Lanier will fly to meet the prospects with the help of Commercial Service officers in the market. "For a very reasonable cost, I can use this virtual Gold Key to facilitate sales to multiple markets simultaneously, knowing I have an experienced team on my side if I run into difficulties," says Lanier.

LESSONS LEARNED

For Lanier, creating LightStream and going global are "the biggest and boldest things of all I've ever done." He's learned several valuable lessons:

- **Move the company's products as close to the customer as possible.** Getting close to the customer means forging alliances in as many markets as possible. U.S. government programs can help your company form partnerships.

- **Strive for a high-quality product.** LightStream is in the process of acquiring a Six Sigma, which equates to 3.2 defects for each million opportunities for defects. Setting a standard for high quality helps a company gain and hold a valuable niche in the marketplace.

- **Remember the importance of personal relationships.** Lanier says, "Through the process of building our worldwide distribution network prior to product release, we were able to learn a great deal that has helped us restructure our organization's plans for regional operation."

ACTION

These ideas can help you find the right partner, agent, or distributor:

- **Use the U.S. Commercial Service.** Consider traveling on a trade mission, or try the Gold Key program.

- **Join business organizations.** Business organizations can help you understand government regulations, promote your industry, and keep up with the latest technical information. To find the best organization for you, consult the U.S. Chamber of Commerce at *www. uschamber.com.*

- **Conduct market research.** The Commercial Service's Country Commercial Guides, found at *www.export.gov/ mrktresearch,* are excellent preliminary resources.

Disease-free drinking water is a luxury in much of the developing world. LightStream of Reston, Virginia, makes technology that purifies water using ultraviolet light.

chapter 6

FINDING QUALIFIED BUYERS

In This Chapter

- U.S. Commercial Service programs to help you find buyers

- Department of Commerce agencies to assist you

- State and local government assistance

FACT:
Most U.S. exporters simply take orders from abroad rather than vigorously marketing their products or services.

INSIGHT:
U.S. government agencies, particularly the U.S. Commercial Service, can help you strategically increase your international sales by identifying and qualifying leads for potential buyers, distributors, and other partners.

B y now, your company has identified its most promising markets and devised a strategy to enter those markets (see Chapters 2 and 3). As discussed earlier, your company may sell directly to a customer or may use the assistance of an in-country representative (agents or distributors) to reach the end user. This chapter describes some of the sources that can help you find buyers, evaluate trade shows and missions, and generate sales.

U.S. DEPARTMENT OF COMMERCE WORLDWIDE BUYER FINDING PROGRAMS

The U.S. Department of Commerce can help exporters identify and qualify leads for potential buyers, distributors, joint venture partners, and licensees from both private and public sources. Along with its experts in various products, countries, and programs, the U.S. Department of Commerce has an extensive network of commercial officers posted in countries that represent 95 percent of the market for U.S. products.

Programs available through the U.S. Department of Commerce, including those of the U.S. Commercial Service, are listed in this section. Exporters should contact the nearest Export Assistance Center for more information or call the Trade Information Center at (800) USA-TRADE (800-872-8723). Information on these programs is also available at the Commercial Service Web site at *www.trade.gov/cs.*

BuyUSA.gov Matchmaking

BuyUSA.gov Matchmaking is a convenient online program of the U.S. Commercial Service that matches U.S. exporters with buyers and importers in overseas markets. On the basis of the profiles that companies send to BuyUSA.gov, U.S. exporters receive the information that they need to contact potential importers in the overseas markets they select. There's no need to search a database or return to check for new importers; when an importer registers with a profile that matches your export objectives, BuyUSA.gov Matchmaking will automatically notify you. Whether you contact the potential importers is up to you, so you won't receive unwanted contacts by registering for the program.

This program is available to current clients of the U.S. Commercial Service with U.S.–made ready-to-export products or services. If your company is not a current client of the U.S. Commercial Service but you are otherwise qualified for this program, find your nearest U.S. Export Assistance Center in Appendix B or at *www.export.gov/eac/* and make an appointment with a trade specialist. To register your company or to receive further information, visit *www.buyusa.gov/matchmaking.*

Commercial News USA

Commercial News USA (CNUSA) is the official U.S. Department of Commerce showcase for American-made products and services. It provides worldwide exposure for U.S. products and services through an illustrated catalog-magazine and through electronic bulletin boards. *CNUSA* is designed to help U.S. companies promote products and services to buyers in more than 145 countries. Each issue of the free bimonthly catalog-magazine reaches an estimated 400,000 readers worldwide. *CNUSA* is mailed directly to qualified recipients and is also distributed by Commercial Service personnel at U.S. embassies and consulates throughout the world.

CNUSA can help your company make sales. Its features include the following:

• **Direct response.** New customers around the world will read about your product or service and will receive information that enables them to contact you directly. Address-coded trade leads make it easy to track results.

• **Built-in credibility.** Distributed by U.S. Commercial Service officials at embassies and consulates, *CNUSA* enjoys exceptional credibility.

• **Follow-up support.** The U.S. Department of Commerce offers free individual export counseling at any of the Export Assistance Centers across the country. For the center nearest you, see Appendix B, call (800) USA-TRADE (800-872-8723), or visit *www.export.gov/eac.*

For more information, visit the *CNUSA* home page at *www.thinkglobal.us/.*

Featured U.S. Exporters

Featured U.S. Exporters (FUSE) is a directory of U.S. products presented on the Web sites of many U.S. Commercial Service offices around the world. It gives your company an opportunity to target markets in specific countries in the local language of business. This service is offered free of charge to qualified U.S. exporters seeking trade leads or representation in certain markets. To find out if your company qualifies and to request a free listing, visit *www.buyusa.gov/home/fuse.html.*

Customized Market Research

Customized market research reports use the Commercial Service's worldwide network to help U.S. exporters evaluate their sales potential in a market, choose the best new markets for their products and services, establish effective marketing and distribution strategies in their target markets, identify the competition, determine which factors are most important to overseas buyers, pinpoint impediments to exporting, and understand many other pieces of critical market intelligence. These customized reports will be built to your specifications. To order a customized market research report, contact your local Export Assistance Center (see Appendix B or *www.export.gov/eac/*).

Gold Key Matching Service

The Gold Key Matching Service is a customized buyer-finding solution offered by the Commercial Service in key export markets around the world. The service includes orientation briefings; market research; appointments with potential partners; interpreter services for meetings; and assistance in closing the deal, shipping the goods, and getting paid. To request a Gold Key Matching Service, contact your local Export Assistance Center (see Appendix B or *www.export.gov/eac/*).

International Company Profiles

An International Company Profile (ICP) is a background report on a specific foreign firm that is prepared by commercial officers of the United States Commercial Service at American embassies and consulates. These reports include the following:

- Information on the firm
- Year established
- Relative size
- Number of employees
- General reputation
- Territory covered
- Language capabilities
- Product lines handled
- Principal owners
- Financial references
- Trade references

Each ICP also contains a general narrative report by the U.S. Commercial Service officer who conducted the investigation concerning the reliability of the foreign firm.

The ICP service is offered in countries that lack adequate private-sector providers of credit and background information on local companies. Credit reports on foreign companies are available from many private-sector sources, including (in the United States) Dun and Bradstreet and Graydon International. For help in identifying private-sector sources of credit reports, contact your nearest Export Assistance Center.

International Partner Search

With the U.S. Commercial Service's International Partner Search, teams of experts in more than 80 countries work to find you the most suitable strategic partners. You provide your marketing materials and background on your company. The Commercial Service uses its strong network of international contacts to interview potential partners and to provide you with a list of up to five prescreened companies. By working only with prescreened firms that are interested in buying or selling your products and services, you save valuable time and money.

The International Partner Search allows you to obtain high-quality market information in 15 days. The search yields information on each potential partner's size, sales, years in business, and number of employees, as well as a statement from each potential partner on the marketability of your product or service. You will also receive complete contact information on key individuals among the potential partners who are interested in your company. To obtain more information or to order an International Partner Search, contact your local Export Assistance Center.

DEPARTMENT OF COMMERCE TRADE EVENT PROGRAMS

Some products, because of their nature, are difficult to sell unless the potential buyer has an opportunity to examine them in person. Sales letters and brochures can be helpful, but an actual presentation of products in the export market may prove more beneficial. One way for your company to actually present its products to an overseas market is by participating in trade events such as trade shows, fairs, trade missions, matchmaker delegations, and catalog exhibitions.

Trade fairs are "shop windows" where thousands of firms from many countries display their goods and services. They serve as a marketplace where buyers and sellers can meet with mutual convenience. Some fairs, especially in Europe, have a history that goes back centuries. Also, it is often easier for buyers from certain regions of the world to gather in Europe than the United States.

Attending trade fairs involves a great deal of planning. The potential exhibitor must take into account the following logistic considerations:

- Choosing the proper fair out of the hundreds that are held every year
- Obtaining space at the fair, along with designing and constructing the exhibit
- Shipping products to the show, along with unpacking and setting up
- Providing proper hospitality, such as refreshments, along with maintaining the exhibit
- Being able to separate serious business prospects from browsers
- Breaking down, packing, and shipping the exhibit home at the conclusion of the fair

A trade magazine or association can often provide information on major shows. Whether privately run or government sponsored, many trade shows have a U.S. pavilion that is dedicated to participating U.S. businesses. For additional guidance, contact your local Export Assistance Center or visit *www.export.gov/tradeevents.* You can find a complete list of trade events online, and you can search by country, state, industry, or date.

Examples of trade shows are Medtrade, which takes place annually and is geared toward the health care services sector, and the Automotive Aftermarket Industry Week, which is also held annually and is attended by companies in various parts of the automotive industry.

International Buyer Program

The International Buyer Program (IBP) supports major domestic trade shows featuring products and services of U.S. industries with high export potential. Commercial Service officers recruit prospective foreign buyers to attend selected trade shows. The shows are extensively publicized in targeted markets through embassy and regional commercial newsletters, catalog-magazines, foreign trade associations, chambers of commerce, travel agents, government agencies, corporations, import agents, and equipment distributors.

As a U.S. exhibitor at an IBP event, you will receive many valuable free benefits, including the following:

• Opportunities to meet with prospective foreign buyers, representatives, and distributors from all over the world who have been recruited by U.S. Commercial Service specialists in more than 150 cities overseas

• Worldwide promotion of your products and services through the *Export Interest Directory,* which is published by the show organizers and distributed to all international visitors attending the show

• Access to hundreds of current international trade leads in your industry

• Hands-on export counseling, marketing analysis, and matchmaking services by country and industry experts from the U.S. Commercial Service

• Use of an on-site international business center, where your company can meet privately with prospective international buyers, sales representatives, and business partners and can obtain assistance from experienced U.S. Commercial Service staff members

Each year, the Commercial Service selects and promotes more than 30 trade shows representing leading industrial sectors, including information technology, environmental products and services, medical equipment and supplies, food processing and services, packaging, building and construction products, sporting goods, and consumer products.

For more information, visit *www.export.gov/ibp.*

Trade Fair Certification Program

The U.S. Department of Commerce Trade Fair Certification Program is a partnership arrangement between private-sector show organizers and the International Trade Administration to assist and encourage U.S. firms to promote their products at appropriate trade fairs abroad. Certification of a U.S. organizer signals to exhibitors, visitors, and the government of the host country that the event is an excellent marketing opportunity and that participants will receive the support of the U.S. government. Certified organizers are authorized to recruit and manage a U.S. pavilion at the show. They are especially focused on attracting small and medium-sized U.S. firms that are new to the market. Certified organizers can help with all aspects of freight forwarding, customs clearance, exhibit design, and on-site services.

Certified organizers receive government assistance, such as the following:

• Designation as the official U.S. pavilion

• Authorized use of an official Commercial Service certification logo

• On-site support and counseling for U.S. exhibitors from the U.S. embassy commercial staff

• Local market information and contact lists

• Press releases and other promotion actions

• Advertising and marketing assistance from Commerce Department Export Assistance Centers

• Support letters from the secretary of commerce and the president of the United States when appropriate

• Exhibitor briefings

• Opening ceremonies, ribbon-cuttings, and dignitary liaison

For more information, visit *www.export.gov/tradeevents.*

Trade Missions

The U.S. Department of Commerce organizes or supports numerous trade missions each year. The missions involve travel to foreign countries by U.S. companies and Commerce Department employees. Participants meet face to face with prescreened international businesspeople in the market they travel to. Trade missions save U.S. companies time and money by allowing them to maximize contact with qualified distributors, sales representatives, or partners. U.S. Commercial Service missions are industry specific and target two to four countries per trip. Commercial Service specialists abroad will prescreen contacts, arrange business appointments, and coordinate logistics in advance. This preparatory effort is followed up by a one-week trip by the U.S. company to personally met with the new prospects. To learn more about trade missions, and for a list of upcoming trade missions, visit *www. export.gov/tradeevents.*

International Catalog Exhibition Program

The U.S. Commercial Service's International Catalog Exhibition Program offers U.S. companies a convenient, affordable way to stimulate interest in their products and services while never leaving the office. Commercial Service trade specialists located in international markets will translate the company profile into the local language, display the company's marketing materials, collect sales leads from interested local buyers, and then assist the U.S. company as it follows up with the local contacts. There are three types of catalog events:

• *Multistate catalog exhibitions* target four or more promising international markets, promote U.S. exports in 20 or more high-demand product and service sectors, and leverage the partnership between the Department of Commerce and state economic development agencies.

• *American Product Literature Centers* target a single promising international market, focus on a single industry sector, and typically take place at a leading industry trade show.

• *U.S. embassy and consulate–sponsored catalog exhibits* target a single promising international market and are managed by a U.S. embassy or consulate.

For all three types of catalog events, the U.S. Commercial Service will coordinate support from local chambers of commerce, industry associations, and other trade groups; provide trade leads generated by each exhibition; and help capitalize on leads by providing any needed export assistance. For a complete list of catalog events, visit *www.export.gov/tradeevents*.

U.S. DEPARTMENT OF AGRICULTURE, FOREIGN AGRICULTURAL SERVICE

Through a network of counselors, attachés, trade officers, commodity analysts, and marketing specialists, the Department of Agriculture's Foreign Agricultural Service (FAS) can help arrange contacts overseas and provide marketing assistance for companies that export agricultural commodities. Extensive information on the FAS is also available on the Internet. Visit the Department of Agriculture FAS Web site at *www.fas.usda.gov*.

U.S. AGENCY FOR INTERNATIONAL DEVELOPMENT

The U.S. Agency for International Development (USAID) administers programs that offer export opportunities for U.S. suppliers of professional technical assistance services and commodities. Opportunities to export commodities are available through the commodity import programs that USAID operates in select USAID-recipient countries and through USAID's direct procurement of commodities. In addition, USAID funds may be available in certain recipient countries to finance developmentally sound projects involving U.S. capital goods and services. For exporters traveling to developing countries where a USAID program is in place, information is available on funds, projects under consideration, and contacts. Talk to someone at the nearest Export Assistance Center or call (800) USAID-4U (800-872-4348). The USAID Web site may be accessed at *www.usaid.gov*.

U.S. TRADE AND DEVELOPMENT AGENCY

The U.S. Trade and Development Agency (TDA) assists in the creation of jobs for Americans by helping U.S. companies pursue overseas business opportunities. Through the funding of feasibility studies, orientation visits, specialized training grants, business workshops, and various forms of technical assistance, TDA helps American businesses compete for infrastructure and industrial projects in emerging markets.

TDA's mission is to help companies get in on the ground floor of export opportunities and to make them competitive with heavily subsidized foreign companies. Because of its focused mission, TDA considers only infrastructure and industrial projects that have the potential to mature into significant export opportunities for American companies and to create jobs in the United States. Projects are typically in the areas of agriculture, energy and power, health care, manufacturing, mining and minerals development, telecommunications, transportation, and environmental services.

To be considered for TDA funding, projects

• Must face strong competition from foreign companies that receive subsidies and other support from their governments

• Must be a development priority of the country where the project is located and have the endorsement of the U.S. embassy in that nation

• Must represent an opportunity for sales of U.S. goods and services that is many times greater than the cost of TDA assistance

• Must be likely to receive implementation financing and have a procurement process open to U.S. firms

Contact TDA at (703) 875-4357, or visit its Web site at *www.tda.gov* for more information.

STATE AND LOCAL GOVERNMENT ASSISTANCE

Most states can provide an array of services to exporters. Many states maintain international offices in major markets; the most common locations are in Western Europe and Japan.

FACT:

According to the World Health Organization, diarrhea causes 1.6 million deaths every year—the vast majority among children under five years. Those deaths are related to unsafe water, sanitation, and hygiene. More than a billion people lack access to a clean water source.

INSIGHT:

By building infrastructure in the developing world, U.S. companies are improving the quality of life of millions of people and are saving lives.

Working closely with the commercial sections of U.S. embassies in those countries, state foreign offices can assist exporters in making contacts in foreign markets, providing such services as the following:

- Specific trade leads with foreign buyers

- Assistance for trade missions, such as itinerary planning, appointment scheduling, travel, and accommodations

- Promotional activities for goods or services, including representing the state at trade shows

- Help in qualifying potential buyers, agents, or distributors

In addition, some international offices of state development organizations help set up and promote foreign buyer missions to the United States, which can be effective avenues of exporting with little effort. Attracting foreign investment and developing tourism are also very important activities of state foreign offices. More and more cities and counties are providing these same services.

PROMOTION IN PUBLICATIONS AND OTHER MEDIA

A large and varied assortment of magazines covering international markets is available to you through U.S. publishers. They range from specialized international magazines relating to individual industries, such as construction, beverages, and textiles, to worldwide industrial magazines covering many industries. Many consumer publications produced by U.S.–based publishers are also available. Several are produced in national-language editions (e.g., Spanish for Latin America), and some offer "regional buys" for specific export markets of the world. In addition, several business directories published in the United States list foreign representatives geographically or by industry specialization.

Publishers frequently supply potential exporters with helpful market information, make specific recommendations for selling in the markets they cover, help advertisers locate sales representation, and render other services to aid international advertisers.

Many of these magazines and directories are available at libraries, Export Assistance Centers, or the U.S. Department of Commerce's reference room in Washington, D.C. State departments of commerce, trade associations, business libraries, and major universities may also provide such publications.

CASE STUDY:

SCIFIT Systems Inc.

"I have the best job in the world. I travel around visiting friends."

—Bo Young, vice president of international sales, SCIFIT Systems Inc.

THE COMPANY

In the late 1980s, Bo Young had an idea for a business and, with some partners, approached venture capitalists in Tulsa, Oklahoma. At first, the business focused on equipment to help people with disabilities in their homes. Young remembers burning through the investment money pretty fast with limited success in building the business. He needed a new approach.

In 1995, Young and his partners formed SCIFIT Systems Inc, with new product lines such as physical therapy equipment and exercise machines. Young and his colleagues predicted that the wellness market was moving toward an emphasis on physical fitness.

THE CHALLENGE

The new formula worked. SCIFIT now has 50 employees, including engineers and other specialists. The main customers are fitness clubs and hospitals. But would SCIFIT find customers overseas?

THE SOLUTION

Rather than waiting until the company was firmly established in its home market, SCIFIT pursued international sales from the beginning. To Young's surprise, his U.S. competitors were not well known overseas. Young found his first international clients by accident: "An Irishman, who'd read about us on our Web site, called me one day from San Francisco. 'I'll pay your expenses if you come to visit us,' I told him." He came, Young paid, and the visitor became a distributor for SCIFIT.

Exporting expanded quickly. Exports now account for nearly 20 percent of sales and are growing by about 15 percent per year. SCIFIT has customers in more than 30 countries.

In these markets, SCIFIT has received assistance from trade specialists at the U.S. Commercial Service. Young recalls working with the Commercial Service years ago, before SCIFIT was an idea: "I was 30 and with a new company. I called the organization. Don't remember why. It was telexes then, and the trade specialist sent a bunch to her colleagues abroad. I got inundated with requests, and I got into all kinds of new markets."

To market SCIFIT abroad, Young sought Commercial Service expertise again. "Thanks to my previous work with the Commercial Service and my own experience, I know a lot about the export process, including financing, trade law, and logistics," he says. "But the Commercial Service saves me time and money, and the legitimacy the U.S. government gives me in market after market is just invaluable."

SCIFIT's fastest market entry was into Brazil. In August 2005, Young did prep work with the Tulsa Commercial Service office and the Commercial Service office in São Paulo. He traveled to São Paulo later that month and attended a fitness trade show there in September. In October, he was selling products.

He was assisted in São Paulo by Commercial Service specialist Patricia Marega, who follows the Brazilian fitness industry and spends time cultivating distributors. Young used the Gold Key Matching Service in São Paulo and Rio de Janeiro and received matches with overseas buyers and distributors. "Patricia did a great job researching the market for us," he says. "We had 20 interviews in four days. The Commercial Service people asked great questions of the candidates. If I wasn't covering my butt, Patricia was."

"Bo was extremely impressed with one of our local clients, Pórtico Artigos Esportivos," says Maregas. "We went to their factory and met their distributor. The fact that the U.S. Commercial Service was accompanying Bo to this meeting made the Brazilians comfortable."

"We settled on one distributor for the entire country," says Young, "because we found that if you have more, they start competing with each other and pretty soon they're cutting the prices on each other." That distributor wanted SCIFIT's equipment for a trade show only a month after closing the deal. A month is normally not enough time to ship large pieces of equipment, but Marega successfully expedited the goods through customs in time for the show.

LESSONS LEARNED

It took three months for SCIFIT to enter Brazil, but six years to enter Japan. Does this mean your business should forget about Japan? No, says Young, you can learn things of value about your business, your products, and yourself from every market you enter. "The Japanese will absolutely improve your product," he says. "They can see more things wrong with what you make than any other culture. They'll check everything. 'On the left side of this piece of equipment you have two different screws. Why?' If our software has 20 stages in it, they'll suggest a way to reduce it to 10. These insights are very valuable to our competitiveness in all markets."

SCIFIT also learned from other markets. In England, SCIFIT partnered with the U.K. government to improve its paint bases and to add instructions in Braille. "Australians helped us identify a new and better tread for our treadmill

machines," Young says. "We tell them, 'Don't be afraid to tell us how we can improve our products.'"

Young learned that international business is about relationships. "We Americans tend to be colder or in too big of a hurry," he observes. "Building relationships has become a mantra in our company. Invite your customers home. Stay in their homes. Send flowers when they're in the hospital. Remember birthdays of wives and children. When my daughter got married, she got gifts from my distributors."

Young laments that U.S. business-people are on the whole "myopic." "Mention a letter of credit and people's eyes glaze over. Most people don't even have passports. If they only knew what's possible. I have the best job in the world. I travel around visiting friends."

ACTION

Here are some ways you can start learning about other markets:

- **Find a Commercial Service office in your target market.** Select the link for your country of interest at *www. buyusa.gov/home/ worldwide_us.html.*

On the country Web sites, you'll find local trade events, directories of specialists in your industry, and links to other useful information. Be sure to visit the Featured U.S. Exporter showcase, which is available on most Commercial Service country Web sites and includes product descriptions and links to the exporter's Web site.

- **Visit trade shows.** Trade shows are a proven way of generating sales. The Commercial Service certifies more than 100 overseas trade shows that have U.S. pavilions, and it recruits international buyer delegations for more than 40 major U.S. trade shows. For a complete list of shows, updated weekly, visit *www.export.gov/ tradeevents.*

Larry Born, chief executive officer (left), poses with Nikki Frasier, international sales coordinator (center), and Bo Young, vice president of inter-national sales (right), at SCIFIT's headquarters in Tulsa, Oklahoma. Young is now selling physical therapy equipment and exercise machines to fitness centers and hospitals worldwide.

chapter 7

USING TECHNOLOGY LICENSING AND JOINT VENTURES

You should consider two alternative ways of obtaining international sales income: technology licensing and joint ventures. Although not necessarily the most profitable forms of exporting, they do offer certain advantages, particularly for small and medium-sized businesses.

TECHNOLOGY LICENSING

Technology licensing is a contractual arrangement in which the licenser's patents, trademarks, service marks, copyrights, trade secrets, or other intellectual property may be sold or made available to a licensee for compensation that is negotiated in advance between the parties. This compensation may be a lump-sum royalty, a running royalty (royalty that is based on volume of production), or a combination of both. U.S. companies frequently license their technology to foreign companies that then use it to manufacture and sell products in a country or group of countries defined in the licensing agreement.

A technology licensing agreement usually enables your firm to enter a foreign market quickly, and it poses fewer financial and legal risks than owning and operating a foreign manufacturing facility or participating in an overseas joint venture. Licensing also permits U.S. firms to overcome many of the tariff and non-tariff barriers that frequently hamper the export of U.S.–manufactured products. For these reasons, licensing can be a particularly attractive method of "exporting" for small companies or companies with little international trade experience, even though small and large firms profitably use this technique. Technology licensing may also be used to acquire foreign technology through cross-licensing agreements or grant-back clauses that award rights to improved technology developed by a licensee. Seek legal advice to determine liability where licensing is involved.

Technology licensing is not limited to the manufacturing sector. Franchising is also an important form of technology licensing used by many service industries (see Box 7.1). In franchising, the franchiser (licenser) permits the franchisee (licensee) to use its trademark or service mark in a contractually specified manner for the marketing of goods or services. The franchiser usually continues to support the operation of the franchisee's business by providing advertising, accounting, training, and related services. In many instances, the franchiser also supplies products needed by the franchisee.

Franchising is not the exclusive domain of well-known brands. Scores of new franchising concepts are converted into profitable businesses every year, and the majority are created in the United States. Among recent franchising concepts that have gone global are personal fitness, flowers and candy, and elder care. Many of the franchises are being created especially for entreprenuers in developing countries and feature relatively affordable license fees and other inputs. Attending the International Franchise Association convention and trade fair is a good way to learn about trends and new franchising concepts. For information, visit *www.franchise.org*.

As a form of "exporting," technology licensing has certain potential drawbacks. One negative aspect of licensing is that your control over the technology is weakened because it has been transferred to an unaffiliated firm. Additionally, licensing usually produces fewer profits for your company than exporting actual goods or services. In certain developing

FACT:
Companies in a wide variety of industries enter joint ventures as a way of obtaining revenue from overseas operations.

INSIGHT:
By forming partnerships or conglomerates, companies can share risk and expertise.

BOX 7.1 ABOUT FRANCHISING

Many new small business owners choose franchising over starting a new business because it provides easy access to an established product, reduces many of the risks involved in opening a new business, gives access to proven marketing methods, and, in some instances, furnishes assistance in obtaining startup capital from financing sources.

BOX 7.2 WHAT YOU SHOULD KNOW ABOUT INTELLECTUAL PROPERTY

Do you have a strategy to protect your company's intellectual property while making sales in international markets?

If not, consider the following:

• A foreign company can appropriate your intellectual property in a foreign country before your company has even marketed in that country or in the United States.

• The processes for applying for intellectual property protection differ from country to country.

Although effective intellectual property management should be a key element of every company's day-to-day business strategy, it is essential when doing business internationally.

countries, there also may be problems in adequately protecting the licensed technology from unauthorized use by third parties (see Box 7.2).

You should make sure to register your patents and trademarks in this country. Copyright is recognized globally, but your patents and trademarks are territorial, meaning that rights are defined and interpreted differently. For this reason, you need to file your patents and trademarks with each country you intend to do business in. An exception is the European Union (EU), because its laws apply to all members. The Patent Cooperative Treaty and the Madrid Protocol allow you to register your patents and trademarks in your home country and apply for protection in the EU as well as in specific countries throughout the world. For more information and instructions for applying, visit *www.stopfakes.gov* and *www.uspto.gov.*

In considering the licensing of technology, remember that foreign licensees may attempt to use the licensed technology to manufacture products in direct competition with the licenser or its other licensees. In many instances, U.S. licensers may wish to impose territorial restrictions on their foreign licensees, depending on U.S. and foreign antitrust laws as well as the licensing laws of the host country. Also, U.S. and foreign patent, trademark, and copyright laws can often be used to bar unauthorized sales by foreign licensees, provided that the U.S. licenser has valid patent, trademark, or copyright protection in the United States or the other countries.

Many countries, particularly the 27 member states of the European Union, also have strict antitrust laws that affect technology licensing. The European Union has issued a detailed regulation, known as the *block exemption regulation,* governing patent and know-how licensing agreements as well as design and model rights and software copyright licenses. The block exemption regulation is Commission Regulation (EC) No. 772/2004 of April 27, 2004, and deals with the application of article 81(3) of the Treaty of Rome to categories of technology transfer agreements. If you are currently licensing or contemplating licensing technology to the European Union, you should carefully consider the regulation.

Because of the potential complexity of international technology licensing agreements, your company should seek qualified legal advice in the United States before entering into such an agreement. In many instances, U.S. licensers should also retain qualified legal counsel in the host country in order to obtain advice on applicable local laws and to receive assistance in securing the foreign government's approval of the agreement. Sound legal advice and thorough investigation of the prospective licensee and the host country will increase the likelihood that your licensing agreement will be a profitable transaction.

JOINT VENTURES

In some cases, joint ventures provide the best partnerlike manner of obtaining foreign trade income. International joint ventures are used in a wide variety of manufacturing, mining, and service industries, and they frequently involve technology licensing by the U.S. company to the joint venture.

Host country laws may require that a certain percentage (often 51 percent or more) of manufacturing or mining operations be owned by nationals of that country, thereby limiting U.S. companies' local participation to minority shares of joint ventures. Despite such legal requirements, as a U.S. firm you may find it desirable to enter into a joint venture with a foreign firm to help spread the high costs and risks frequently associated with foreign operations. The local partner will likely bring to the joint venture its knowledge of the customs and tastes of local consumers, an established distribution network, and valuable business and political contacts.

There are some possible disadvantages to international joint ventures. A major potential drawback, especially in countries that limit foreign companies to minority participation, is the loss of effective managerial control. As a result, you may experience reduced profits, increased operating costs, inferior product quality, exposure to product liability, and environmental litigation and fines. U.S. firms that wish to retain effective managerial control

FACT:
Domestic and overseas trade shows can help small firms find technology licensing and joint venture opportunities, and U.S. government assistance is also available at many of them.

INSIGHT:
German trade shows, both vertical and horizontal, are among the biggest international shows in the world.

will find this issue important in negotiations with the prospective joint venture partner and the host government.

Because of the complex legal issues frequently raised by international joint venture agreements, you should seek legal advice from qualified U.S. counsel before entering into such an agreement. Many of the export counseling sources discussed in Chapter 4 can help direct you to legal counsel suitable for your needs.

U.S. companies contemplating international joint ventures should consider retaining experienced counsel in the host country as well. You may be at a disadvantage if you rely on your potential joint venture partners to negotiate host government approvals and to advise you on legal issues, because the interests of the prospective partners may not always coincide with your own. Qualified foreign counsel can be very helpful in obtaining government approvals and providing ongoing advice regarding the host country's intellectual property, tax, labor, corporate, commercial, antitrust, and exchange control laws.

Spancrete Machinery Corporation

"There's just no doubt that selling overseas has made SMC a more effective exporter and our products more competitive."

—Terry Dittrich, international sales manager, Spancrete Machinery Corporation

Construction quality in China is improving, and some of the credit for better building goes to U.S. firms like Wisconsin-based Spancrete Machinery Corporation (SMC), makers of machines that produce precast reinforced concrete floor and wall panels. How SMC engineered its way into China provides a model that may benefit other U.S. firms eager to sell to this booming market of 1.3 billion consumers.

THE COMPANY

SMC, a division of the Spancrete Group, employs 45 people in its Waukesha, Wisconsin, production facility. The firm, founded by Henry Nagy, manufactured the first precast hollow-core slabs in North America in 1952. SMC, which sells its equipment worldwide under license agreements and direct sales, is a client of the U.S. Commercial Service Export Assistance Center in Milwaukee.

SMC entered China in the late 1980s. It wanted to incorporate licensing agreements, but the Chinese government forbade such arrangements. SMC opted to sell the machinery outright. Nevertheless, SMC's hollow-core machines were the first foreign equipment of that type sold in China.

THE CHALLENGE

The early years were challenging, concedes Terry Dittrich, SMC's international sales manager: "Our customers were state-owned enterprises, and the Chinese government encouraged them to expand into the precast construction business, despite their limited knowledge of that sector."

THE SOLUTION

Those companies started by producing floor slabs, SMC's most basic product, but local architects and engineers had limited experience with precast products of this type. Even in a state-controlled economic system, companies need effective marketing to generate sales. To better support the companies, SMC began assisting with seminars for these state-owned enterprises and the construction community in general.

SMC's next achievement was to establish the China Spancrete Association, probably the first organization of its kind. The association is a non-profit support organization for SMC's Chinese customers, assisting them in technical, production, and marketing procedures. "At first, the Chinese didn't understand the concept of a professional association," explains Dittrich. "They said, 'Why should we pay dues to belong to something like this? Why should we cooperate with people outside of our own enterprise?' It's not how they operated. Now they can see the value and continue to expand the association's efforts."

Working through the association, SMC pooled the existing knowledge for the benefit of all members. The association tackled the lack of codes and standards, making recommendations on matters like the loads that floors can safely carry and conducting research on seismic and fire-safety issues. Ultimately, SMC, with the association, achieved the registration of Spancrete–China products in the national building and design code.

Business processes are changing rapidly in China, and competitors are getting more aggressive. Also, the economic boom has moved south and west of where it started, creating more opportunities and challenges. Recently, Dittrich used the Commercial Service's Gold Key Service and Single Company Promotion program in seven Chinese cities. The Commercial Service identified local companies interested in purchasing SMC equipment systems and coordinated meetings with key government officials. Dittrich expects significant new sales because of the introductions provided by the Commercial Service.

However, the Commercial Service alone will not ensure success. SMC must continue to build relationships, help customers succeed by finding creative solutions to their problems, and adapt its products and services to meet the needs of a dynamic marketplace.

Dittrich claims that experience in international markets has made him a more effective professional and the company more competitive. "There's just no doubt that selling overseas has made SMC a more effective exporter and our products more competitive. Our key personnel have grown from the international experience, and we continuously bring ideas back home and apply them throughout the company."

"Competition is tough in these markets, "Dittrich says, "but that's where the opportunities are. Exporting is no longer an option, and America's export future lies in these markets."

LESSONS LEARNED

For U.S. companies attempting to sell in China, Dittrich has these recommendations:

- **Find good representation.** Connections are key, as evidenced in the Chinese expression guanxi, meaning "personal relationship."

- **Try to secure payment in advance.** Equity stakes can be a problem, given the limitations of the Chinese legal framework and challenges of business transparency, and Americans need to conduct thorough due diligence.

- **Keep the product simple.** The more complex the product, the more things can go wrong.

- **Talk to your Chinese business partners about taking a long-term perspective.** American companies need to make a long-term and sustained commitment to these emerging markets if they are to successfully build lasting relationships. Encourage your Chinese partners to take a similar long-term perspective.

ACTION

Here's what you can do to help your business succeed in China:

- **Visit the China Business Information Center**. For useful, comprehensive information on the Chinese market, go to *www.export.gov/china*. Of particular interest is the self-assessment, which asks, "Are you China ready?"

- **Investigate Web sites for manufacturers.** Manufacturing firms should check out the National Association of Manufacturers export portal at *www.nam.org*. If you're seeking help to make your manufacturing processes more competitive, learn about the services of the U.S. Department of Commerce's Manufacturing Extension Program at *www.mep.nist.gov*.

Spancrete Machinery Corporation of Waukesha, Wisconsin, has found China to be a key market for its machinery that produces precast concrete floors and wall panels. Terry Dittrich (center), international sales manager, is pictured here with other senior SMC managers and Chinese business partners.

PREPARING YOUR PRODUCT FOR EXPORT

Selecting and preparing your product for export require not only product knowledge but also knowledge of the unique characteristics of each target market. Market research and contacts with foreign partners, buyers, customers, and others should give your company an idea of what products can be sold and where. However, before the sale can occur, your company may need to modify a particular product to satisfy buyer tastes, needs in foreign markets, or legal requirements for the foreign destination.

The extent to which your company will be willing to modify products sold for export markets is a key policy issue to be addressed by management. Some exporters believe that their domestic products can be exported without significant changes. Others seek to consciously develop uniform products that are acceptable in all markets. It is very important to do research and to be sure of the right strategy to pursue. For example, you may need to redesign an electrical product to run on a different level of voltage for a particular destination, or you may need to redesign packaging to meet labeling standards or cultural preferences.

If your company manufactures more than one product or offers many models of a single product, you should start by exporting the one best suited to the targeted market. Ideally, your company may choose one or two products that fit the target market without major design or engineering modifications. Doing so works best when your company

- Deals with international customers that have the same demographic characteristics or the same specifications for manufactured goods

- Supplies parts for U.S. goods that are exported to other countries without modifications

- Produces a unique product that is sold on the basis of its status or international appeal

• Produces a product that has few or no distinguishing features and that is sold almost exclusively on a commodity or price basis

QUESTIONS TO CONSIDER

You must consider several issues when you are thinking of selling overseas, including the following:

• What foreign needs does your product satisfy?

• What products should your company offer abroad?

• Should your company modify its domestic-market product for sale abroad? Should it develop a new product for the foreign market?

• What specific features, such as design, color, size, packaging, brand, labels, and warranty, should your product have? How important are language or cultural differences?

• What specific services are necessary abroad at the presale and postsale stages? Warranties? Spare parts?

• Are your firm's service and repair facilities adequate?

PRODUCT ADAPTATION

To enter a foreign market successfully, your company may have to modify its product to conform to government regulations, geographic and climatic conditions, buyer preferences, or standards of living. Your company may also need to modify its product to facilitate shipment or to compensate for possible differences in engineering and design standards. Foreign government product regulations are common in international trade and are expected to expand in the future. These regulations can take the form of high tariffs, or they can be non-tariff barriers, such as industrial regulations or product specifications. Governments impose these regulations

• To protect domestic industries from foreign competition

• To protect the health and safety of their citizens

• To force importers to comply with environmental controls

• To ensure that importers meet local requirements for electrical or measurement systems

• To restrict the flow of goods originating in or having components from certain countries

• To protect their citizens from cultural influences deemed inappropriate

Detailed information on regulations imposed by foreign countries is available from the Trade Information Center at (800) USA-TRADE (800-872-8723) or from your local Export Assistance Center. When a foreign government imposes particularly onerous or discriminatory barriers, your company may be able to obtain help from the U.S. government to press for their removal. Your firm should contact an Export Assistance Center or the Office of the U.S. Trade Representative (USTR). The USTR office can be contacted at (202) 395-3230 or at *www.ustr.gov.*

Buyer preferences in a foreign market may also lead you to modify your product. Local customs, such as religious practices or the use of leisure time, often determine whether a product is marketable. The sensory impression made by a product, such as taste or visual effect, may also be a critical factor. For example, Japanese consumers tend to prefer certain kinds of packaging, leading many U.S. companies to redesign cartons and packages that are destined for the Japanese market.

Market potential must be large enough to justify the direct and indirect costs involved in product adaptation. Your firm should assess the costs to be incurred and, though it may be difficult, should determine the increased revenues expected from adaptation. The decision to adapt a product is based partly on the degree of commitment to the specific foreign market; a firm with short-term goals will probably have a different perspective than a firm with long-term goals.

FACT:
Language and cultural factors have played an important role in the success or failure of many exporting efforts.

INSIGHT:
Be careful to look into the meanings that your company's (or product's) name may have in other markets. You don't want to discover too late that they are inappropriate in the local language or culture.

chapter **8**

PREPARING YOUR PRODUCT

ENGINEERING AND REDESIGN

In addition to adaptations related to cultural and consumer preference, your company should be aware that even fundamental aspects of products may require changing. For example, electrical standards in many foreign countries differ from U.S. electrical standards. It's not unusual to find phases, cycles, or voltages (for both residential and commercial use) that would damage or impair the operating efficiency of equipment designed for use in the United States. Electrical standards sometimes vary even within the same country. Knowing the requirements, the manufacturer can determine whether a special motor must be substituted or if a different drive ratio can be achieved to meet the desired operating revolutions per minute.

Similarly, many kinds of equipment must be engineered in the metric system for integration with other pieces of equipment or for compliance with the standards of a given country. The United States is virtually alone in its adherence to a non-metric system, and U.S. firms that compete successfully in the global market realize that conversion to metric measurement is an important detail in selling to overseas customers. Even instruction or maintenance manuals should take care to give dimensions in centimeters, weights in grams or kilos, and temperatures in degrees Celsius. Information on foreign standards and certification systems is available from the National Center for Standards and Certificates Information, National

Institute of Standards and Technology, U.S. Department of Commerce, 100 Bureau Dr., M.S. 2150, Gaithersburg, MD 20899-2150. You may also contact the center by telephone at (301) 975-4040 or online at *www.nist.gov.*

BRANDING, LABELING, AND PACKAGING

Consumers are concerned with both the product itself and the product's secondary features, such as packaging, warranties, and service. Branding and labeling products in foreign markets raise new considerations for your company, such as the following:

• Are international brand names important to promote and distinguish a product? Conversely, should local brands or private labels be used to heighten local interest?

• Are the colors used on labels and packages offensive or attractive to the foreign buyer? For example, in some countries certain colors are associated with death.

• Can labels and instructions be produced in official or customary languages if required by law or practice?

• Does information on product content and country of origin have to be provided?

• Are weights and measures stated in the local unit? Even with consumer products, packaging and describing contents in metric measurements (e.g., kilograms, liters) can be important.

• Must each item be labeled individually? What is the language of the labeling? For example, "Made in U.S.A." may not be acceptable; the product may need to be labeled in the language spoken by the country's consumers. There may be special labeling requirements for foods, pharmaceuticals, and other products.

• Are local tastes and knowledge considered? A cereal box with the picture of a U.S. athlete on it may not be as attractive to overseas consumers as the picture of a local sports hero.

INSTALLATION

Another element of product preparation that your company should consider is the ease of installing the product overseas. If technicians or engineers are needed overseas to assist in

FACT:
Freight charges are usually assessed by weight or volume.

INSIGHT:
Consider shipping items unassembled to reduce delivery costs. Shipping unassembled goods also facilitates movement on narrow roads or through doorways and elevators. Remember, however, that while shipping your items unassembled can save your firm shipping costs, it could delay payment if the sale is contingent on receipt of an assembled product.

installation, your company should minimize their time in the field if possible. To do so, your company may wish to preassemble or pretest the product before shipping or to provide training for local service providers through the Web, training seminars, or DVDs.

Your company may consider disassembling the product for shipment and reassembling it abroad. This method can save your firm shipping costs, but it may delay payment if the sale is contingent on an assembled product. Your company should be careful to provide all product information, such as training manuals, installation instructions (even relatively simple instructions), and parts lists, in the local language.

WARRANTIES

Your company should consider carefully the terms of a warranty on the product (and be very specific as to the warranty's coverage), because the buyer will expect a specific level of performance and a guarantee that it will be achieved. Levels of expectation and rights for a warranty vary by country, depending on the country's level of development, its competitive practices, the activism of consumer groups, the local standards of production quality, and other factors. Product service guarantees are important because customers overseas typically have service expectations as high or greater than those of U.S. customers.

CASE STUDY:
Falcon Waterfree Technologies

"With a small team, you can accomplish great things."

—Ditmar Gorges, executive vice president, Falcon Waterfree Techologies

THE COMPANY

A water shortage spurred the idea. Perhaps 5 percent of fresh water is literally flushed away in urinals around the world. There had to be a better way—so thought Ditmar Gorges, co-inventor of a water-free urinal. Now, thanks to his company, Falcon Waterfree Technologies, the little cartridges that absorb urine without the need for water are becoming a staple in male restrooms across the globe.

It took more than a good idea to build a successful business and a patented product, says Gorges, a mechanical engineer by training who went back to school for a master's degree in economics. "We began," says Gorges, "with the intent of retrofitting toilets and saving users a lot of money in water and sewer fees. Water is scarce and becoming scarcer in many parts of the world, and it's too costly in economic and environmental terms to flush it down the drain."

From these small beginnings, Falcon Waterfree now has offices in Grand Rapids, Michigan, and Los Angeles, California, where the research and development are done, and its products sell in 48 countries worldwide.

THE CHALLENGE

Falcon Waterfree began selling in foreign countries in 1995. The company has two competitors in the United States, six in Europe, and so far none in Asia, where it is hurrying to take advantage of an open playing field: a 100 percent market share of retrofitted waterless urinals and infinite growth in public restrooms. Gorges said Falcon Waterfree's number one position seems secure for the moment because "our technology is different than the competition's, and customers tell us that ours is easier to use." Falcon Waterfree's sales worldwide are bubbling up smartly at about 140 percent per year.

But Gorges is far from complacent. "Our technology seems bullet proof at the moment, but we need to constantly improve. We are working to make the cartridges last longer and to be 100 percent recyclable. That's the next innovation—within the next few years."

THE SOLUTION

Gorges credits the U.S. Commercial Service with helping a small firm like his enter and find buyers in multiple markets around the world. For example, when Gorges targeted the Philippines, he received word from the Commercial Service office in Manila that the McDonald's franchiser there wanted to overhaul bathrooms in all the Manila restaurants. "Somehow, the Commercial Service got wind of this, knew our product, and called us with the lead," says Gorges. "Meetings were arranged for us, introductions were made, and it wasn't long before we had the contract."

Other benefits followed. The McDonald's put a sign over the urinals touting their environmental friendliness. The owner of a five-star hotel in Manila was so impressed that he ordered them installed in the hotel's public restrooms.

And that wasn't all. The McDonald's chain asked if Falcon Waterfree could put the gold arches logo on the urinal ceramic bowl. Gorges said, "Why not?" And soon male customers were asking if they could buy the golden arches waterless urinal at the counter along with their Big Macs. They couldn't, but the importance of word of mouth and the market intelligence capabilities of the Commercial Service were not lost on Gorges.

Gorges signed up with the Commercial Service office in Japan for long-term technical assistance that included research on building codes, meetings with government officials, and introductions to the best people to talk to in companies that could make suitable business partners. "Companies in Asia and elsewhere in the world seem to respect the U.S. government presence in our meetings. You get the sense that they are on their best behavior," says Gorges.

A Commercial Service representative attended 24 meetings between Falcon Waterfree and a Japanese urinal manufacturer that became the leading suitor. In the end, a deal was signed, and Falcon Waterfree now has a strong foothold in this important market. Says Gorges, "The Commercial Service was invaluable to us. They gave us insight on the business culture and how the Japanese viewed the terms of the contract. They had unbelievable market intelligence. In market after market, they knew. No one else did."

Gorges was particularly pleased when his Japanese partners told him later, "The Japanese government doesn't provide us this level of assistance. When we go to places like China, we are on our own. You Americans have the edge. You are lucky."

But Gorges knows that he has the edge only if he uses it, and he aims to—everywhere he can. His product seems to be cleaning up in some surprising places, including India's Taj Mahal, where a solution was needed that didn't require installing piping in ancient walls, and the Austrian Alps, where he had

the distinction of outfitting the highest restroom in the world.

LESSONS LEARNED

Gorges finds that adapting his product to new markets has been among the most useful lessons he's learned. Different cultures have different "bathroom cultures," and recognizing these differences was key to adapting the product. Gorges explains that urinals are round in European countries and square in Asian countries. Also, different cultures clean toilets differently. Europeans use sponges and cloth wipes, but Japanese prefer to keep their distance from the cleaning surfaces and tend to use brushes. These differences are important when writing instruction manuals for use of the products.

He also learned that different cultures have shorter time horizons for getting to know you and deciding to buy. In Europe and some Asian countries, this process can happen quickly. But other places take more time. In Japan, for example, it took Falcon Waterfree five years to make its first major sale.

A final lesson is how quickly and profitably a small company, which has grown to 167 employees, was able to generate sales in international markets. Gorges says of his company's many accomplishments, "With a small team, you can accomplish great things."

ACTION

How can your company accomplish great things? Here are some ideas:

- **Let the Commercial Service help you find international partners.** Visit *www.export.gov/tradeleads*.
- **Research the countries.** For more information about best prospects in Austria, China, India, Japan, and the Philippines, consult the Country Commercial Guides in the Market Research Library at *www.export.gov/mrktresearch*. In addition, you can link to the Commercial Service Web sites in these and more than 80 other countries at *www.export.gov*.

China is a growing market for Falcon Waterfree Technologies, which manufactures waterless urinals. Ditmar Gorges (center), executive vice president, is pictured along with Wang Yi (left) and David Gossack (right) of the U.S. Commercial Service in China.

chapter 9

EXPORTING SERVICES

In This Chapter

- Role of the service sector in the United States and in world economies

- Differences between service and product exporting

- Places where service exporters can find assistance

FACT:
More than two-thirds of U.S. small and medium-sized exporters are non-manufacturers.

INSIGHT:
You don't have to be a manufacturer to export.

The United States is the world's premier producer and exporter of services. As the largest component of the U.S. economy, the service sector includes all private-sector economic activity other than agriculture, mining, construction, and manufacturing. The service sector accounts for nearly 80 percent of the private-sector gross domestic product (GDP) and for 90 million jobs.

In the future, the service sector will loom even larger in the U.S. economy. Small and medium-sized entrepreneurial firms—those employing fewer than 500 employees—overwhelmingly lead this service-driven business expansion. There are more than 4 million small service companies that account for more than 16 million jobs. Although small service firms make up most of the service sector, many of the most prominent U.S. service exporters are large firms. Seven of the 30 companies that constitute the widely cited Dow Jones Industrial Average are service firms.

The dominant role that services play throughout the U.S. economy translates into leadership in technology advancement, growth in skilled jobs, and global competitiveness. U.S. service exports more than doubled between 1990 and 2000—increasing from $148 billion in 1990 to $299 billion in 2000. Growth continued to $404 billion in 2006.

In 2004, U.S. service exports exceeded imports by $80 billion, offsetting 10 percent of the deficit in merchandise trade. U.S. services compete successfully worldwide. Major markets for U.S. services include the European Union ($140 billion), Japan ($41 billion), and Canada ($39 billion). At $22 billion, Mexico is the largest emerging market for U.S. service exports.

SERVICE EXPORTS WITH HIGH GROWTH POTENTIAL

The following sectors have grown most rapidly because of technology development and have particularly high export potential:

- **Travel and tourism.** The largest single category within the U.S. service sector encompasses all travel- and tourism-related businesses. As such, recreational and cultural services are included. The industry is diverse and encompasses services in transportation, lodging, food and beverage, recreation, and purchase of incidentals consumed while in transit. Export sales for this sector in 2006 were $86 billion.

- **Environmental services.** The *environmental technologies industry* is defined generally as all goods and services that generate revenue associated with environmental protection, assessment, compliance with environmental regulations, pollution control, waste management, remediation of contaminated property, design and operation of environmental infrastructure, and provision and delivery of environmental resources. The industry has evolved in response to growing concern about the risks and costs of pollution and to the enactment of pollution control legislation in the United States and around the world. The United States is the largest producer and consumer of environmental technologies in the world.

- **Transportation services.** This sector encompasses aviation, ocean shipping, inland waterways, railroads, trucking, pipelines, and intermodal services, as well as ancillary and support services in ports, airports, railyards, and truck terminals. Transportation is the indispensable service for international trade in goods, moving all manufactured, mining, and agricultural products to market as well as transporting people engaged in business, travel, and tourism. For 2006, total export sales for transportation services were more than $68 billion.

- **Banking, financial, and insurance services.** U.S. financial institutions are very competitive internationally, particularly when offering account management, credit card operations, and collection management. U.S. insurers offer valuable services, ranging from underwriting and risk evaluation to insurance operations and management contracts in the international marketplace. This sector was a $52 billion export market in 2006.

FACT: In the coming decade, the service sector is forecast to account for almost all net gains in U.S. employment, with small, medium-sized, and large companies all playing key roles in capital formation, business expansion, and new jobs.

INSIGHT: Small firms make up most of the service sector, and small service firms will play a vital role in job growth.

- **Telecommunications and information services**. This sector includes companies that generate, process, and export electronic commerce activities, such as e-mail, funds transfer, and data interchange, as well as data processing, network services, electronic information services, and professional computer services. The United States leads the world in marketing new technologies and enjoys a competitive advantage in computer operations, data processing and transmission, online services, computer consulting, and systems integration. Export sales in this sector also totaled more than $16 billion in 2006.

- **Education and training services**. Management training, technical training, and English-language training are areas in which U.S. expertise remains unchallenged. The export market for such training is almost limitless, encompassing most industry sectors for products and services. Export sales were almost $15 billion in 2006 for this sector.

- **Commercial, professional, and technical services**. This sector encompasses accounting, advertising, and legal and management consulting services. The international market for those services is expanding at a more rapid rate than the U.S. domestic market. Organizations and business enterprises all over the world look to U.S. firms as leaders in these sectors for advice and assistance. This sector represented $13 billion in export sales in 2006.

- **Entertainment**. U.S.–filmed entertainment and U.S.–recorded music have been very successful in appealing to audiences worldwide. U.S. film companies license and sell rights to exhibit films in movie theaters, on television, on videocassettes, and on DVDs and CDs. U.S. music has been successful in both English-speaking and non-English-speaking countries. The entertainment sector had more than $11 billion in export sales in 2006.

- **Architectural, construction, and engineering services**. The vast experience and technological leadership of the U.S. construction industry, as well as special skills in operations, maintenance, and management, frequently give U.S. firms a competitive edge in international projects. U.S. firms with expertise in specialized fields, such as electric-power utilities, construction, and engineering services, are similarly competitive. Exports for this sector were about $5 billion in 2006.

- **E-business**. This sector, which can be service or product oriented, is expected to grow dramatically. It is estimated that there are already 400 million Internet users worldwide—but that figure represents only about 7 percent of the world's population.

ASPECTS OF SERVICE EXPORTS

Services can be crucial in stimulating goods exports and are critical in maintaining those transactions. Many U.S. merchandise exports would not take place if they were not supported by service activities such as banking, insurance, and transportation. There are many obvious differences between services and products, including differences in tangibility and customer involvement (see Box 9.1). Because services are intangible, you may find that communicating a service offer is more difficult than communicating a product offer. Also, services frequently must be tailored to the specific needs of the client. Such adaptation often necessitates the client's direct participation and cooperation. Involving the client requires the service provider to possess interpersonal skills and cultural sensitivity.

The intangibility of services makes financing somewhat more difficult—given that no form of collateral is involved—and financial institutions may be less willing to provide financial support to your company. However, many public and private institutions will provide financial assistance to creditworthy service exporters. Trade organizations offer two important finance services under various terms and conditions. One is a guarantee program that requires the participation of an approved lender; the other program provides loans or grants to the exporter or a foreign government. Exporters who insure their accounts receivable against commercial credit and political risk loss are usually able to secure financing from commercial banks and other institutions at lower rates and on a more liberal basis than would otherwise be the case.

MARKETING SERVICES ABROAD

Because service exports may be delivered in support of product exports, you might find it sensible to follow the path of complementary product exports. For years, many large accounting and banking firms have exported by following their major international clients abroad and continuing to assist them in their international activities. Smaller service exporters who cooperate closely with manufacturing firms are operating internationally and aim to provide service support for those manufacturers abroad.

Also, your service firm may seek affiliation with a foreign firm. An agent, representative, or joint venture relationship could prove beneficial to your firm. An indigenous service

BOX 9.1 THE UNIQUE CHALLENGES OF EXPORTING SERVICES

The most obvious way in which exporting services differs from exporting goods is that you are exporting something invisible or intangible. Most likely, this will mean

• **More travel.** Without a tangible product, you may have to make special efforts to elevate the profile of your company and the credibility of its services.

• **Awareness of labor requirements.** You may be in-country for an extended period of time, or you may need to hire local workers. Be aware of your legal obligations, such as securing work permits.

• **More intensive market research.** Market research methodologies and business opportunity indicators are unique for service firms, often requiring more in-depth and detailed activities, information, and intelligence than are routine for exporting goods.

firm already has knowledge of the various aspects of marketing in a particular country, such as regulations, restrictions, primary participants, potential clients, and competitors. The indigenous firm will also have market research, exposure, and contacts that you can use to your advantage.

OBTAINING GOVERNMENT SUPPORT FOR SERVICE EXPORTS

The Manufacturing and Services unit of the Department of Commerce's International Trade Administration provides support to U.S. services exporters by conducting policy research and industry analysis, coordinating advisory committees, and advocating for U.S. interests in trade negotiations. More information is available on the Web at *http://trade.gov/mas.*

The U.S. Commercial Service, through the network of domestic U.S. Export Assistance Centers, provides counseling and assistance to services exporters. A list of Export Assistance Centers appears in Appendix B. For more information, call the Trade Information Center at 1-(800)-USA-TRADE (1-800-872-8723) or go to the U.S. government export portal, *www.export.gov.*

Two Men and a Truck

"From a practical standpoint, going international protects our brand globally and it lends credibility to the domestic market."

—Melanie Bergeron, president and chief operating officer, Two Men and a Truck

THE COMPANY

Mary Ellen Sheets never imagined herself being in the moving business—that is, until her sons Brig and Jon scraped together some money to buy a truck to help raise extra cash for college. Although they soon left the nest to attend school, Sheets knew a good idea when she saw one. In 1985, with $350, she started a company called—what else?— Two Men and a Truck. She wouldn't have to worry about moving again and, more important, neither would her customers.

"Believe it or not, moving is ranked as the third most stressful event, after death and divorce, so there is a real demand for a service that makes the customer king," says Sheets. "Our goal is to do things right the first time. The most important concern customers have about moving is that the moving company be there when it says it will."

With its emphasis on putting the customer first, it wasn't long before the Lansing, Michigan, firm was expanding its franchising concept across the United States, with Sheets serving as its founder and chief operating officer. By 2001, with her daughter, Melanie Bergeron running

day-to-day operations as president and chief operating officer, Sheets was ready to take the franchise concept internationally.

THE CHALLENGE

One of the biggest challenges for Sheets and Bergeron was that they were only just breaking into the export market. Fortunately, they had attended an International Franchise Association training seminar in Minneapolis, where they connected with Bill Edwards, president of Edwards Global Services, a consultancy company specializing in international franchising expansion. "The biggest challenges for franchisers in going global is getting accurate market research and identifying potential master franchisees," Edwards says. "In the case of Two Men and a Truck, they faced a third challenge known as market differentiation—otherwise, with plenty of moving businesses out there, why should a potential master franchisee in another country sign on with Two Men and a Truck? What makes it a cut above the rest?"

The company already had an answer to that question, as it placed an

exceptional focus on customer service and sophisticated Web-based tracking systems. Those systems would enable Two Men and a Truck's potential master franchisees to monitor quality control and to improve performance measures such as labor costs and the time it takes to complete a move. The company's tracking systems created a potentially larger profit margin as compared with other moving companies. What Two Men and a Truck needed now was solid market research and a list of highly qualified prospects to convey their business model to potential master franchisees.

THE SOLUTION

Edwards Global Services was a long-term client of the Commercial Service's Newport Beach U.S. Export Assistance Center and had used the center's export counseling and other services to help several premier franchise brands enter international markets. Among these programs was the Gold Key Service, which arranges business appointments abroad with potential foreign partners, all set up and prescreened by the Commercial Service. Would Two Men and a Truck be Edwards Global Services' next success?

By 2003, Two Men and a Truck, through Edwards Global Services, worked with the Export Assistance Center to search for a franchise partner in Ireland. The company was assisted by the U.S. Commercial Service post in Ireland, whose commercial specialists provided key market research and designed a customized search strategy that included reaching out to databases of existing and potential master licensees. An advertisement was also placed in a local business newspaper highlighting the company's search for a master licensee. Then, in December 2003, Edwards met with nine qualified prospects in Dublin. Partially as a result of those meetings and ongoing follow-up by the Commercial Service and Edwards Global Services, Two Men and a Truck signed a master license for Ireland in May 2006 with DMG Services. The agreement was valued in excess of $300,000, and it included the rights for the U.K. market.

"From a practical standpoint, going international protects our brand globally and it lends credibility to the domestic market," Bergeron says. "Exporting also makes us more competitive and allows us to diversify our portfolio and weather changes in the economy."

LESSONS LEARNED

Edwards, whose franchising clients have benefited from many Commercial Service programs over many years, has some important suggestions for franchisers looking to go global:

- **Don't cast a wide net when looking for potential partners.** Instead, use the Commercial Service to target the best prospects. "Being able to meet with reputable, motivated prospects really helped us in targeting our search efforts," he says. "Not only was it cost-effective for us, but it would have taken months longer on our own to narrow down the best prospects. The Commercial Service is a source of information, market research, and due diligence that we know we can depend on when doing business around the world."

- **Register your trademark.** "Not enough people do this, and if you don't, it can really cost you a lot of money in the long run," he says. He also recommends that franchisers invest in good market research and personnel training to increase their chances for international franchising success as buyers are becoming very sophisticated.

- **Know the culture where you are going to do business.** For example, Bergeron says that when it comes to moving there are differences. "Americans have so much stuff and bigger houses, while people in emerging markets have much less," she says. "In emerging markets, many families live together, but we are seeing a growing trend in the use of moving services as people don't wish to trouble their relatives in helping them move."

ACTION

- **Contact a business consultant.** A business consultant that is experienced in the international market can offer invaluable advice. The U.S. Commercial Service is also an excellent place to start exploring your exporting potential.

- **Use the Gold Key Service.** The Commercial Service offers this customized service in key export markets around the world. From making appointments with potential partners, to providing interpreter services for meetings, to helping you close the deal, ship the goods, and get paid, the Gold Key Service offers top-of-the-line assistance. Contact your local Export Assistance Center for more information.

Mary Ellen Sheets (left to right), founder and chief executive officer of Two Men and a Truck, is pictured along with Brig Sorber, vice president; Melanie Bergeron, president and chief operating officer; and Jon Sorber, vice president. The Lansing, Michigan, firm completed 335,000 moves last year and recently entered the Irish market.

Customs

Custom

Conn

INTERNATIONAL LEGAL CONSIDERATIONS

EXPORT REGULATIONS

The Export Administration Regulations (EAR) govern the export and reexport of items for reasons of national security, non-proliferation, foreign policy, and short supply. A relatively small percentage of exports and reexports require the submission of a license application to the U.S. Department of Commerce's Bureau of Industry and Security (BIS). Licensing is dependent on an item's technical characteristics, destination, end use, and end user (see Box 10.1). Once a classification has been determined, exporters may use a single chart, set forth in the EAR, to decide if a license is needed to export to a particular country. The regulations include answers to frequently asked questions, detailed step-by-step instructions for finding out if a transaction is subject to the regulations, instructions for requesting a commodity classification or advisory opinion, and directions for applying for a license. If you have questions about whether your products require a license, call your local Export Assistance Center or (800) USA-TRADE (800-872-8723).

Antidiversion Clause

To help ensure that U.S. exports go only to legally authorized destinations, the U.S. government requires a destination control statement on shipping documents. The commercial invoice and bill of lading (or air waybill) for nearly all commercial shipments leaving the United States must display a statement notifying the carrier and all foreign parties (the ultimate and intermediate consignees and purchaser) that the U.S. material has been approved for export only to certain destinations and may not be diverted. The minimum antidiversion statement

BOX 10.1 HOW THE EAR DEFINES PRODUCTS SUBJECT TO LICENSING

The EAR groups items (commodities, software, and technology) into 10 categories, each containing numerous entries that bear Export Control Classification Numbers (ECCNs). These entries are found in Supplement No. 1 to Part 774 of the EAR, or the Commerce Control List (CCL). The CCL and the Country Chart (Supplement No. 1 to Part 738) together define items subject to export controls solely on the basis of the technical parameters of the item and the country of ultimate destination. Items that are on the CCL but that do not require a license by reason of the Country Chart and items classified as EAR99 (see section 734.3(c) of the EAR, titled "Scope of the EAR") are designated as "NLR," or "no license required."

for goods exported under U.S. Department of Commerce authority says, "These commodities, technology, or software were exported from the United States in accordance with the Export Administration Regulations. Diversion contrary to U.S. law is prohibited."

Exceptions to the use of the destination control statement are listed in Part 758.6 of the EAR. Advice on the appropriate statement to use can be provided by the U.S. Department of Commerce, an attorney, or the freight forwarder.

Antiboycott Regulations

The United States has an established policy of opposing restrictive trade practices or boycotts fostered or imposed by foreign countries against other countries friendly to the United States. This policy is implemented through the antiboycott provisions of the Export Administration Act (enforced by the U.S. Department of Commerce) and through a 1977 amendment to the Tax Reform Act of 1976 (enforced by the U.S. Department of the Treasury). In general, these laws prohibit U.S. persons from participating in foreign boycotts or taking actions that further or support such boycotts. The antiboycott regulations carry out this general purpose by

• Prohibiting U.S. agencies or persons from refusing to do business with blacklisted firms and boycotted friendly countries pursuant to foreign boycott demands

• Prohibiting U.S. persons from discriminating against, or agreeing to discriminate against, other U.S. persons on the basis of race, religion, gender, or national origin in order to comply with a foreign boycott

• Prohibiting U.S. citizens from furnishing information about business relationships with boycotted friendly foreign countries or blacklisted companies in response to boycott requirements

• Providing for public disclosure of requests to comply with foreign boycotts

• Requiring U.S. persons who receive requests to comply with foreign boycotts to report receipt of the requests to the U.S. Department of Commerce and to disclose publicly whether they have complied with such requests

Foreign Corrupt Practices Act

Under the Foreign Corrupt Practices Act (FCPA), it is unlawful for a U.S. person or firm (as well as any officer, director, employee, or agent of a firm or any stockholder acting on behalf of the firm) to offer, pay, or promise to pay (or to authorize any such payment or promise) money or anything of value to any foreign official (or foreign political party or candidate for foreign political office) for the purpose of obtaining or retaining business. It is also unlawful to make a payment to any person while knowing that all or a portion of the payment will be offered, given, or promised—directly or indirectly—to any foreign official (or foreign political party or candidate for foreign political office) for the purposes of assisting the firm in obtaining or retaining business. "Knowing" includes the concepts of "conscious disregard" and "willful blindness." The FCPA also covers foreign persons or firms that commit acts in furtherance of such bribery in the territory of the United States. U.S. persons or firms, or covered foreign persons or firms, should consult an attorney when confronted with FCPA issues.

FACT:
Failure to understand and fully comply with laws and regulations related to restricted or prohibited exports may result in substantial penalties.

INSIGHT:
You must be diligent in your efforts to comply. Contact the U.S. Commercial Service's Trade Information Center to learn more about restricted or prohibited exports by calling (800) USA-TRADE (800-872-8723).

chapter 10

LEGAL CONSIDERATIONS

For further information from the U.S. Department of Justice about the FCPA and the FCPA Opinion Procedure, contact the Deputy Chief, Fraud Section, Criminal Division, U.S. Department of Justice, 10th and Constitution Ave., NW, Bond Building, 4th Floor, Washington, DC 20530, or call (202) 514-1721. Specific questions should be faxed to the Foreign Corrupt Practices Act coordinator, Department of Justice, Criminal Division, Fraud Section at (202) 514-7021. You may obtain more information on the act online at *www.usdoj. gov/criminal/fraud/fcpa.*

Although the U.S. Department of Commerce has no enforcement role with respect to the FCPA, it supplies general guidance to U.S. exporters who have questions about the law and about international developments concerning it. For further information, contact the Office of Chief Counsel for International Commerce at (202) 482-0937 or view the Web site at *www.osec.doc.gov/ogc/occic/tabi.html.*

IMPORT REGULATIONS OF FOREIGN GOVERNMENTS

Import documentation requirements and other regulations imposed by foreign governments vary from country to country. As an exporter, you must be aware of the regulations that apply to your own operations and transactions. For instance, many governments require consular invoices, certificates of inspection, health certification, and various other documents. For sources of information about foreign government import regulations, see Chapter 4.

NORTH AMERICAN FREE TRADE AGREEMENT

The North American Free Trade Agreement (NAFTA) was negotiated among the United States, Mexico, and Canada and came into effect on January 1, 1994. It provides for the elimination of tariffs on most goods originating in the three countries over a maximum transition period of 15 years. An excellent source of information on all aspects of NAFTA is the U.S. Commercial Service's Trade Information Center at (800) USA-TRADE (800-872-8723).

Tariffs will be eliminated only on goods that originate in one of the four ways defined in article 401 of the NAFTA:

• Goods wholly obtained or produced entirely in the NAFTA region

• Goods meeting a specific Annex 401 origin rule

• Goods produced entirely in the NAFTA region exclusively from originating materials

• Unassembled goods and goods whose content does not meet the Annex 401 rule of origin but contains NAFTA regional value of 60 percent according to the transaction value method or 50 percent according to the net-cost method

Article 502 of the NAFTA requires that importers base their claims of the country of origin on the exporters' written certificate of origin, which may be the U.S.–approved certificate of origin (CF 434), the Canadian certificate of origin (Form B-232), or the Mexican certificate of origin (*Certificado de Origen*). The certificate may cover a single shipment, or it may be used as a blanket declaration for a period of 12 months. In either case, the certificate must be in the importer's possession when the importer is making the claim.

U.S. FOREIGN-TRADE ZONES

As an exporter, your company should also consider the customs privileges of U.S. foreign-trade zones (FTZs). These zones are domestic U.S. sites that are considered outside U.S. customs territory and are available for activities that might otherwise be carried on overseas for customs reasons. For export operations, the zones provide accelerated export status for purposes of excise tax rebates. There is no issue of drawback because duties are not collected when the goods are in the FTZ. For import and reexport activities, no customs duties, federal excise taxes, or state or local ad valorem taxes are charged on foreign goods moved into FTZs unless and until the goods or products made from them are moved into U.S. customs territory. Thus, FTZs can be profitable for operations involving foreign dutiable materials and components being assembled or produced here for reexport. Also, no quota restrictions ordinarily apply to export activity.

As of January 2006, there were 268 approved FTZs in communities throughout the United States. Associated with these FTZs are more than 400 subzones. These facilities are available for operations involving storage, repacking, inspection, exhibition, assembly, manufacturing, and other processing. The value of merchandise handled by FTZs exceeds $170 billion.

Information about the zones is available from the zone manager, from local Export Assistance Centers, or from the Executive Secretary, Foreign-Trade Zones Board, International Trade Administration, United States Department of Commerce, 1401 Constitution Ave., NW, Suite 4100W, Washington, DC 20230. You may also access information at *www.ia.ita.doc.gov/ftzpage/*.

EXPORT PROCESSING ZONES

To encourage and facilitate international trade, countries all over the world have established many types of export processing zones (EPZs), which include free trade zones, special economic zones, bonded warehouses, free ports, and customs zones. EPZs have evolved from initial assembly and simple processing activities to include high-tech and science parks, finance zones, logistics centers, and even tourist resorts. They now include not only general-type zones but also single-industry zones and single-commodity zones. Both the number of EPZs and the number of countries hosting them have expanded rapidly. There are now more than 600 EPZs in more than 100 countries. Many U.S. manufacturers and their distributors use these zones for receiving shipments of goods that are reshipped in smaller lots to customers throughout the surrounding areas. For further information, contact your local Export Assistance Center or the Trade Information Center at (800) USA-TRADE (800-872-8723).

CUSTOMS-BONDED WAREHOUSES

A customs-bonded warehouse is a building or other secured area in which dutiable goods may be stored, may be manipulated, or may undergo manufacturing operations without payment of duty. Authority for establishing bonded-storage warehouses is set forth in Title 19, *United States Code* (*U.S.C.*), section 1555. Bonded manufacturing and smelting and refining warehouses are established under Title 19, *U.S.C.,* sections 1311 and 1312.

When goods enter a bonded warehouse, the importer and warehouse proprietor incur financial and legal liability under a bond. The liability is canceled when the goods are

- Exported
- Withdrawn for supplies to a vessel or aircraft in international traffic
- Destroyed under U.S. Customs supervision
- Withdrawn for consumption within the United States after payment of duty

Your company could enjoy several advantages by using a bonded warehouse. No duty is collected until merchandise is withdrawn for consumption. An importer has control over use of money until the duty is paid on withdrawal of merchandise from the bonded warehouse. If no domestic buyer is found for the imported articles, the importing company can sell merchandise for exportation, thereby canceling the importer's obligation to pay duty.

Many items subject to quota or other restrictions may be stored in a bonded warehouse. Check with the nearest U.S. Customs office, however, before placing such merchandise in a bonded warehouse.

Duties owed on articles that have been manipulated are determined at the time of withdrawal from the bonded warehouse.

INTELLECTUAL PROPERTY CONSIDERATIONS

Intellectual property refers to a broad collection of rights relating to works of authorship, which are protected under copyright law; inventions, which are protected under patent law; marks, which are protected by trademark law; and designs and trade secrets. No international treaty completely defines these types of intellectual property, and countries' laws differ in significant respects. National intellectual property laws create, confirm, or regulate a property right without which others could use or copy a trade secret, an expression, a design, or a product or its mark and packaging.

The rights granted by a U.S. patent, trademark registration, copyright, or mask work (design of a semiconductor chip) registration extend only throughout the United States and its territories and possessions. They confer no protection on your company's product in a foreign country. There is no such thing as an international patent, trademark, or copyright. To secure patent or mask rights in any country, you must apply for the patent or register the mask work in that country. While most countries require registration of trademarks in order to secure protection, others grant rights that are based on priority of use in that country. Copyright protection depends on national laws, but registration is typically not required. There is no real shortcut to worldwide protection of intellectual property. However, some advantages and minimum standards for the protection and enforcement of intellectual property exist under treaties or other international agreements (see Box 10.2).

BOX 10.2 STRATEGY TARGETING ORGANIZED PIRACY

Developed in 2004, the Strategy Targeting Organized Piracy (STOP!) is the most comprehensive initiative yet advanced to help small businesses secure and enforce their rights in overseas markets.

The initiative established a hotline at (866) 999-HALT (866-999-4258) that provides a "one-stop" shop for businesses wanting to protect their intellectual property at home and abroad.

STOP! also educates small businesses on best practices and the risks of global piracy and counterfeiting to help them protect their rights.

For more information about STOP!, visit *www.stopfakes.gov*.

International Agreements

The oldest treaty relating to patents, trademarks, and unfair competition is the Paris Convention for the Protection of Industrial Property. The United States and more than 160 other countries are parties to this treaty. The Paris Convention sets minimum standards of protection and provides two important benefits: the right of national treatment and the right of priority.

In a general sense, *national treatment* means that a Paris Convention country will not discriminate against nationals of another Paris Convention country in granting patent or trademark protection. The rights provided by a foreign country may be greater or less than those provided under U.S. law, but the rights given will be the same as that country provides to its own citizens.

Before the existence of the Paris Convention, it was difficult to obtain protection for industrial property rights in the various countries of the world because of the diversity of their laws. Furthermore, patent applications had to be made roughly at the same time in all countries in order to avoid publication in one country destroying the novelty of the invention in the other countries. In addition, a delay in filing a patent or trademark application left open the possibility that those rights would be lost because of intervening acts such as sale of the invention or registration of the trademark by another person. The Paris Convention's right of priority provides a solution to that problem by establishing an alternative to filing applications in many countries simultaneously. It allows the applicant one year from the date of the first application filed in a Paris Convention country (six months for a design or trademark) in which to file in other countries. Publication or sale of an invention, or use of a mark, after first filing will therefore not jeopardize patentability in countries that grant a right of priority to U.S. applicants as long as they submit an application before the end of the priority period.

Not all countries adhere to the Paris Convention, but similar benefits may be available under another treaty or bilateral agreement. These substantive obligations have been incorporated into the World Trade Organization (WTO) Agreement on Trade-Related Aspects of Intellectual Property Rights (TRIPs) and must be adhered to by WTO members.

The United States is also a party to the Patent Cooperation Treaty (PCT), which provides procedures for filing patent applications in its member countries. The PCT allows you to file one international application that designates member countries in which a patent is sought. Filing the international application extends the period in which you have to fulfill the national requirements for each country by 18 months. This additional time can be very useful for evaluating the chances of obtaining patents and of exploiting your invention commercially in various designated countries. It is also useful for assessing both the technical value of your invention and the continued need for protection in those countries. Only after you have decided whether, and with respect to which countries, you wish to proceed further with your application must you fulfill the various national requirements for entry into the national phase. These requirements include paying national fees and, in some cases, filing translations of the application as filed or as amended.

The international copyright regulations that the United States abides by are governed principally by the Berne Convention for the Protection of Literary and Artistic Works, to which about 160 other nations adhere. The United States is also a member of the Universal Copyright Convention (UCC) and has special bilateral relations with a number of foreign countries. Under the Berne Convention, works created by a national of a Berne Union country or works first or simultaneously published in a Berne country are automatically eligible for protection in every other country of the Berne Union, without registration or compliance with any other formality of law.

These rules hold true of works first published in the United States on or after March 1, 1989, the date on which the United States acceded to the Berne Convention. Works first published before March 1989 were protected in many countries under the UCC—if the works were published with the formalities specified in that convention. Older works may also be protected as a consequence of simultaneous publication in a Berne country or by virtue of bilateral obligations. In any event, the requirements and protection vary from country to country; you should investigate them before seeking publication anywhere.

North American Free Trade Agreement and Agreement on Trade-Related Aspects of Intellectual Property Rights

Both NAFTA and TRIPs establish minimum standards for the protection of intellectual property and the enforcement of those standards. Neither agreement bestows rights on U.S. intellectual property owners. Rather, both agreements ensure that a member state that is party to one or both of the agreements provides a certain level of protection to those individuals or companies protected under that member state's laws.

Patent Law

U.S. patent law differs from the patent laws of most other countries in several important aspects. U.S. patent law grants a patent to the first inventor, even if another person independently makes the invention and files an application first. Most other countries award the patent to the inventor who first files a patent application. The United States also provides a one-year grace period that does not preclude an inventor from obtaining protection after an act such as publishing, offering for sale, or using the invention that would make the invention public. Many countries, including most European countries, lack a grace period that allows an inventor to so disclose an invention before filing a patent application. In countries with an absolute novelty rule, the inventor must file a patent application before making the invention public anywhere. Hence, even the publication of an invention in a U.S. patent grant is a disclosure that can defeat the right to obtain foreign patents unless the applicant is entitled to claim the right of priority under the Paris Convention, as described.

Unlike the United States, many countries require that an invention be worked locally to retain the benefit of the patent. Working a patent may require commercial-scale manufacture within the country, or it may be met by importation of goods covered by the patent, depending on the law of a particular country. The Paris Convention permits penalties for abuses of patent rights, such as not working a patent—for example, the right to a compulsory license at a reasonable royalty followed by possible forfeiture of the patent when the grant of a compulsory license was not sufficient to prevent abuses.

For an invention made in the United States, U.S. law prohibits filing abroad without a foreign filing license from the Patent and Trademark Office unless six months have elapsed since a U.S. application was filed. This prohibition protects against transfers of information that might damage the national security. The penalties for filing abroad without following these requirements range from loss of U.S. patent rights to possible imprisonment if classified information is released. In addition, other export control laws require you to obtain a license before exporting certain technologies, even if no patent application is filed—or they may bar the exporting of certain technologies altogether.

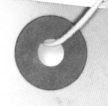

FACT:
Trademark laws impose no deadline for registering a mark.

INSIGHT:
A business should, as a practical matter, register promptly to avoid having its mark registered by someone else.

Trademark Law

A *trademark* is a word, symbol, name, slogan, or combination thereof that identifies and distinguishes the source of sponsorship of goods and may serve as an index of quality. *Service marks* perform the same function for businesses dealing in services rather than goods. For example, an airplane manufacturer might register its service mark. In the United States, rights to trademarks, service marks, and other marks (such as collective marks) are acquired through use in commerce within the United States. (A company may register its mark in the United States based on such use.) Additionally, the United States provides for protection of a mark, registered or not, if that mark has become well known through domestic or international use. However, in most countries, trademark rights are acquired only through registration, and many countries require local use of the registered mark to maintain the registration. Whether a given mark can be registered in a particular country will depend on the law of that country. For example, some countries do not protect service marks. The United States is not a member of any agreement under which a single filing will provide international protection, although the right of priority under the Paris Convention confers a substantial benefit.

If your business is expanding, you may face a period of time in which your mark may be known and perhaps registered in the United States, but you are not quite ready to do business abroad. It is prudent to decide early where you will need trademark protection and to protect your rights by filing in those countries. Where to file is a business decision, balancing the expense of registration against its benefit. At a minimum, you will want to file in countries in which you will do business. You may also find it desirable to file in countries that are known sources of counterfeit goods, although some require local use to maintain a registration. Although trademark laws impose no deadlines for registering a mark, a business should, as a practical matter, register promptly to avoid having its mark registered by someone else.

Although you are not legally required to do so, you may find it helpful to investigate the connotation of a trademark, trade name, number, or trade dress before making a major investment in another country. A different language or culture may have unfavorable, silly, or even rude meanings for words or symbols with neutral or favorable connotations in the United States. Even packaging colors may connote different meanings in different countries. For example, white may imply purity in the United States, but it is the color of mourning in most of the Far East.

Trade names are also protected on a country-by-country basis. Although the Paris Convention requires protection of trade names, they are not necessarily registered as they are in the United States. Each country protects trade names in accordance with its own business practices.

Copyright Law

A *copyright* protects original works of authorship. In the United States, this protection gives the owner the exclusive right to reproduce the work, to prepare derivative works, to distribute copies, or to perform or display the work publicly.

In the United States, original works of authorship include literary, dramatic, musical, artistic, and certain other intellectual works. A computer program, for example, is considered a literary work protected by copyright in the United States and in a large and increasing number of foreign countries.

In most countries, the place of first publication determines if copyright protection is available. Some countries require certain formalities to maintain copyright protection. Many other countries, particularly member countries of the Berne Union, offer copyright protection without these formalities. Still others offer little or no protection for the works of foreign nationals. Before publishing a work anywhere, you should investigate the scope of protection available, as well as the specific legal requirements for copyright protection in countries where you desire copyright protection.

For more information on intellectual property rights and the Strategy Targeting Organized Piracy (STOP!) initiative, visit *www.stopfakes.gov.*

CASE STUDY:
Tierra Dynamic

"Our success internationally over the past 10 years is a direct result of the substantial help ... provided by the Commercial Service."

—J. Dan Kelley, chief executive officer, Tierra Dynamic

THE COMPANY

J. Dan Kelley is chief executive officer of Tierra Dynamic, a Phoenix-based environmental firm specializing in removing toxins from soil and water. Kelley's firm cultivates bacteria that occur naturally, and a special process induces them to eat spilled hydrocarbons at an accelerated rate. "We increased their appetite," says Kelley. Tierra Dynamic has negotiated the rights to another patented technology that destroys PCBs (polychlorinated biphenyls)—a particularly lethal source of carcinogens.

THE CHALLENGE

A few years ago, Kelley and his 30 employees set their sights on entering some emerging markets. The move was a matter of common sense. The U.S. environmental industry is very competitive. In contrast, Kelley says, "The environmental industry is new to many developing countries, and we can compete better over there than we can in more developed countries." He explains that competitors with similar technologies tend to be bigger firms for which a $300,000 contract isn't worth the effort. "There's a big void in the market, and we're happy to fill it." But Tierra needed guidance.

THE SOLUTION

With help from the U.S. Commercial Service, Kelley's international business has gone from nothing to 25 percent of annual revenues. In the process, his key assumptions about the viability of developing markets were challenged.

Tierra Dynamic began its international business in Latin America and Southeast Asia in the late 1990s. Those markets were booming at the time but soon experienced recession and currency devaluation. Business, which began well, evaporated not only because of economic conditions but also because countries in those regions lacked laws requiring companies to clean up their environmental messes and lacked the basic infrastructure that needed cleaning, such as sewage systems.

Faced with an unacceptable level of uncertainty, Kelley headed to Western Europe, where the legal system recognizes third-party liability for environmental damage. He participated in a Commercial Service trade mission to Italy and Spain. Encouraged by interest expressed by potential partners and purchasers, Kelley later returned to Italy to participate in a trade show and to close some deals. "The Commercial Service in Milan found the partners for us," says Kelley. "We couldn't have done it without them." In fact, he adds, "Our success internationally over the past 10 years is a direct result of the substantial help ... provided by the Commercial Service."

Kelley says Tierra has signed one contract worth $1 million and is negotiating another of similar value. The company will do soil and water remediation at a solvent plant and a pharmaceutical factory. Those projects, which are expected to be long term, will add 10 percent to the company's total revenue for the year.

LESSONS LEARNED

Kelley has this advice to other U.S. businesses contemplating entering international markets:

- **Spread the risk.** Kelley learned it's best to have a presence in dissimilar markets. Then, if one goes south, the other may not.

- **Look at lower-risk options in higher-risk markets.** In Argentina, Tierra Dynamic lowered its risks by doing business with an international development bank.

- **Don't rule out a market by assuming it is mature.** It may not be as competitive as you think. "Ultimately, we found ourselves doing very good business in Italy," Kelley says.

- **Focus in one core area rather than try to deliver different services in different markets.** "We were trying to do air pollution monitoring in Singapore, water systems management in Malta, and something else in Argentina," Kelley explains. "Now we do the one thing we do best—site remediation services."

- **Find a good partner."** Your partner will go through the rigmarole of helping find clients," Kelley advises, "and this will greatly accelerate market entry."

- **Respect your customer.** Kelley notes, "You can never go wrong by showing a client too much respect—even if it means wearing a suit and tie … on an impossibly hot summer afternoon in some dusty place."

- **Adapt to the culture."** We Americans like to cut to the chase in business," Kelley observes. "Other cultures like to orate more than we do, and only eventually get around to what they want."

- **Be patient.** Kelley believes that "Americans think in quarters. If nothing happens in three months, 'I'm out of here.' You need to invest some money and time developing new markets."

- **Enjoy the intangible benefits.** "International work experience has allowed me to live and work on six continents, among diverse cultures," Kelley says. "I've learned five languages and developed a worldview that no educational training could ever provide. It has given me a sense of self and a self-confidence that have served me very well in the business world, allowing me to develop a keen insight into the commonality of man."

In his travels, Kelley found that "'Made in the U.S.A.' means everything. It means the best." But more motivates Tierra Dynamic than pride of place and any competitive advantage associated with it. "This is an idealistic business. At the end of the day, I want to say I got this paycheck for doing something good for somebody else."

ACTION

How can you make the "Made in the U.S.A." label work for you?

- **Travel to overseas trade shows.** They are a good place to meet buyers and business partners. The Commercial Service certifies more than 100 overseas shows representing many different industries each year. Typically, a U.S. pavilion at each show features exhibition space and assistance from Commercial Service specialists. The pavilion offers U.S. companies exhibition space at a lower cost than if they purchase it directly. For more information, visit *www.export.gov/ tradeevents.*

- **Register on Export.gov.** Comprising 19 federal agencies, the Export.gov community is involved in opening foreign markets and promoting U.S.

exports. These agencies are known as the Trade Promotion Coordinating Committee (TPCC). Export.gov is the TPCC's gateway for a broad range of export assistance, export finance, and trade advocacy services. By registering on Export.gov, you will enable TPCC agencies to contact you with targeted information on trade opportunities, market research, and government services. Registration also allows you to access a vast library of country and industry market research reports and trade leads. To register, visit *www. export.gov.*

J. Dan Kelley (left), chief executive officer of Tierra Dynamics, is pictured with Dr. Oscar Cuper (right), his partner in Argentina. The Phoenix, Arizona, company specializes in removing toxins from soil and water by inducing bacteria to eat spilled hydrocarbons at an accelerated rate.

GOING ONLINE: E-EXPORTING TOOLS FOR SMALL BUSINESSES

In This Chapter

- **E-commerce defined**

- **Your company's readiness**

- **Steps to going online**

lobal Web use is booming, and millions of new buyers are logging on each year. Electronic commerce, especially business-to-consumer (B2C) e-commerce, reflects this growth.

The Internet's global reach is a cost-effective means for marketing products and services overseas. Companies that establish a corporate Web site publicizing their products and services are able to create an electronic mechanism for safe and secure electronic transactions, to track orders, to provide customer service interface, and to list products' technical specifications. Small and medium-sized companies can broaden their market presence internationally by adopting e-commerce or electronic business practices that are user friendly for non-English-speaking users.

What is electronic commerce? It is buying and selling online through the Internet. The transaction is completed through an electronic network featuring computer systems—the vendor's, a Web host's, and the buyer's—all of which are linked to the Internet.

USE OF ELECTRONIC COMMERCE FOR INTERNATIONAL BUSINESS AND TRADE

Using the Internet to transact business in the global marketplace offers significant advantages to the small or medium-sized company seeking new outlets for its products and services. More than 1 billion people throughout the world have access to the Internet. This presence offers a tremendous potential customer base for the entrepreneur. At the same time, business-to-business (B2B) e-commerce has also surged. Corporations in Africa, Asia, Europe, and Latin America are increasingly migrating many of their marketing programs online to seek new business in regions and countries that they had previously thought to be beyond their resources. They also seek new supply sources and services to meet their internal needs and partners to share manufacturing and marketing responsibilities. Some companies, such as GE, have migrated all their sourcing and bidding processes to the Internet.

For certain industries, products, and services, going online reduces variable costs associated with international marketing. Handling tasks such as order processing, payment, after-sales service, marketing (direct e-mail), and advertising online may lower the international market development costs that an enterprise would incur had it used conventional "brick-and-mortar" market penetration strategies. You should be aware of one important caveat: although English is spoken in many countries, it is still important to consider using the languages prevalent in the countries targeted in your company's e-business strategy. Your Web site should be designed to reach the widest audience in the languages of that audience.

In the context of the Internet, electronic commerce needs to be viewed beyond the traditional commercial arena. E-commerce affects marketing, production, and consumption. Information gathered from customers through Internet stores can be used to customize products, to forecast demand, and to prepare business strategies. Consumers not only pay online for products and services but also search for information about products, negotiate with vendors, and reveal their preferences through their purchasing patterns.

E-commerce offers much promise to U.S. firms interested in using the Internet as another vehicle for exporting. However, you should be familiar with the steps necessary to make your firm's Web site e-export capable. Many U.S. companies have a Web site that fulfills one or more marketing functions tailored to their business specialties. These sites feature at least one of the following characteristics:

• **Transactional site.** A transactional site may be an electronic storefront for a brick-and-mortar retailer or a catalog business, or it may be a showroom for a manufacturer wishing to sell directly to the public. Transactional sites conduct full "end-to-end" transactions through the Web site, allowing customers to search for, order, and pay for products online, as well as allowing them to contact the company for after-sales service. The most sophisticated sites create efficiencies by integrating the transaction process with back-office systems such as accounting, inventory, service, and sales.

• **Information delivery site.** This kind of site generates sales by promoting corporate awareness rather than facilitating online transactions. Its function is similar to a brochure that provides information about the product or service and gives contact information on how to proceed with a purchase. Because such a site is often static and doesn't require the software systems necessary for online transactions, it is less expensive to design and maintain than a transactional site. An information delivery site is ideal for companies that market products and services that cannot be provided online or goods that cannot be sold online. A modified version of this kind of site permits the buyer to shop online for the best price from competing vendors providing the identical product—for example, authorized car manufacturers. Information on options available for a particular model allows the buyer to visualize the configuration and obtain an estimated price for the vehicle.

• **E-marketplaces.** These sites are market-makers because they bring buyers and sellers together to facilitate transactions. Participation in a brokerage often provides an efficient way of finding a customer without the expense of building a proprietary transactional Web site. Types of brokerages include auctions, virtual malls, and matching services.

MARKET DEVELOPMENT ON THE WEB

As with brick-and-mortar enterprises, market development is an essential ingredient for all types of Web sites and must be an integral part of your firm's e-business presence on the Internet. Your company should consider and evaluate the advantages of advertising online as an extension and a component of your corporate growth strategies. Advertising messages often appear on portals or on other Web sites that draw viewers with content (e.g., news and information) and services (e.g., e-mail, chat, and forums). You may seek to advertise on search engines that attract high traffic volume or to target a specialized demographic. Some portals sell favorable link positioning or advertising keyed to particular search terms in a user query. Companies may also consider using an advertising network that feeds ads to a network of sites, thereby enabling large marketing campaigns. These options are available in the United States and internationally in English or in other languages.

Direct e-mail is an inexpensive and efficient way to reach thousands of potential customers. Direct e-mail can be used to promote and enhance Web presence, depending on the market, product, or service. However, several countries have legislation affecting unsolicited commercial e-mail that direct marketers must be aware of. The Direct Marketing Association suggests that direct e-mail messages should have (a) an honest subject line; (b) no forged headers or technological deceptions; (c) the identity of the sender, which includes a physical address; and (d) a visible opt-out clause that is easy to use. Before using direct e-mail to promote Web presence, your company should be aware of the potential for backlash against unsolicited e-mails by consumers who feel overwhelmed by the number of such e-mails they receive. Companies should consult the Controlling the Assault of Non-Solicited Pornography and Marketing (CAN-SPAM) Act of 2003 to ensure full compliance with the law (see Box 11.1).

TOOLS TO ASSESS YOUR FIRM'S READINESS TO GO ONLINE

Companies that have decided to have a Web presence must assess whether they have the most efficient information technology (IT) solutions to execute their online exporting pro-

FACT: Business-to-business e-commerce in China is expected to increase 81 percent by 2008. India's predicted growth is even higher at 88 percent.

INSIGHT: As e-commerce grows throughout the world, your company will want to be ready to reap the benefits.

BOX 11.1 THE CAN-SPAM ACT

The CAN-SPAM Act establishes requirements for senders of commercial e-mail to consumers. The act became effective on January 1, 2004. Enforced by the Federal Trade Commission, the act includes heavy penalties for violators. The main provisions are as follows:

• Header information—routing information and information in the "From" and "To" lines—cannot be false or misleading.

• Subject lines cannot mislead recipients about the contents of the message.

• A return e-mail address or other mechanism must be included to allow recipients to opt out of receiving future messages, and these requests from recipients must be honored.

• A clear notice must be included that notifies recipients that the message is an advertisement and that provides a valid physical postal address for the sender.

For more information, visit *www.ftc.gov/spam/*.

grams and objectives. IT embodies a range of computer systems and software applications for managing a firm's Web site. With more and more cyber attacks on government and corporate sites, your company should consider investing in security technologies to protect you and your customers from identify theft and denial of service.

An IT assessment should answer the following questions:

• What is your firm's current IT usage? Is it at capacity, and what are the plans for additional IT investment to upgrade existing systems?

• What business applications are best suited to move online for B2B or B2C e-commerce?

• Have you done a cost-benefit analysis of all possible projects involving IT?

• Have you identified current and future security issues, and do you have an action plan for correcting problems?

The U.S. Department of Commerce, through the National Institute of Standards and Technology, has created a tool to assist companies with IT assessment. Called the eScan Security Assessment, the tool is available free of charge at *https://www.mepcenters.nist.gov. escan*. It assesses the electronic security infrastructure of a small or medium-sized business and provides an action plan for improvement. It asks specific questions regarding the following:

• Virus protection

• Physical environment

• Mechanical failure

• Information technology and security policies

• Internet and e-commerce transactions

- File permissions
- Back-up policies and contingency planning
- International concerns
- Operating systems

Once the questions have been answered, the eScan Security Assessment tool produces a detailed report on how well an organization scores in all of those critical security areas. The tool recommends specific steps to correct uncovered security holes, thus enabling companies to build a more secure business model for future Internet strategies.

STEPS TO GOING ONLINE

You must lay the groundwork before your company can transact business on the Internet (see Box 11.2). Potential customers must know who you are and how to reach you. Then, if they want to buy what your company has to sell, you have to facilitate the exchange of money for your product.

Selecting a Domain Name

A key component to establishing a Web presence is choosing a uniform resource locator (URL) and a domain name. As with URLs aimed toward the domestic market, a URL for an online exporter's Web site should be short, simple, descriptive, and memorable to customers in the target market. URL registration is concurrent with domain name registration. Every country (plus a few territories) has a reserved, two-letter country-code domain (e.g., the United Kingdom has the domain ".uk"). An online exporter may choose domain names localized for the target markets. Locally branded domain names may increase brand awareness and Web site address recall, and they may even influence brand sales and loyalty. In addition, most local search engines display only locally relevant content by filtering the search results to include only local country-code domains. If your company wants to have a local domain name, you must research the rules for the particular country, as registration requirements vary.

If your company is seeking foreign customers, you may also consider an internationalized or multilingual domain name. Such domain names are Web addresses written in characters other than the Roman alphabet. For example, a company called Bright Light Bulbs that wishes to sell in China could have a domain name that would use the Chinese characters for Bright Light Bulbs in its Web site address. Internationalized or multilingual domain names allow customers to search and access sites in their native language.

Registering at Search Engines

Most people use search engines to find information on the Internet, so Web site registration with multiple search engines is key to visibility. Search engines range from those that are

BOX 11.2 ARE YOU READY TO GO ONLINE?

Here are some points to consider:

- Who are your target customers? Do they use the Internet?
- What information would your Web site provide? How can your customers use it?
- How does your e-commerce strategy fit into your overall exporting objectives?
- How effectively can you provide service that is personalized and customized?

global in scope to search tools that are focused on small areas of information. Online exporters should register with search engines that are popular with the target audience in their target markets.

Choosing a Web Host

A Web host is a company with a server that maintains the files of Web sites. A variety of free and subscription-based Web-hosting services are available, including those offered by many Internet service providers. Web-hosting services often go beyond Web site maintenance to include domain name registration, Web site design, and search engine registration. For some online exporters, it may be most feasible to use a Web host in their target market to take advantage of all the localized services the host offers. The location or nationality of the Web site host does not affect accessibility of the site; however, when choosing a host, your company should ensure that the host's servers reside within a stable infrastructure and are maintained for optimal reliability.

Localizing and Internationalizing Web Site Content

Companies seeking foreign audiences with their Web sites will want to either localize or internationalize their sites. They may also provide a mixture of both processes. Localization consists of adapting one's Web site to meet the linguistic, cultural, and commercial requirements of a targeted market. Internationalizing a Web site enables a company to be multilingual and sensitive to cultural conventions without the need for extensive redesign. Localization or internationalization must be part of the online exporter's corporate strategy for Web site and business development. Among the features that your company should consider are the following:

- Language
- Cultural nuances, such as differences in color association and symbols
- Payment preferences

- Pricing in the appropriate currency
- Currency converter
- Metric measurements

You can find more information on localization and internationalization at the Web site for the Localization Industry Standards Association at *www.lisa.org*.

Promoting Your Site

Setting up shop is no guarantee that customers will come flooding in. If you want a successful site, you can't wait for people to stumble across it. There are a number of ways to promote your site without spending a lot of money:

- Consider purchasing an ad for a nominal cost on BuyUSA.gov, a network of Web sites operated by the U.S. Commercial Service and targeted at foreign buyers.

- Depending on the business you are in, send brief stories about your company and Web site to trade publications that serve the larger industry or business sector in the country market you are targeting.

- Put your domain name on business cards, letterheads, envelopes, packaging, and promotional materials of all kinds.

- Ask foreign visitors if they'd like to receive occasional "opt-in" ads, which are essentially e-mails promoting upcoming sales or new products. Encourage those visitors who consent to receiving the opt-in ads to e-mail them to a friend or relative. People who agree to receive opt-in ads tend to purchase up to seven times as frequently as other visitors.

- Consider sending people who visited or registered on your Web site but didn't buy anything a follow-up e-mail with a coupon for a discount on your products and services.

EXECUTING ORDERS AND PROVIDING AFTER-SALES SERVICE

Guidelines for order execution and after-sales service are similar for offline and online transactions. Therefore, companies planning to export through the Internet should be knowledgeable about the topics discussed in previous chapters. Companies engaging in e-commerce should also consider the following pertinent issues:

Payment Modes and Terms

Companies that use the Internet to reach overseas customers frequently use their Web site to process orders and accept payments. Payment practices vary from country to country. It

FACT:
Web sites that take an international audience into account make more international sales.

INSIGHT:
Consider these points:
- Include a currency converter.
- Use the language of your target audience.
- Make navigation simple and visual.

is important that you identify and incorporate the prevalent payment mechanisms into the order-processing component of the Web site:

- **Credit cards.** For B2C transactions, many overseas customers use credit cards for online purchases, but credit cards are not a universally common method of online payment. To offer credit card payment services, a company must establish a credit card merchant account with a bank. The bank will process the transactions in exchange for a fee. Companies should compare the fee structures of banks to determine which works best for the size and number of transactions expected. The transactions may be fast, but credit cards carry their own risks. Chargebacks can be very costly for online exporters. Common chargeback reasons are fraud, dispute over the quality of merchandise, non-receipt of merchandise, or incorrect amount charged to the card. If your company accepts online credit card transactions, you should be knowledgeable about the credit card issuer's and your bank's policies toward chargebacks and how to avoid them.

- **Account-to-account transfers.** Account-to-account (A2A) transfers, in which money is transferred electronically between the customer's and merchant's banks, are popular in many countries. A2A transactions offer the advantages of occurring in real time and of reducing the potential for fraud and chargebacks. Unfortunately, because A2A transactions are rare in the United States, few U.S. banks offer this service.

- **Person-to-person transfers.** Many companies offer person-to-person (P2P) transfers, in which funds are sent electronically to a third party, which in turn deposits the funds in the merchant's account. An example of a P2P service provider that conducts cross-border transactions is PayPal. PayPal lets anyone with an e-mail address securely send and receive online payments using his or her credit card or bank account. PayPal will also conduct currency exchange, allowing the customer and merchant to operate in their preferred currency. Google Checkout offers similar service. Other P2P providers, such as Western Union's BidPay, accept a credit card payment from the payer and send a money order to the payee.

Shipping and Pricing

The process of shipping and pricing goods purchased over the Internet is identical to the process for goods purchased by other means, except for digital products (e.g., music, videos, games, or software) that are downloaded from a Web site. See Chapter 12 for information about shipping and Chapter 13 for information about pricing, quotations, and terms.

Customer Service

As with offline exporters, online exporters must have an effective customer service program to build and maintain a customer base. Online business poses unique challenges and opportunities for customer service. Customer service should be integral to Web site design and overall business strategy. Online exporters should consider providing the following information and services:

- A list of frequently asked questions (FAQs)
- An online interface for customers to track orders
- Clearly posted contact information (e.g., address, phone number, and e-mail)
- Delivery of timely (e.g., four hours), personalized responses to customer inquiries
- Customer testimonials
- Contact information fields to collect foreign address contact information
- Toll free phone numbers that include Canada
- Information presented in languages other than English

Taxation

Taxation is as relevant to online merchants as to brick-and-mortar businesses. In general, for most overseas markets, a company must have a permanent establishment in a foreign country before that country can subject the company to its general tax jurisdiction. Thus, an American online vendor of digitally or physically delivered goods that does not have equipment or personnel in Japan would not be subject to Japanese taxation. However, there are important exceptions to this general rule. On July 1, 2003, the European Union (EU) member states began taxing sales of electronically supplied goods and services from non-EU firms to customers located in the European Union. Non-EU providers of electronic goods and services are now required to register with a tax authority in the member state of their choosing and to collect and remit value added tax (VAT) at the VAT rate of the member state where their customer is located. Although the EU countries have been the first to move toward a system of taxing electronic sales according to customer location (regardless of where the vendor is established), other countries may soon follow suit. Therefore, if your company exports online, you must know about the tax requirements of your target market. You can find more information about online taxation at the Web site for the Department of Commerce's Office of Technology and Electronic Commerce at *web.ita.doc.gov/ITI/itiHome.nsf/(hotNews)/HotNews.*

OTHER IMPORTANT SALES CONSIDERATIONS

For an international Web site, there are a number of additional factors to consider, particularly as they relate to foreign legal and regulatory requirements.

Privacy

U.S. organizations that collect personally identifiable information online should display their privacy policies prominently and offer choices to their data subjects (e.g., customers, employees, and other business contacts) about how their personal information is used. Customers should have the opportunity to refuse having their personal information shared with others or used for promotional purposes. Many countries have privacy laws, and organizations should take care to comply or they may face prosecution. For example, the European Union prohibits the transfer of personal data to non-EU nations that do not meet the EU "adequacy" standard for privacy protection. The U.S. Department of Commerce, in consultation with the European Commission and the private sector, has developed a safe-harbor framework that provides U.S. organizations with a streamlined means to comply with the EU requirements. Companies may self-certify to the safe harbor through the safe-harbor Web site at *www.export.gov/safeharbor/*.

Security

Consumers often cite security concerns for not placing orders over the Internet. Compared with other forms of consumer purchasing, the Internet is safe as long as the online merchant takes prudent business precautions. If your company operates a transactional Web site as part of its exporting business, you should post a security statement to reassure customers.

Electronic Signatures

In legal terms, an online sale is an enforceable contract, a valid and binding agreement. However, in some overseas markets, a contract is only enforceable if it is signed "in writing." Such jurisdictions do not recognize electronic signatures and, in the event of a dispute, would not enforce an agreement made by e-mail or through a Web site. Although many countries have modified their laws to recognize electronic signatures, online exporters should check to be sure their target markets accept electronic signatures. If they do, the next step is to determine which signatures are restricted and which technologies are legally valid. You can find more information on electronic signatures at the Department of Commerce's Office of Technology and Electronic Commerce Web site at *web.ita.doc.gov/ITI/itiHome.nsf/(hotNews)/HotNews.*

Unsolicited Commercial E-Mail

Unsolicited commercial e-mail (UCE), also known as *unsolicited bulk e-mail* (UBE) or *spam,* is relevant to international e-commerce because its use is controversial. Many businesses see UCE as a quick and cheap way to promote goods and services to a broad range of potential customers. However, UCE costs individuals and businesses significant amounts of time, money, equipment, and productivity. Many domestic and international jurisdictions have laws about UCE, and violation may result in penalties. (See Box 11.1 for information about U.S. law.) In addition, many e-mail service providers, such as America Online and Yahoo!, have rules of conduct that forbid using their service to send UCE. Visit the Direct Marketing Association Web site at *www.the-dma.org/* for more guidance on UCE.

Advertising Content

Most countries have laws about advertising content, which may be applied to Web sites, banner ads, and marketing e-mails sent from the United States. Online exporters should research the advertising laws of their target market before initiating a marketing campaign. If you are an exporter of heavily regulated products and services, such as pharmaceuticals or insurance, you may anticipate disclosure requirements and limitations on claims. Companies should avoid the following:

• Comparative advertising (that is, comparing your company's goods or services with those of a competitor)

• Advertising aimed at children

• Use of images or sounds that may be considered intellectual property and may require the permission of the artist

• Use of lotteries, competitions, contests, games, and betting as part of a promotional offer

The International Chamber of Commerce has guidelines on advertising and marketing on the Internet that are available at *www.iccwbo.org*.

Jurisdiction

Online exporters must be aware that they are doing business in a foreign jurisdiction, which means the laws and regulations of the target market apply to the goods and services being sold. For example, an online exporter of medical equipment should ensure that the equipment has been approved for use in the foreign market. Companies should also be aware that the transaction itself may be under the jurisdiction of the foreign market. In other words, the foreign market's laws regarding contracts may apply.

Good Faith

Dealing in good faith is perhaps more important for online businesses than for brick-and-mortar operations because customers rely heavily on reputation. Moreover, it is illegal in most countries to behave otherwise. If you engage in online business, your company must do the following:

• Use fair business, advertising, and marketing practices.

• Provide accurate, clear, and easily accessible information about the company and its goods and services.

• Disclose full information about the terms, conditions, and costs of the transaction.

• Ensure that consumers know they are making a commitment before closing the deal.

• Address consumer complaints and difficulties quickly and fairly.

For more guidance on online good faith commerce, see the Federal Trade Commission's guide for business at *www.ftc.gov/bcp/conline/pubs/alerts/ecombalrt.shtm*.

Evertek Computer Corp.

"Any company in the U.S. with sales of $5 million per year should be exporting. And they should be using the U.S. Commercial Service to help them do it."

—John Ortley, international sales manager, Evertek Computer Corp.

THE COMPANY

Established in 1990, San Diego–based Evertek Computer Corp. specializes in overstocked, discontinued, and factory refurbished computers, peripherals, and consumer electronics. The demand for "obsolete" products is large and growing because buyers around the world don't need the latest and most expensive equipment. They want cheap. Match these folks with people who want to make a few bucks off their used personal computers, printers, and monitors, and you have a business with serious growth potential.

THE CHALLENGE

Evertek international sales manager John Ortley wanted to grow the global side of the business. Given the company's small sales staff, Ortley thought Evertek should emphasize e-commerce Web sites and portals. To scale up fast and keep ahead of the competition, Ortley elected to focus on countries with lower gross national products.

THE SOLUTION

Although Evertek has an established sales channel, a multilingual sales staff, an e-commerce Web site, and representation on several portal sites, Ortley still sought to increase Evertek's market penetration and enlisted the assistance of the U.S. Commercial Service.

The Export Assistance Center in San Diego helped Ortley pick the best overseas trade shows to attend to promote Evertek's products. One such show, CeBIT in Germany, generated $1 million in orders—well worth the plane fare and hotel room. "Any company in the U.S. with sales of $5 million per year should be exporting," says Ortley. "And they should be using the U.S. Commercial Service to help them do it."

In just a few years, Ortley was able to add four new salespeople. International sales zoomed to $34 million last year, an increase of 84 percent from the previous year. He thinks future annual sales of $100 million are attainable, especially since he now sells to customers in 105 countries, including Iraq, Ukraine, and several countries in Africa and Eastern Europe. Approximately 30 percent of Evertek's international customers are in South America, with 20 percent in Europe

and 20 percent in the Middle East and North Africa.

International sales are good for Evertek not only because of the volume and balancing business cycles, but also because gross margins are higher and merchandise returns have been "next to nil." Ortley says the return rate for domestic sales is between 3 and 5 percent.

Payment also has not been an issue for Evertek. The firm uses a combination of wire transfers, credit cards, and letters of credit. "For certain high-risk countries, we only ship upon receipt of a wire transfer to our bank," says Ortley.

LESSONS LEARNED

The chief lesson Ortley learned is that a small sales department can use the Internet to find and sell to customers all over the world. Because multiple channels are a key to growth, Ortley has a presence on e-commerce portals such Alibaba.com and Singapore-based Exporters.sg. About half of Evertek's international sales are generated through the Internet and half through trade shows and other methods more suited to "an older-style sales company," explains

Ortley. He adds that even e-commerce sales are seldom entirely devoid of human contact because of the need to deal with documentation issues and the desire of many foreign customers to have a personal relationship with the company they are buying from.

Ortley spends hours on the phone, adjusting his calls for different time zones. Speaking directly with the client is still an essential part of the business process, he believes, because it forges closer ties. "I sit there making calls with the CIA's *World Factbook* on my computer screen. It's important to know something about the country you're doing business in. The buyers really appreciate it if you can talk to them about issues of importance to them."

Ortley also uses an array of free and low-cost help to build his international business. Trade leads from the Commercial Service are one good source of reliable buyers. Advertising in *Commercial News USA,* the Commercial Service's magazine, is another. U.S. embassies across the globe distribute the magazine, which features editions in English, Spanish, and Chinese.

Ortley's enthusiasm for doing business abroad has helped Evertek realize that a big part of its business is going to be international: "For me it started with being curious about the world. I enjoy learning about other cultures and respecting people who have a different background than mine." Ortley says the company's owners were always open to doing business globally, but he has been able to deliver results that have positioned the company as a major exporter.

Ortley advises companies to consider the potential rewards of exporting and of working with the Commercial Service. "We are in part an e-commerce business and we're thriving. The world is shrinking, and it's getting easier and less expensive to do business on a global basis."

ACTION

Here are some tips for taking your e-commerce business global:

- **Answer purchasing inquiries from overseas, even if unsolicited.** The Commercial Service advises that you respond to such inquiries if only to request additional information about the potential buyer. If you are concerned about the legitimacy of the buyer, the Commercial Service can do a background check or provide other useful information that can help your company make its decision.

- **Advertise in *Commercial News USA.*** This bimonthly catalog-style magazine helps American companies promote products and services to buyers in more than 145 countries. The magazine, which is free, is mailed directly to qualified recipients and distributed by Commercial Service personnel at U.S. embassies and consulates worldwide. Each issue reaches an estimated 400,000 readers.

- **Get online.** Companies that have decided to sell their products online must assess whether they have the most efficient information technology (IT) solutions to execute their online exporting programs. The U.S. Department of Commerce has created a tool to assist companies with IT assessment. It is available free on the Internet. The eScan Security Assessment, at *www.mepcenters.nist. gov/escan/*, assesses the electronic-security infrastructure of a small or medium-sized business and provides an action plan for improvement. You can also visit the E-Export Toolbox Web site at *www.export.gov/sellingonline* for information about the resources the Department of Commerce and other U.S. government agencies offer to U.S. businesses interested in using the Internet to increase exports.

John Ortley is international sales manager of Evertek Computer Corporation. The company is filling a large worldwide market niche for selling both new and refurbished computers and parts through e-commerce Web sites and portals.

SHIPPING YOUR PRODUCT

T he hurdles you have to clear don't end with the sale and the Web site. You still have to get the goods to the buyer, who is often located thousands of miles away where different rules may apply. When shipping a product overseas, you must be aware of packing, labeling, documentation, and insurance requirements and regulations. Make sure that the merchandise is

• Packed correctly so that it arrives in good condition

• Labeled correctly to ensure that the goods are handled properly and arrive on time at the right place

• Documented correctly to meet U.S. and foreign government requirements, as well as proper collection standards

• Insured against damage, loss, pilferage, and delay

Because of the multitude of considerations involved in physically exporting goods, exporters often receive assistance from their air carrier or freight forwarder to perform those services.

FREIGHT FORWARDERS

An international freight forwarder is an agent for moving cargo to an overseas destination. These agents are familiar with the import rules and regulations of foreign countries, the export regulations of the U.S. government, the methods of shipping, and the documents related to foreign trade. Freight forwarders are licensed by the International Air Transport Association (IATA) to handle air freight and the Federal Maritime Commission to handle ocean freight.

Freight forwarders assist exporters in preparing price quotations by advising on freight costs, port charges, consular fees, costs of special documentation, insurance costs, and the freight forwarders' own handling fees. They recommend the packing methods that will protect the merchandise during transit, or they can arrange to have the merchandise packed at the port or put in containers. If the exporter prefers, freight forwarders can reserve the necessary space on a vessel, aircraft, train, or truck. The cost for their services is a factor that should be included in the price charged to the customer.

Once the order is ready for shipment, freight forwarders should review all documents to ensure that everything is in order. This review is of particular importance with letter-of-credit payment terms. Freight forwarders may also prepare the bill of lading and any special required documentation. After shipment, they can route the documents to the seller, the buyer, or a paying bank. Freight forwarders can also make arrangements with customs brokers overseas to ensure that the goods comply with customs import documentation regulations. A *customs broker* is an individual or company that is licensed to transact customs business on behalf of others. Customs business is limited to those activities involving transactions related to the entry and admissibility of merchandise; its classification and valuation; the payment of duties, taxes, or other charges assessed or collected; and the refund, rebate, or drawback of those charges.

For more information, visit the National Customs Brokers and Freight Forwarders Association of America at *http://ncbfaa.org.*

PACKING

Your company should be aware of the demands that international shipping puts on packaged goods. You should also keep four potential problems in mind when designing an export shipping crate: breakage, moisture, pilferage, and excess weight.

Buyers are often familiar with the port systems overseas, so they will sometimes specify packaging requirements. If the buyer does not provide such specifications, be sure the goods are prepared using these guidelines:

• Pack in strong containers that are adequately sealed and filled when possible.

• Make sure the weight is evenly distributed to provide proper bracing in the container, regardless of size.

• Put goods on pallets and, when possible, place them in containers.

• Make packages and packing filler out of moisture-resistant material.

• To avoid pilferage, avoid writing contents or brand names on packages.

• Use straps, seals, and shrink-wrap to safeguard goods.

• Observe any product-specific hazardous materials packing requirements.

• Verify compliance with wood-packaging documentation and markings for fumigation and chemical treatment.

One popular method of shipment is to use containers obtained from carriers or private leasing companies. These containers vary in size, material, and construction. They accommodate most cargo but are best suited for standard package sizes and shapes. Also, refrigerated and liquid-bulk containers are usually readily available. Some containers are no more than semitrailers lifted off their wheels, placed on a vessel at the port of export, and then transferred to another set of wheels at the port of import.

Normally, air shipments require less heavy packing than ocean shipments, though they should still be adequately protected, especially if they are likely to attract pilferage. In many instances, standard domestic packing is acceptable if the product is durable and there is no concern for display packaging. In other instances, high-test (at least 250 pounds per square inch) cardboard or tri-wall construction boxes are preferable.

Finally, transportation costs are determined by volume and weight. Specially reinforced and lightweight packing materials have been developed for exporting to minimize volume and weight while reinforcing the packaging. The proper materials may save money as well as ensure that the goods are properly packed. You should hire a professional firm to pack the products if you are not equipped to do so. This service is usually provided at a moderate cost.

LABELING

Specific marking and labeling are used on export shipping cartons and containers. This labeling

• Meets shipping regulations

• Ensures proper handling

• Conceals the identity of the contents

• Helps receivers identify shipments

• Ensures compliance with environmental and safety standards

The overseas buyer usually specifies which export marks should appear on the cargo for easy identification by receivers. Products may require many markings for shipment. For example, exporters need to put the following markings on cartons to be shipped:

• Shipper's mark

• Country of origin (in your case, "U.S.A.")

• Weight marking (in pounds and kilograms)

• Number of packages and size of cases (in inches and centimeters)

• Handling marks (i.e., international pictorial symbols)

• Cautionary markings, such as "This Side Up" or "Use No Hooks" (in English and in the language of the destination country)

• Port of entry

• Labels for hazardous materials (i.e., universal symbols adopted by the International Air Transport Association and the International Maritime Organization)

• Ingredients (if applicable, also included in the language of the destination country)

DOCUMENTATION

Your company should seriously consider having the freight forwarder handle the documentation that exporting requires. Forwarders are specialists in this process. The following documents are commonly used in exporting, but which of them are necessary in a particular transaction depends on the requirements of the U.S. government and the government of the importing country:

• Air freight shipments are covered by *air waybills,* which can never be made in negotiable form (see Sample Form 12.1).

• A *bill of lading* is a contract between the owner of the goods and the carrier (as with domestic shipments). For shipment by vessel, there are two types: a straight bill of lading, which is not negotiable and does not give title to the goods, and a negotiable, or shipper's order, bill of lading. The latter can be bought, sold, or traded while the goods are in transit. The customer usually needs an original bill of lading as proof of ownership to take possession of the goods. See Sample Form 12.2 for an example of a straight bill of lading short form and Sample Form 12.3 for an example of a liner bill of lading.

• A *commercial invoice* is a bill for the goods from the seller to the buyer (Sample Form 12.4). Many governments use commercial invoices to determine the true value of goods when assessing customs duties. Governments that use the commercial invoice to control imports will often specify the invoice's form, content, number of copies, language to be used, and other characteristics.

• A *consular invoice*, a required document in some countries, describes the shipment of goods and shows information such as the consignor, consignee, and value of the shipment. Certified by the consular official of the foreign country, it is used by the country's customs officials to verify the value, quantity, and nature of the shipment.

• A *certificate of origin*, also a required document in certain nations, is a signed statement as to the origin of the export item (Sample Form 12.5). Certificates of origin are usually validated by a semiofficial organization, such as a local chamber of commerce. A certificate may be required even if the commercial invoice contains the same information. See Box 12.1 for more information about certificates of origin.

BOX 12.1 A WORD ON CERTIFICATES OF ORIGIN

Specific certificates of origin are sometimes required for countries involved in special trade agreements, such as the North American Free Trade Agreement (NAFTA), which was signed by Canada, Mexico, and the United States.

For instance, the NAFTA certificate of origin validates that a good originated in a NAFTA country and is eligible for the preferential duty rate. The U.S.–Israel Free Trade Area also has its own certificate of origin.

• A *NAFTA certificate of origin* is required for products traded among the signatory countries of the North American Free Trade Agreement (Canada, Mexico, and the United States) if the goods are NAFTA qualified and the importer is claiming zero-duty preference under NAFTA.

• An *inspection certification* is required by some purchasers and countries to attest to the specifications of the goods shipped. The inspection is usually performed by a third party, often an independent testing organization.

• A *dock receipt* and a *warehouse receipt* are used to transfer accountability when the domestic carrier moves the export item to the port of embarkation and leaves it with the shipping line for export.

• A *destination control statement* appears on the commercial invoice and on the air waybill or bill of lading to notify the carrier and all foreign parties that the item can be exported only to certain destinations.

• A *shipper's export declaration* (SED) is used to control exports and is a source document for official U.S. export statistics. SEDs, or their electronic equivalent, are required for shipments when the value of the commodities, classified under any single Schedule B number (the four-digit U.S. extension to the six-digit code under the Harmonized Tariff System—see Box 12.2), exceeds $2,500. SEDs must be prepared and submitted for all shipments, regardless of value, that require an export license or are destined for countries restricted by the Export Administration Regulations (see Chapter 10). SEDs are prepared by the exporter or the exporter's agent and are delivered to the exporting carrier (e.g., the post office, airline, or vessel line). The exporting carrier will present the required number of copies to the U.S. Customs Service at the port of export. Sample Form 12.6 is an example of the reformatted SED, whose use became mandatory on July 18, 2003. The U.S. Census Bureau's Foreign Trade Division is the controlling agency for this document. The bureau made electronic filing of the SED mandatory on September 1, 2008, using AESDirect. AESDirect is a Web-based application that is available to exporters free of charge. It permits the SED to be filed electronically. You can obtain more information on registering as an AESDirect filer and all filing options at *www.aesdirect.gov*. Often, the SED is prepared as a by-product of another

BOX 12.2 THE HARMONIZED SYSTEM

The World Customs Organization developed the Harmonized System (HS) to describe products for customs purposes. The HS is recognized by 179 countries, customs bureaus, or economic unions, representing 98 percent of world trade.

HOW IT WORKS

Six-digit codes are assigned that represent general categories of goods. Countries that use

HS numbers are allowed to define commodities at a more detailed level but must "harmonize" the first six digits to the HS framework.

WHAT THIS MEANS FOR YOU

Using these codes ensures that customs officials are referring to the same item when classifying the product and applying the tariff rate.

document, the shipper's letter of instructions (see Sample Form 12.7).

• An *export license* is a government document that authorizes the export of specific goods in specific quantities to a particular destination. This document may be required for most or all exports to some countries. For other countries, it may be required only under special circumstances.

• An *export packing list* is considerably more detailed and informative than a standard domestic packing list. It itemizes the material in each package and indicates the type of package, such as a box, crate, drum, or carton. It also shows the individual net, tare, and gross weights and measurements for each package (in both U.S. and metric systems). Package markings should be shown along with references to identify the shipment. The shipper or forwarding agent uses the list to determine the total shipment weight and volume and whether the correct cargo is being shipped. In addition, U.S. and foreign customs officials may use the list to check the cargo (see Sample Form 12.8).

• An *insurance certificate* is used to assure the consignee that insurance will cover the loss of or damage to the cargo during transit (see Sample Form 12.9).

Documentation must be precise because slight discrepancies or omissions may prevent merchandise from being exported, may result in non-payment, or may even result in the seizure of the exporter's goods by U.S. or foreign customs officials. Collection documents are subject to precise time limits and may not be honored by a bank if the time has expired. Most documentation is routine for freight forwarders and customs brokers, but as the exporter, you are ultimately responsible for the accuracy of the necessary documents.

The number and kinds of documents that the exporter must deal with vary according to the destination of the shipment. Because each country has different import regulations, the exporter must be careful to provide all proper documentation. The following sources also provide information pertaining to foreign import restrictions:

• Export Assistance Centers—find listings for offices in Appendix B and at *www.export.gov/eac.*

• Trade Information Center—call (800) USA-TRADE (800-872-8723) or visit *www.export.gov/exportbasics/ticredirect.asp.*

• Foreign government embassies and consulates in the United States—go online to *www.state.gov.*

SHIPPING

The handling of transportation is similar for domestic and export orders. Export marks are added to the standard information on a domestic bill of lading. These marks show the name of the exporting carrier and the latest allowed arrival date at the port of export. Instructions for the inland carrier to notify the international freight forwarder by telephone on arrival should also be included. You may find it useful to consult with a freight forwarder to determine the method of international shipping. Because carriers are often used for large and bulky shipments, you can reserve space on the carrier well before actual shipment date. This reservation is called the *booking contract.*

International shipments are increasingly made on a bill of lading under a multimodal contract. The multimodal transit operator (frequently one of the transporters) takes charge of and responsibility for the entire movement from factory to final destination.

The cost of the shipment, delivery schedule, and accessibility to the shipped product by the foreign buyer are all factors to consider when determining the method of international shipping. Although air carriers may be more expensive, their cost may be offset by lower domestic shipping costs (e.g., using a local airport instead of a coastal seaport) and quicker delivery times. These factors may give the U.S. exporter an edge over other competitors.

Before shipping, your firm should check with the foreign buyer about the destination of the goods. Buyers may want the goods to be shipped to a free trade zone or a free port, where they are exempt from import duties (see Chapter 10).

INSURANCE

Damaging weather conditions, rough handling by carriers, and other common hazards to cargo make insurance an important protection for U.S. exporters. If the terms of sale make you responsible for insurance, your company should either obtain its own policy or insure the cargo under a freight forwarder's policy for a fee. If the terms of sale make the foreign buyer responsible, you should not assume (or even take the buyer's word) that adequate insurance has been obtained. If the buyer neglects to obtain adequate coverage, damage to the cargo may cause a major financial loss to your company.

Shipments by sea are covered by marine cargo insurance. Air shipments may also be covered by marine cargo insurance, or insurance may be purchased from the air carrier. Export shipments are usually covered by cargo insurance against loss, damage, and delay in transit. International agreements often limit carrier liability. Additionally, the coverage is substantially different from domestic coverage. Arrangements for insurance may be made by either the buyer or the seller in accordance with the terms of sale. Exporters are advised to consult with international insurance carriers or freight forwarders for more information. Although sellers and buyers can agree to different components, coverage is usually placed at 110 percent of the CIF (cost, insurance, freight) or CIP (carriage and insurance paid to) value.

TARIFFS

Because tariffs, port handling fees, and taxes can be high, it is very important for you to consider their effects on your product's final cost. Typically, the importer pays the tariffs. Nevertheless, these costs will influence how much the buyer is willing to pay for your product.

MAJOR SHIPPERS

International shipping companies have become an excellent resource for exporters. In addition to transporting bulk freight, they now offer assistance with shipping documentation, warehousing in the foreign market, and—in some cases—payment collection from the foreign buyer.

SAMPLE FORM 12.1 AIR WAYBILL

© 2001 UNZ & CO.

House Air Waybill Number

Shipper's Name and Address	Shipper's Account Number

Not negotiable

Air Waybill
(Air Consignment note)
Issued by

Copies 1, 2 and 3 of this Air Waybill are originals and have the same validity

Consignee's Name and Address	Consignee's Account Number

It is agreed that the goods described herein are accepted in apparent good order and condition (except as noted) for carriage SUBJECT TO THE CONDITIONS OF CONTRACT ON THE REVERSE HEREOF. THE SHIPPER'S ATTENTION IS DRAWN TO THE NOTICE CONCERNING CARRIERS' LIMITATION OF LIABILITY. Shipper may increase such limitation of liability by declaring a higher value for carriage and paying a supplemental charge if required.

These commodities licensed by the United States for ultimate destination

Diversion contrary to

United States law prohibited.

Airport of Departure (Addr. of first Carrier) and requested Routing

To	By first Carrier	Routing and Destination	Air Waybill Number	Currency	CHGS Code	WT/VAL		Other		Declared Value for Carriage	Declared Value for Customs
						PPD	COLL	PPD	COLL		

Airport of Destination	Flight/Date	For Carrier Use only	Flight/Date	Amount of Insurance	INSURANCE: If Carrier offers insurance and such insurance is requested in accordance with conditions on reverse hereof, indicate amount to be insured in figures in box marked "amount of insurance".

Handling Information

No. of Pieces RCP	Gross Weight	kg lb	Rate Class / Commodity Item No.	Chargeable Weight	Rate / Charge	Total	Nature and Quantity of Goods (incl. Dimensions or Volume)

Prepaid	Weight Charge	Collect	Other Charges

Valuation Charge

Tax

Total other Charges Due Agent

Total other Charges Due Carrier

Shipper certifies that the particulars on the face hereof are correct and that insofar as any part of the consignment contains dangerous goods, such part is properly described by name and is in proper condition for carriage by air according to the applicable Dangerous Goods Regulations.

....
Signature of Shipper or his Agent

Total prepaid	Total collect

Currency Conversion Rates	cc charges in Dest. Currency

Executed on (Date)   at   (Place)   Signature of Issuing Carrier or its Agent

House Air Waybill Number

Form No. 16-810 Printed and Sold by UNZ&CO 201 Circle Drive N, Suite 104, Piscataway, NJ 08854 (800) 631-3098 www.unzco.com

Source: Unz & Co.

chapter 12

SHIPPING YOUR PRODUCT

STRAIGHT BILL OF LADING – SHORT FORM – ORIGINAL – NOT NEGOTIABLE

RECEIVED, subject to the classifications and tariffs in effect on the date of the issue of this Bill of Lading, the property described above in apparent good order, except as noted (contents and condition of contents of packages unknown), marked, consigned, and destined as indicated above which said carrier (the word carrier being understood throughout this contract as meaning any person or corporation in possession of the property under the contract) agrees to carry to its usual place of delivery at said destination, if on its route, otherwise to deliver to another carrier on the route to said destination. It is mutually agreed as to each carrier of all or any of said property over all or any portion of said route to destination and as to each party at any time interested in all or any said property, that every service to be performed hereunder shall be subject to all the bill of lading terms and conditions in the governing classification on the date of shipment.

Shipper hereby certifies that he is familiar with all the bill of lading terms and conditions in the governing classification and the said terms and conditions are hereby agreed to by the shipper and accepted for himself and his assigns.

From _____ **(1)**

At _____ **(2)** __ 20 __ **(3)**   DESIGNATE WITH AN (X)
BY TRUCK ☐ FREIGHT ☐ **(4)**

Shipper's No. _____ **(5)**

Carrier _____ **(6)**

Agent's No. _____ **(7)**

(Mail or street address of consignee–For purposes of notification only.)

Consigned to _____ **(8)**

Destination _____ **(9)** State of _____ County of _____

Route _____ **(10)**

Delivering Carrier _____ **(11)** Vehicle or Car Initial _____ **(12)** No. _____

No. Packages **(13)**	Kind of Package, Description of Articles, Special Marks, and Exceptions **(14)**	*Weight (Sub. to Cor.) **(15)**	Class or Rate **(16)**	Check Column

Subject to Section 7 of conditions of applicable bill of lading, if this shipment is to be delivered to the consignee without recourse on the consignor, the consignor shall sign the following statement:

The carrier shall not make delivery of this shipment without payment of freight and all other lawful charges. **(17)**

Per _____
(Signature of Consignor.)

If charges are to be prepaid, write or stamp here, "To be Prepaid." **(18)**

Received $ _____ **(19)**
to apply in prepayment of the charges on the property described hereon.

_____
Agent or Cashier

Per _____
(The signature here acknowledges only the amount prepaid.)

Charges Advanced: _____ **(20)**

C.O.D. SHIPMENT
Prepaid ☐
Collect ☐ $ _____ **(21)**

Collection Fee _____

Total Charges _____

*If the shipment moves between two ports by a carrier by water, the law requires that the bill of lading shall state whether it is "Carriers or Shippers weight."

†Shipper's imprint in lieu of stamp; not a part of bill of lading approved by the Department of Transportation.

NOTE–Where the rate is dependent on value, shippers are required to state specifically in writing the agreed or declared value of the property.

THIS SHIPMENT IS CORRECTLY DESCRIBED. CORRECT WEIGHT IS _____ LBS. **(22)**
DECLARED VALUE IF SO STATED
$ _____

Subject to verification by the Respective Weighing and Inspection Bureau According to Agreement.

Per _____

If lower charges result, the agreed or declared value of the within described containers is hereby specifically stated to be not exceeding 50 cents per pound per article.

This is to certify that the above-named materials are properly classified, described, packaged, marked and labeled and are in proper condition for transportation according to the applicable regulations of the Department of Transportation.

_____ SIGNATURE **(27)**

TOTAL PIECES

The fibre containers used for this shipment conform to the specifications set forth in the box maker's certificate thereon, and all other requirements of Rule 41 of the Uniform Freight Classification and Rule 5 of the National Motor Freight Classification. Shipper's imprint in lieu of stamp, not a part of bill of lading approved by Interstate Commerce CCommission.

_____ **(23)** Shipper, Per _____

_____ **(24)** Agent, Per _____ **(25)**

Permanent post-office address of shipper _____ **(26)**

1

Form No. 35-644 Printed and Sold by UNZ&CO 201 Circle Drive N, Suite 104, Piscataway, NJ 08854 (800) 631-3098 www.unzco.com

Source: Unz & Co.

1. Shipper (from). Enter the company name and address of the shipper (consignor).

2. Point of origin (at). Enter the city and state of the actual shipping point.

3. Date of shipment. Enter the date of the shipment (the date the carrier took control of the merchandise).

4. Truck or freight. Check the "truck" box if shipment is to move by truck. Check the "freight" box if the shipment is to move by rail.

5. Shipper's number. Enter a unique control number to reference the shipment with the carrier.

6. Carrier. Enter the name of the company that will take initial control of the shipment and cause its delivery to the consignee.

7. Agent's number. Enter the carrier's control number, if known or required.

8. Consigned to. Enter the full name of the final recipient of the shipment (the ultimate consignee). Also enter the mailing address of the ultimate consignee, if different from the destination, for carrier notification purposes.

9. Destination. Enter the street address, city, and postal code where the carrier will make delivery to the consignee in Field 8.

10. Route. If applicable, enter the route the carrier will take to the consignee. This field may also be used to specify docks, warehouses, and so forth and to specify any intermediate carriers.

11. Delivering carrier. If applicable, specify the carrier that will deliver the shipment to the ultimate consignee at the destination, but only if different from the carrier entered in Field 6.

12. Vehicle or car initial or number. Enter any vehicle identifying initials or numbers, if applicable.

13. Number of packages. Enter the total number of packages per line item.

If the packages are consolidated on a pallet or in an outer container, note this information on a second line (for example, 112 pkgs. 3 pall.).

14. Description of shipment. Enter the description of each line item, noting the type of package (carton, barrel, etc.) and quantity per package. Because correct freight classification is essential in describing an item, there must be a separate line item for each freight classification description. If more than one type of packaging is used per freight classification, a separate entry must be used for each type. Enter any special package markings, special handling requirements, and delivery instructions. For hazardous material items, special provisions must be met in completing this field.

15. Weight. Enter the total gross weight, in pounds, for each line item. For bulk shipments, the tare and net weights should also be referenced in the description field. For package shipments, include the weights of pallets and skids. The total weight of the merchandise should be shown after the last line item, with pallet and dunnage weights shown separately.

16. Class or rate. Enter either the five-digit class (per the Uniform Freight Classification or the National Motor Freight Classification) or a two-digit class rate (a percentage of the first-class 100 rate) per line item. This information may be determined by contacting the carrier.

17. Without recourse statement. Per standard bill of lading terms, the shipper is ultimately liable for freight charges, even when the shipment is sent on a collect basis to the consignee. By signing this statement, the shipper is released from the liability of freight charges for collect shipments delivered by the carrier to the consignee without the carrier's collecting the freight charges. For prepaid shipments, leave blank.

18. Prepaid shipments. Enter "To Be Prepaid" if shipment is to be paid for by the shipper. If this field is left blank, the carrier will seek to collect the charges from the consignee (see Field 17).

19. Prepayments received. The carrier's agent will enter any payments received in advance from the shipper for the shipment.

20. Charges advanced. The carrier's agent will enter any charges advanced for the shipment, if applicable.

21. C.O.D. shipment. First, check the box indicating whether the freight charges are prepaid (the carrier bills the shipper) or collect (the carrier deducts the freight charges from the amount collected from the consignee). Second, enter the amount to be collected for the merchandise itself—be sure to include the freight charges. Third, enter any collection fees applicable. Then enter total charges to be collected by carrier.

22. Shipment declared value. When the weight charged by the carrier depends on the value of the shipment, the dollar value per unit of measure (e.g., $100.00/pound) must be stated by the shipper. Enter this information in Field 14.

23. Shipper. Enter the company name of the shipper.

24. Shipper's agent. Enter the signature of the individual preparing the shipment for the shipper.

25. Carrier's agent. The carrier's agent will sign here before taking control of the shipment.

26. Permanent address. Enter the permanent (business) mailing address of the shipper. This information may be the same as for Field 1.

27. Certification. A signature is required by the U.S. Department of Transportation after this statement for all shipments of hazardous material.

Page 1

Shipper (full style and address)	**BIMCO LINER BILL OF LADING** **CODE NAME: "CONLINEBILL 2000"**
	Amended January 1950; August 1952; January 1973; July 1974; August 1976; January 1978; November 2000.

Consignee (full style and address) or Order	B/L No.	Reference No.
	Vessel	

Notify Party (full style and address)	Port of loading
	Port of discharge

PARTICULARS DECLARED BY THE SHIPPER BUT NOT ACKNOWLEDGED BY THE CARRIER

Container No./Seal No./Marks and Numbers	Numbers and kind of packages; description of cargo	Gross weight, kg	Measurement, m³

SHIPPED on board in apparent good order and condition (unless otherwise stated herein) the total number of Containers/Packages or Units indicated in the Box opposite entitled "Total number of Containers/Packages or Units received by the Carrier" and the cargo as specified above, weight, measure, marks, numbers, quality, contents and value unknown, for carriage to the Port of discharge or so near thereunto as the vessel may safely get and lie always afloat, to be delivered in the like good order and condition at the Port of discharge unto the lawful holder of the Bill of Laiding, on payment of freight as indicated to the right plus other charges incurred in accordance with the provisions contained in this Bill of Laiding. In accepting this Bill of Laiding the Merchant* expressly accepts and agrees to all its stipulations on both Page 1 and Page 2, whether written, printed, stamped or otherwise incorporated, as fully as if they were all signed by the Merchant.
One original Bill of Laiding must be surrendered duly endorsed in exchange for the cargo or delivery order, whereupon all other Bills of Laiding to be void.
IN WITNESS whereof the Carrier, Master or their Agent has signed the number of original Bills of Laiding stated below right, all of this tenor and date.

Total number of Containers/Packages or units received by the Carrier	
Shipper's declared value	Declared value charge
Freight details and charges	

Carrier's name/principal place of business	Date shipped on board	Place and date of issue
	Number of original Bills of Laiding	
	Pre-carriage by**	

Signature

.... Carrier
or, for the Carrier

.... as Master
(Master's name/signature)

.... as Agents
(Agent's name/signature)

Place of receipt by pre-carrier**

Place of delivery by on-carrier**

*As defined hereinafter (Cl.1)
**Applicable only when pre-/on-carriage is arranged in accordance with Clause 8

Form 35-121 Printed and *UNZCO*

201 Circle Drive N, Piscataway, NJ 08854
(800) 631-3098 www.unzco.com

Source: Unz & Co.

COMMERCIAL INVOICE

SELLER:

1

SOLD TO:

2

SHIP TO (if different than Sold To):

3

INVOICE No.	**4**	DATE
CUSTOMER REFERENCE No.	**5**	DATE
TERMS OF SALE	**6**	
TERMS OF PAYMENT	**7**	
CURRENCY OF SETTLEMENT	**8**	
MODE OF SHIPMENT	**9**	BILL OF LAIDING / AWB

QTY	DESCRIPTION	UNIT OF MEASURE	UNIT PRICE	TOTAL PRICE
10	**11**	**12**	**13**	

PACKAGE MARKS:

15

TOTAL COMMERCIAL VALUE:	**14**
MISC. CHARGES: (packing, insurance, etc.)	**16**
TOTAL INVOICE VALUE:	

CERTIFICATIONS:

17

I certify that the stated export prices and description of goods are true and correct:

_____
(SIGNED)

TITLE: _____

Form No. 10-327 Printed and Sold by *UNZ&CO* 201 Circle Drive N, Suite 104, Piscataway, NJ 08854   (800) 631-3098 www.unzco.com

chapter
12

SHIPPING YOUR PRODUCT

Source: Unz & Co.

1. Seller. Enter the name and address of the principal party responsible for effecting export from the United States (i.e., the exporter as named on the export license).

2. Sold to. Enter the name and address of the person or company to which the goods are shipped for the designated end use, or the party so designated on the export license.

3. Ship to (if different than sold to). Enter the intermediate consignee— that is, the name and address of the party that effects delivery of the merchandise to the ultimate consignee, or the party so named on the export license or forwarding agent (i.e., the name and address of the duly authorized forwarder acting as agent for the exporter).

4. Invoice number. Enter the invoice number assigned by the exporter.

5. Customer reference number. Enter the overseas customer's reference or order number.

6. Terms of sale. Enter the delivery and payment terms of the sales agreement.

7. Terms of payment. Describe the terms and conditions as agreed upon by the seller and buyer per the pro forma invoice, customer purchase order, or the letter of credit.

8. Currency of settlement. Enter the currency agreed upon by seller and buyer as payment.

9. Mode of shipment. Indicate air, ocean, or surface.

10. Quantity. Record the total number of units per description line.

11. Description. Provide a full description of the items shipped; the type of container (carton, box, pack, etc.); the gross weight per container; and the quantity and unit of measure of the merchandise.

12. Unit of measure. Record the total net weight and total gross weight (includes weight of container) in kilograms per description line.

13. Unit price and total price. Record the unit price of the merchandise per the unit of measure. Compute the extended total value of the line.

14. Total commercial value. Compute the total value of the invoice.

15. Package marks. Record in this field, as well as on each package, the package number (for example, "1 of 7," "3 of 7," etc.); shipper's company name; country of origin (for example, "Made in U.S.A."); destination port of entry; package weight in kilograms; package size (length × width × height); and shipper's control number (optional).

16. Miscellaneous charges. Record any miscellaneous charges that are to be paid by the customer, such as export transportation, insurance, export packaging, and inland freight to pier.

17. Certifications. Enter any certifications or declarations required of the shipper regarding any information recorded on the commercial invoice.

SAMPLE FORM 12.5 CERTIFICATE OF ORIGIN

CERTIFICATE OF ORIGIN

SHIPPER/EXPORTER
1

COMMERCIAL INVOICE NO.
5

DATE

CUSTOMER PURCHASE ORDER NO.
6

B/L, AWB NO.
7

COUNTRY OG ORIGIN
8

DATE OF EXPORT
9

CONSIGNEE
2

EXPORT REFERENCES
10

NOTIFY: INTERMEDIATE CONSIGNEE
3

FORWARDING AGENT
4

AIR/OCEAN PORT OF EMBARKATION
11

EXPORTING CARRIER/ROUTE
12

QUANTITY	NET WT. (Kilos)	GROSS WT. (Kilos)	DESCRIPTION OF MERCHANDISE
13	**14**	**15**	**16**

PACKAGE MARKS:
17

The undersigned _____ **18** _____ (Owner or Agent), does hereby declare for the above named shipper, the goods as described above were shipped on the above date and consigned as indicated and are products of the United States of America.

Dated at _____ **19** _____ on the _____ day of _____ 20 _____

Sworn to before me this _____ day of _____ 20 _____

_____

_____
SIGNATURE OF OWNER OR AGENT
20

The _____ **21** _____ , a recognized Chamber of Commerce under the laws of the

State of _____ , has examined the manufacturer's invoice or shipper's affidavit concerning the origin of the merchandise, and, according to the best of its knowledge and belief, finds that the products named originated in the United States of America.

Secretary _____ **22** _____

Source: Unz & Co.

INSTRUCTIONS FOR SAMPLE FORM 12.5, CERTIFICATE OF ORIGIN

1. Shipper or exporter. Enter the name and address of the principal party responsible for effecting export from the United States.

2. Consignee. Enter the name and address of the party receiving the merchandise.

3. Notify: intermediate consignee. Enter the name and address of the party in a foreign country that effects the delivery of the merchandise.

4. Forwarding agent. Enter the name and address of the freight forwarder.

5. Commercial invoice number. Enter the number assigned by the exporter.

6. Customer purchase order number. Enter the number assigned by the exporter.

7. Bill of lading or air waybill number. Enter the number provided by the freight forwarder or carrier.

8. Country of origin. Enter the actual country of origin of the goods.

9. Date of export. Enter the date of actual export from the United States.

10. Export references. Include any special reference numbers assigned by the exporter.

11. Air or ocean port of embarkation. Enter the port from which the goods are shipped.

12. Exporting carrier and route. Enter the name of the air carrier or vessel and flight number or voyage number.

13. Quantity. Enter the total number of packages, cartons, boxes, skids, and so forth, per description line.

14. Net weight. Enter the total weight of all packages per description line, excluding the outer packaging but including inner packaging, in kilograms.

15. Gross weight. Enter the total weight of all packages, including the shipping container, outer packaging, and inner packaging, in kilograms.

16. Description of merchandise. Fully describe the items shipped, type of container, gross weight per container, and unit of measure of the merchandise. Cross-references to purchase order or commercial invoice numbers may be included.

17. Package marks. Describe the marks recorded on each package, usually including shipper's company name; country of origin (for example, "Made in U.S.A."); destination port of entry; and customer's company name. They may also include a shipper's control number and the customer's import license number. "Number" refers to the numbering of the packages in the shipment (for example, "1 of 30," "2 of 30," etc.).

18. The undersigned. Enter the name of the individual completing and signing the certificate (see Field 20). The signer may be the exporter or an agent of the exporter.

19. Date. Enter the date on which the certificate of origin was prepared and signed.

20. Signature. The owner, employee, or agent appearing in Field 18 should sign here.

21. Chamber of commerce. Enter the name of the local chamber of commerce (and state) certifying the origin of the merchandise.

22. Secretary. The authorized signature of the local chamber of commerce secretary and that organization's seal should be added here.

SAMPLE FORM 12.6 SHIPPER'S EXPORT DECLARATION

U.S. DEPARTMENT OF COMMERCE – Economics and Statistics Administration – U.S. CENSUS BUREAU – BUREAU OF EXPORT ADMINISTRATION

FORM **7525-V** (7-18-2003)   **SHIPPER'S EXPORT DECLARATION**   OMB No. 0607-0152

1a. U.S. PRINCIPAL PARTY IN INTEREST (USPPI)(Complete name and address)	
ZIP CODE	**2.** DATE OF EXPORTATION **3.** TRANSPORTATION REFERENCE NO.
b. USPPI'S EIN (IRS) OR ID NO. **c.** PARTIES TO TRANSACTION ☐ Related ☐ Non-related	
4a. ULTIMATE CONSIGNEE *(Complete name and address)*	
b. INTERMEDIATE CONSIGNEE *(Complete name and address)*	
5a. FORWARDING AGENT *(Complete name and address)*	

5b. FORWARDING AGENT'S EIN (IRS) NO.	**6.** POINT (STATE) OF ORIGIN OR FTZ NO.	**7.** COUNTRY OF ULTIMATE DESTINATION
8. LOADING PIER *(Vessel only)* **9.** METHOD OF TRANSPORTATION *(Specify)*	**14.** CARRIER IDENTIFICATION CODE	**15.** SHIPMENT REFERENCE NO.
10. EXPORTING CARRIER **11.** PORT OF EXPORT	**16.** ENTRY NUMBER	**17.** HAZARDOUS MATERIALS ☐ Yes ☐ No
12. PORT OF UNLOADING *(Vessel and air only)* **13.** CONTAINERIZED *(Vessel only)* ☐ Yes ☐ No	**18.** IN BOND CODE	**19.** ROUTED EXPORT TRANSACTION ☐ Yes ☐ No

20. SCHEDULE B DESCRIPTION OF COMMODITIES *(Use columns 22–24)*

D/F or M (21)	SCHEDULE B NUMBER (22)	QUANTITY – SCHEDULE B UNIT(S) (23)	SHIPPING WEIGHT (Kilograms) (24)	VIN/PRODUCT NUMBER/ VEHICLE TITLE NUMBER (25)	VALUE (U.S. dollars, omit cents) (Selling price or cost if not sold) (26)

27. LICENSE NO./LICENSE EXCEPTION SYMBOL/AUTHORIZATION	**28.** ECCN *(When required)*	
29. Duly authorized officer or employee	The USPPI authorizes the forwarder named above to act as forwarding agent for export control and customs purposes.	

30. I certify that all statements made and all information contained herein are true and correct and that I have read and understand the instructions for preparation of this document, set forth in the **"Correct Way to Fill Out the Shipper's Export Declaration."** I understand that civil and criminal penalties, including forfeiture and sale, may be imposed for making false or fraudulent statements herein, failing to provide the requested information or for violation of U.S. laws on exportation (13 U.S.C. Sec. 305; 22 U.S.C. Sec. 401; 18 U.S.C. Sec. 1001; 50 U.S.C. App. 2410).

Signature	**Confidential –** Shipper's Export Declarations (or any successor document) wherever located, shall be exempt from public disclosure unless the Secretary determines that such exemption would be contrary to the national interest (Title 13, Chapter 9, Section 301 (g)).
Title	Export shipments are subject to inspection by U.S. Customs Service and/or Office of Export Enforcement.
Date	**31.** AUTHENTICATION *(When required)*
Telephone No. (Include Area Code)	E-mail address

This form may be printed by private parties provided it conforms to the official form. For sale by the Superintendent of Documents, Government Printing Office, Washington, DC 20402, and local Customs District Directors. The **"Correct Way to Fill Out the Shipper's Export Declaration"** is available from the U.S. Census Bureau, Washington, DC 20233.

Source: U.S. Department of Commerce.

1a. U.S. PRINCIPAL PARTY IN INTEREST (USPPI)(Complete name and address)

(1)

ZIP CODE

b. USPPI'S EIN (IRS) OR ID NO. | **c.** PARTIES TO TRANSACTION
☐ Related   ☐ Non-related

4a. ULTIMATE CONSIGNEE *(Complete name and address)*

(7)

b. INTERMEDIATE CONSIGNEE *(Complete name and address)*

(8)

5a. FORWARDING AGENT *(Complete name and address)*

(9)

5b. FORWARDING AGENT'S EIN (IRS) NO. **(10)**

8. LOADING PIER *(Vessel only)* **(13)** | **9.** METHOD OF TRANSPORTATION *(Specify)* **(14)**

10. EXPORTING CARRIER **(15)** | **11.** PORT OF EXPORT **(16)**

12. PORT OF UNLOADING *(Vessel and air)* **(17)** | **13.** CONTAINERIZED *(Vessel only)* **(18)**
☐ Yes   ☐ No

INLAND CARRIER **(2)**   SHIP DATE   PRO NO.

2. DATE OF EXPORTATION **(3)** | **3.** TRANSPORTATION REFERENCE NO. **(4)**

SPECIAL INSTRUCTIONS

SHIP VIA **(5)**
☐ AIR   ☐ OCEAN | **(6)** ☐ CONSOLIDATE   ☐ DIRECT

**SHIPPER'S LETTER
OF INSTRUCTIONS**

6. POINT (STATE) OF ORIGIN OR FTZ **(11)** | **7.** COUNTRY OF ULTIMATE DESTINAT... **(12)**

14. CARRIER IDENTIFICATION CODE **(19)** | **15.** SHIPMENT REFERENCE NO. **(20)**

16. ENTRY NUMBER **(21)** | **17.** HAZARDOUS MATERIALS **(22)**
☐ Yes   ☐ No

18. IN BOND CODE **(23)** | **19.** ROUTED EXPORT TRANSACTION **(24)**
☐ Yes   ☐ No

---

20. SCHEDULE B DESCRIPTION OF COMMODITIES *(Use columns 22–24)*

D/F or M (21)	SCHEDULE B NUMBER (22)	QUANTITY – SCHEDULE B UNIT(S) (23)	SHIPPING WEIGHT (Kilograms) (24)	VIN/PRODUCT NUMBER/ VEHICLE TITLE NUMBER (25)	VALUE (U.S. dollars, omit cents) (Selling price or cost if not sold) (26)
(25)	**(26)**	**(28)**	**(29)**	**(30)**	**(31)**
	(27)				

27. LICENSE NO./LICENSE EXCEPTION SYMBOL/AUTHORIZATIO... **(32)** | **28.** ECCN *(When required)* **(33)**

29. Duly authorized officer or employee **(35)** | The USPPI authorizes the forwarder named above to act as forwarding agent for export control and customs purposes.

30. I certify that all statements made and all information contained herein are true and correct and that I have read and understand the instructions for preparation of this document, set forth in the **"Correct Way to Fill Out the Shipper's Export Declaration."** I understand that civil and criminal penalties, including forfeiture and sale, may be imposed for making false or fraudulent statements herein, failing to provide the requested information or for violation of U.S. laws on exportation (13 U.S.C. Sec. 305; 22 U.S.C. Sec. 401; 18 U.S.C. Sec. 1001; 50 U.S.C. App. 2410).

Signature **(36)**

Confidential – Shipper's Export Declarations (or any successor document) wherever located, shall be exempt from public disclosure unless the Secretary determines that such exemption would be contrary to the national interest (Title 13, Chapter 9, Section 301 (g)).

Title

Export shipments are subject to inspection by U.S. Customs Service and/or Office of Export Enforcement.

Date | **31.** AUTHENTICATION *(When required)*

Telephone No. (Include Area Code) | E-mail address

SHIPPER MUST CHECK **(34)**
☐ PREPAID OR
☐ COLLECT

C.O.D. AMOUNT $

SHIPPER'S INSTRUCTIONS IN CASE OF INABILITY TO DELIVER CONSIGNMENT AS CONSIGNED:

☐ ABANDON   ☐ RETURN TO SHIPPER
☐ DELIVER TO   **(37)**

SHIPPER'S REQUESTS INSURANCE **(38)**
☐ Yes $ _____   ☐ No

If Shipper has requested insurance as provided for at the left hereof, shipment is insured in the amount indicated (recovery is limited to actual loss) in accordance with the provisions as specified in the Carrier's Tariffs. Insurance is payable to Shipper unless payee is designated in writing by the shipper.

BE SURE TO PICK UP TOP SHEET AND SIGN THE FIRST
BUFF EXPORT DECLARATION WITH PEN & INK.

Form 19-305 Printed and Sold by UNZ&CO 201 Circle Drive N, Suite 104, Piscataway, NJ 08854
(800) 631-3098 www.unzco.com

Source: Unz & Co.

INSTRUCTIONS FOR SAMPLE FORM 12.7, SHIPPER'S LETTER OF INSTRUCTIONS

1(a). U.S. principal party in interest (USPPI). Provide the name and address of the USPPI. The USPPI is the person in the United States that receives the primary benefit, monetary or otherwise, of the export transaction. Generally that person is the U.S. seller, manufacturer, order party, or foreign entity. The foreign entity must be listed as the USPPI if in the United States when the items are purchased or obtained for export. Report only the first five digits of the ZIP code.

1(b). USPPI's employer identification number (EIN) or ID number. Enter the USPPI's Internal Revenue Service EIN, or Social Security Number (SSN) if no EIN has been assigned.

1(c). Parties to transaction. Indicate if this is a related or non-related party transaction. A related party transaction is a transaction between a USPPI and a foreign consignee (for example, a parent company or sister company), where there is at least 10 percent ownership of each by the same U.S. or foreign person or business enterprise.

2. Inland carrier. If you have shipped this material to the United States by inland carrier, provide the inland carrier's name, shipping date, and receipt or progressive number (pro. no.), if available.

3. Date of exportation. Enter the date on which the merchandise is scheduled to leave the United States for all methods of transportation. If the actual date is not known, report the best estimate of departure. The date format should be MM/DD/YYYY.

4. Transportation reference number. Report the booking number for ocean shipments. The booking number is the reservation number assigned by the carrier to hold space on the vessel for the cargo being shipped. For air shipments, the air waybill number must be reported. For other methods of transportation, leave blank.

5. Ship via air or ocean. Indicate the mode of shipment.

6. Consolidate or direct shipping. Indicate how the forwarder is to instruct the carrier to ship the goods.

7. Ultimate consignee. Enter the name and address of the foreign party actually receiving the merchandise for the designated end use or the party so designated on the export license. For overland shipments to Mexico, also include the Mexican state in the address.

8. Intermediate consignee. Enter the name and address of the party in a foreign country that delivers the merchandise to the ultimate consignee or the party so named on the export license.

9. Forwarding agent. Enter the name and address of the forwarding or other agent authorized by a principal party in interest.

10. Forwarding agent's EIN or ID number. Enter the forwarding agent's Internal Revenue Service EIN. Ender the nine-digit numerical code as reported on the latest employer's quarterly federal tax return (Treasury Form 941).

11. Point (state) of origin or foreign-trade zone (FTZ) number. If from an FTZ, enter the FTZ number for exports; otherwise enter the two-digit U.S. Postal Service abbreviation of the state in which the merchandise actually starts its journey to the port of export, the state of the commodity of the greatest value, or the state of consolidation.

12. Country of ultimate destination. Enter the country in which the merchandise is to be consumed, further processed, or manufactured; the final country of destination as known to the exporter at the time of shipment; or the country of ultimate destination as shown on the export license. Two-digit (alpha character) International Organization for Standardization (ISO) codes may also be used.

13. Loading pier. For vessel shipments only, enter the number or name of the pier at which the merchandise is laden aboard the exporting vessel.

14. Method of transportation. Enter the method of transportation by which the merchandise is exported (or exits the border of the United States). Specify the method by name, such as vessel, air, rail, or truck.

15. Exporting carrier. Enter the name of the carrier transporting the merchandise out of the United States. For vessel shipments, give the name of the vessel.

16. Port of export. For overland shipments, enter the name of the U.S. Customs port at which the surface carrier (truck or railcar) crosses the border. For vessel and air shipments, enter the name of the U.S. Customs port where the merchandise is loaded on the carrier (airplane or ocean vessel) that is taking the merchandise out of the United States. For postal shipments, enter the U.S. post office from which the merchandise is mailed.

17. Port of unloading. For vessel shipments between the United States and foreign countries, enter the foreign port and country at which the merchandise will be unloaded from the exporting earner. For vessel and air shipments between the United States and Puerto Rico, enter the Schedule C code, "U.S. Customs District and Port Code."

18. Containerized cargo. For vessel shipments only, check the "Yes" box for cargo originally booked as containerized cargo and for cargo that has been placed in containers at the vessel operator's option.

19. Carrier identification code. For vessel, rail, and truck shipments, enter the four-character Standard Carrier Alpha Code (SCAC) of the carrier. For air shipments, enter the two- or three-character International Air Transport Association (IATA) code of the carrier. In a consolidated shipment, if the ultimate carrier is unknown, the consolidator's carrier ID code may be reported.

20. Shipment reference number. Enter the unique reference number assigned by the filer of the Shipper's Export Declaration (or SED; see Sample Form 12.6) for identification purposes. This shipment reference number must be unique for five years.

21. Entry number. Enter the import entry number when the export transaction is used as proof of export for import transactions such as in-bond, temporary import bond, drawbacks, and so forth. Also, an entry number is required for merchandise that is entered as an import (CF 7501 or Automated Broker Interface entries) and is then exported out of the United States.

22. Hazardous materials. Check the appropriate "Yes" or "No" indicator that identifies the shipment as hazardous as defined by the U.S. Department of Transportation.

23. In-bond code. Report one of the two-character in-bond codes listed in Part IV of Appendix C of the Foreign Trade Statistics Regulations (15 CFR Part 30) to indicate whether the shipment is being transported under bond.

24. Routed export transaction. Check the appropriate "Yes" or "No" indicator that identifies the transaction as a routed export transaction. A routed export transaction is one in which the foreign principal party in interest authorizes a U.S. forwarding or other agent to export the merchandise out of the United States.

25. "D" (domestic), "F" (foreign), or "M" (foreign military sales). Domestic exports (D) consist of merchandise that is grown, produced, or manufactured in the United States (including imported merchandise that has been enhanced in value or changed from the form in which imported by further manufacture or processing in the United States). Foreign exports (F) consist of merchandise that has entered the United States and is being reexported in the same condition as when imported. Foreign military sales (M) consist of exports of merchandise that are sold under the foreign military sales program.

26. Schedule B number. Enter the commercial description of the commodity being exported and the 10-digit commodity number as provided by the Census Bureau in Schedule B, "Statistical Classification of Domestic and Foreign Commodities Exported from the United States."

27. Schedule B description of commodities. Use columns 22–24 to enter the commercial description of the commodity being exported, its Schedule B number, the quantity in Schedule B units, and the shipping weight in kilograms. Enter a sufficient description of the commodity as to permit verification of the Schedule B commodity number or the commodity description as shown on the validated export license. Include marks, numbers, or other identification shown on the packages and the numbers and kinds of packages (boxes, barrels, baskets, etc.).

28. Quantity (Schedule B units). Report whole units as specified in the Schedule B commodity classification code. Report also the unit specified on the export license if the units differ.

29. Shipping weight. For all methods of transportation, enter the gross shipping weight in kilograms for each Schedule B number, including the weight of containers, but excluding carrier equipment.

30. Vehicle identification number (VIN) or product number, and vehicle title number. Report the following items of information for used self-propelled vehicles as defined in Customs regulations 19 CFR 192.1: (a) the unique VIN in the proper format, or the product identification number (PIN) for those used self-propelled vehicles for which there are no VINs, and (b) the vehicle title number.

31. Value (U.S. dollars). Enter the selling price—or, if not sold, cost—including freight, insurance, and other charges to U.S. port of export, but excluding unconditional discounts and commissions (nearest whole dollar; omit cents). The value to be reported on the SED is the USPPI's price—or, if not sold, cost—to the foreign principal party in interest. Report one value for each Schedule B number.

32. License number, license exception symbol, and authorization. Whenever an SED or Automated Export System (AES) record is required, do the following:

(a) Enter the license number on the SED or AES record when you are exporting under the authority of a Department of the Treasury, Office of Foreign Assets Control (OFAC) license (enter either the general or specific OFAC license number); a Department of Justice, Drug Enforcement Agency (DEA) permit; or any other export license number issued by a federal government agency. Export information for items identified on the Commerce Department's Commerce Control List

(CCL) or the State Department, Office of Defense Trade Controls, U.S. Munitions List, must be filed through the AES.

(b) Enter the correct license exception symbol (for example, LVS, GBS, or CIV) on the SED or AES record when you are exporting under the authority of a license exception. See §740.1, §740.2, and §758.1 of the Export Administration Regulations (EAR) for an explanation of the LVS, GBS, and CIV symbols.

(c) Enter the "no license required" (NLR) designator when you are exporting items under the NLR provisions of the EAR and the items being exported are subject to the EAR but are not listed on the CCL (that is, items that are classified as EAR99).

33. Export Control Classification Number (ECCN). Whenever an SED or AES record is required, you must enter the correct ECCN on the SED or AES record for all exports authorized under a license or license exception, as well as items being exported under the NLR provisions of the EAR that are listed on the CCL and that are controlled for reasons other than antiterrorism.

34. Shipper must check prepaid or collect. This field specifies whether the shipper (prepaid) or the consignee (collect) will pay freight charges. If the shipment is to be paid for C.O.D. by the consignee, specify amount in the "C.O.D. Amount" field.

35. Duly authorized officer or employee. Provide the signature of the USPPI authorizing the named forwarding or agent to effect the export when that agent does not have a formal power of attorney or written authorization.

36. Signature and certification. Provide the signature of the USPPI or authorized forwarding or other agent certifying the truth and accuracy of the information on the SED, the title of the USPPI or authorized agent, the date of signature, the telephone number of the USPPI or authorized agent who prepared the SED and can best answer questions regarding the SED, and the e-mail address of the USPPI or authorized agent.

37. Shipper's instructions. This field instructs the forwarder how to dispose of the shipment in the event it proves to be undeliverable abroad.

38. Insurance. Use this field when insurance is required and the shipper wishes to use an insurer chosen by the forwarder. The amount insured is usually 110 percent of the shipment value.

PACKING LIST

© Copyright 2001 Unz & Co.

_____ 19 _____
Place and Date of Shipment

To

Gentlemen:

Under your Order No. _____ the material listed below
was shipped   via
To

_____

Shipment consists of:	Marks
_____ CasesPackages _____ Packages	
_____ CratesCartons _____ Cartons	
_____ Bbls.Drums _____ Drums	
_____ Reels	

* LEGAL WEIGHT IS WEIGHT OF ARTICLE PLUS PAPER, BOX, BOTTLE, ETC., CONTAINING THE ARTICLE AS USUALLY CARRIED IN STOCK.

PACKAGE NUMBER	WEIGHTS IN LBS. or KILOS			DIMENSIONS			QUANTITY	CLEARLY STATE CONTENTS OF EACH PACKAGE
	GROSS WEIGHT EACH	*LEGAL WEIGHT EACH	NET WEIGHT EACH	HEIGHT	WIDTH	LENGTH		

Form No. 30-036 Printed and Sold by UNZ&CO 201 Circle Drive N, Suite 104, Piscataway, NJ 08854   (800) 631-3098 www.unzco.com

Source: Unz & Co.

ORIGINAL

OPEN POLICY NO.	CERTIFICATE NO.
A2310	2952305

FOREMAN'S FUND INSURANCE COMPANY
SAN FRANCISCO, CALIFORNIA
ATLANTIC DIVISION, 110 WILLIAM STREET
NEW YORK, NEW YORK 10038

$ 125,000.000

The company named above in consideration of premium in the amount of and at rates as arranged and subject to the Conditions and Warranties specified and/or attached hereto, does by this policy insure

ASSURED **Metalworking Machines, Inc.**

as well in their own name as in that of those to whomsoever the subject matter of this Policy does, may, or shall appertain.

IN THE SUM OF **One hundred twenty-five thousand and 00/100---------------------------------**

UPON **steel grinders with accessories**

CONTAINER-HOUSE/HOUSE ☐
CONTAINER-PORT/PORT ☐
CONTAINER-OTHER ☐
NON-CONTAINER ☐

VALUED AT SUM OR SUMS INSURED

LADEN (UNDER DECK) ON BOARD THE VESSEL/AIRLINE: **S/L Adventurer**

(LOST OR NOT LOST) AT AND FROM (INITIAL POINT/PORT): **Interior USA via Baltimore**

LOSS IF ANY PAYABLE TO THE ORDER OF THE ASSURED AT: **destination**

B/L OR SAILING DATE: 9-30-2006

TO (FINAL POINT/PORT): Taipei Taiwan via Kaoshiung

Insured against all risks of physical loss or damage from any external cause irrespective of percentage, but excluding the risks excluded by the "F.C.&S." and/or "S.R.&C.C." warranties on the reverse side of this policy except to the extent that such risks may be specifically covered by endorsement also warranted free from any claim arising out of the inherent price of the goods insured or consequent upon loss of time or market.

This insurance attaches from the time the goods leave the warehouse at the place named in the policy for the commencement of the transit and continues during the ordinary course of transit until the goods are delivered to the final warehouse at the destination named in the policy.

It is a condition of this insurance that there shall be no interruption or suspension of transit unless due to circumstances beyond the control of the Assured.

The risks covered by this policy include loss, damage, or expense resulting from explosion howsoever or wheresoever occurring, irrespective of percentage, but it is especially understood and agreed that this wording is not intended to cover any of the risks excluded by the F.C.&S. and/or S.R.&C.C. Warranties set forth elsewhere in the policy.

In the event of the vessel, wharf, warehouse, conveyance, or other cargo being fumigated by order of property constituted authority and damage arises therefrom to the goods insured hereunder, this Company agrees to indemnify the Assured for such damage irrespective of percentage.

General Average and Salvage Charges payable according to United States laws and usage and/or as per Foreign Statement and/or as per York-Antwerp Rules (as prescribed in whole or in part) in accordance with the Contract of Affreightment.

In cases of any loss or misfortune, it shall be lawful and necessary for the Assured, his or their factors, servants and assigns, to sue, labor, and travel for, in, and about the defense, safeguard, and recovery of the interest insured, or any part thereof, without prejudice to this insurance; to the charges whereof this Company shall contribute according to the rate and quantity of the sum hereby insured; nor shall the acts of the Assured or the Company in recovering, saving, or preserving the property insured, in case of disaster, be considered as a waiver or acceptance of abandonment.

In case of any agreement, act, or omission of the Assured, prior or subsequent to loss, whereby any right of recovery of the Assured for loss or damage to any property insured hereunder against any Carrier or Bailee, is released, impaired, or lost, which would on acceptance of abandonment or payment of loss by this Company have inured to its benefit, but for such agreement, act, or omission, this Company shall pay for the loss only to the extent its right of recovery was not released, impaired, or lost.

This insurance is subject to the American Institute Marine Extension Clauses (1943) and the following American Institute Clauses as if the current form of each were endorsed hereon:

South America 60-Day Clause   S.R.&C.C. Endorsement   War Risk Insurance

It is hereby understood and agreed that in case of loss and damage to the property insured under this policy, same shall be immediately reported as soon as the goods are landed, or the loss is known or expected, to the nearest agent of this Company as designated on the reverse side hereof.

(See reverse side for further terms and conditions which are hereby made a part of this Policy.)

NOTE—It is necessary for the assured to give prompt notice to underwriters when he becomes aware of an event for which he is "held covered" under this policy and the right to such cover is dependent on compliance with this obligation.

In witness whereof the company named above has caused this policy to be signed by its duty authorized officers, but this policy shall not be valid unless countersigned by an authorized representative of this Company or the Assured.

Secretary   President

Endorsement –

Counteragreed at	Baltimore MD	9-30-2006
		Date

chapter
12
SHIPPING YOUR PRODUCT

Certified Worldwide LLC

> *"We recognized that by not exporting, we were not tapping our full sales potential—sort of like leaving money on the table."*
>
> —Hal Selim, director of business development, Certified Worldwide, LLC

THE COMPANY

Did you have a strenuous and tiring work week? Then maybe you could use some nutritional supplements. Certified Worldwide LLC (CW) has made health and nutrition its business. Hal Selim, director of business development for CW, says his company's success doesn't just hinge on the more than 10,000 products and 500 lines of over-the-counter medicines, vitamins, supplements, and sports nutrition; it also depends on great worldwide customer service.

Located in Moorpark, California, CW started in 1999 with sales to distributors and to online customers in the United States through its e-commerce Web site (*www.medicalprovisions. com*). CW then began to pursue international opportunities by identifying overseas distributors who could help streamline the selling process abroad. "We recognized that by not exporting, we were not tapping our full sales potential—sort of like leaving money on the table," says Selim.

THE CHALLENGE

Equipped with freight forwarders and potential overseas buyers, Selim focused his attention on making export sales a reality. He soon began learning the ins and outs of import regulations for foreign countries and Food and Drug Administration (FDA) export certification issues, such as obtaining the health certificates that many foreign countries require for health-related products. Addressing these issues was key to navigating the export process.

Selling health-related products in the international market also requires extensive market and economic research. Each market has its own consumer tastes and ways of doing business. For example, in Asia, people might want joint pain and muscle relief, whereas in other countries, people might have heart-related needs. To supplement his marketing strategy, Selim tracked down specific information on health industries in Europe, the Far East, the Middle East, and other regions.

"When you think about the documentation required and other areas where we needed assistance, it was sort of daunting as to where we would begin," Selim says. "But we knew through our business acquaintances that we could count on the U.S. Commercial Service to help."

THE SOLUTION

During his initial meeting with Selim, Gerald Vaughn, director of the U.S. Export Assistance Center in Ventura, set up a plan to assist CW. First, Vaughn contacted key Commercial Service trade specialists on the Health Care Technologies Team. Tony Michalski and Julieanne Hennessy were familiar with FDA and could connect with the right people. Next, Vaughn gained insight into the FDA approval process. Shortly thereafter, Vaughn contacted the Commercial Service's health care trade specialists overseas and discussed certificate issues, thus laying the foundation for obtaining the required health documents. Vaughn then introduced Selim to the Commercial Service's Country Commercial Guides, which provide detailed market research on different industries and countries.

"Without the experience and on-the-ground support of the U.S. Commercial Service, we would not have surpassed the export challenges that we met early on when we began exporting," Selim says. "Had we tried this on our own, we would not be as well positioned in international markets as we are today."

LESSONS LEARNED

Early on, CW learned that the best way to build a good business is to get background information on potential distributors beforehand. CW receives payment up front in the form of bank wire transfer or letter of credit. A typical scenario is to receive a 30 percent deposit when the customer places the order and the remaining 70 percent balance before shipping the order. "Getting paid is a key part to running a business, and unless a company has the right payment policies in place, that company is more likely to be subjected to payment scams," says Selim.

CW also learned that the cost of freight can make or break a deal. Selim has worked extensively on building key relationships with freight forwarders. His efforts have resulted in great air and ocean rates for customers. CW's freight forwarders can ship almost anywhere. "Seek out your local Commercial Service office, contact and interview different freight forwarders, and remember that the company chosen will be responsible for shipping your product," says Selim. Airlines are a great source for finding freight forwarders. Their cargo departments work directly with freight forwarders and can recommend which ones to use for the product line. "Also," Selim advises, "depending on the size of the shipment, freight damage and theft insurance is vital."

The more business you give your freight forwarder, the more valuable you become. As shipments grow, you can set up agreements to obtain better rates. Also, you can shop for competitive rates. If you find a better rate than what you already have, see if your freight forwarder can match it. Your customer overseas may also be able to find a better rate. "The better the rate, the better the savings for your customer, which translates into more business in the future," says Selim.

Selim says the following elements are crucial in an export operation:

- Large selection of competitively priced products
- Fresh products with a long expiration date
- Continuous promotions and discounts
- Competitive freight charges
- Quick lead time for shipments
- Thorough product inspection before shipping
- Quick response to customer demands for additional documentation
- Quick response to new customer inquiries and follow-up after delivery

Feasibility studies are vital as you develop overseas markets. When conducting the study, address factors such as market size, market growth, accessibility, competition, business practices, and economic stability. Exporting overseas has introduced CW to many different cultures, business practices, and legal systems and has made CW's management team more flexible and creative.

ACTION

Are you ready to promote your product in other countries? Here are some tips:

- **Build rapport with your customers.** Smaller orders will build rapport and give you a feel for the market. Orders will increase as your company progresses.

- **Participate in trade shows.** Trade shows are one of the best ways to generate trade leads. "Walk the show floor and observe exhibitors and buyers—and after attending a few shows, you might be ready to set up an exhibit of your own and pursue new market opportunities," Selim advises.

- **Take advantage of seminars.** Selim says that seminars are where businesses can learn the rules, regulations, and policies associated with export controls, financing, customs, and other issues.

Hal Selim is director of business development for Certified Worldwide LLC. Based in Moorpark, California, the company is a major distributor and exporter of vitamins, supplements, and over-the-counter medicines.

PRICING, QUOTATIONS, AND TERMS

Pricing your product properly, giving complete and accurate quotations, choosing the terms of the sale, and selecting the payment method are four critical elements in selling a product or service overseas. Of the four, pricing can be the most challenging, even for an experienced exporter. (Methods of payment are covered in Chapter 14.)

PRICING CONSIDERATIONS

These considerations will help you determine the best price for your product overseas:

• At what price should your firm sell its product in the foreign market?

• What type of market positioning (that is, customer perception) does your company want to convey from its pricing structure?

• Does the export price reflect your product's quality?

• Is the price competitive?

• What type of discount (for example, trade, cash, quantity) and allowances (for example, advertising, trade-offs) should your firm offer its foreign customers?

• Should prices differ by market segment?

• What should your firm do about product-line pricing?

• What pricing options are available if your firm's costs increase or decrease? Is the demand in the foreign market elastic or inelastic?

• Is the foreign government going to view your prices as reasonable or exploitative?

• Do the foreign country's antidumping laws pose a problem?

As in the domestic market, the price at which a product or service is sold directly determines your firm's revenues. It is essential that your company's market research include an evaluation of all the variables that may affect the price range for your product or service. If your firm's price is too high, the product or service will not sell. If the price is too low, export activities may not be sufficiently profitable or may actually create a net loss.

The traditional components for determining proper pricing are costs, market demand, and competition. Each component must be compared with your company's objective in entering the foreign market. An analysis of each component from an export perspective may result in export prices that are different from domestic prices.

It is also very important that you take into account additional costs that are typically borne by the importer. They include tariffs, customs fees, currency fluctuation, transaction costs, and value added taxes (VATs). These costs can add substantially to the final price paid by the importer, sometimes resulting in a total that is more than double the U.S. domestic price.

Foreign Market Objectives

An important aspect of your company's pricing analysis is the determination of market objectives. For example, you may ask whether your company is attempting to penetrate a new market, seeking long-term market growth, or looking for an outlet for surplus production or outmoded products.

Marketing and pricing objectives may be generalized or tailored to particular foreign markets. For example, marketing objectives for sales to a developing nation, where per capita income may be one-tenth of that in the United States, are necessarily different than marketing objectives for sales to Europe or Japan.

Costs

The computation of the actual cost of producing a product and bringing it to market is the core element in determining if exporting is financially viable. Many new exporters calculate their export price by the cost-plus method. In that calculation, the exporter starts with the domestic manufacturing cost and adds administration, research and development, overhead, freight forwarding, distributor margins, customs charges, and profit.

The effect of this pricing approach may be that the export price escalates into an uncompetitive range. Table 13.1 provides a sample calculation. It clearly shows that if an export product has the same ex-factory price as the domestic product has, its final consumer price is considerably higher once exporting costs are included.

Marginal cost pricing is a more competitive method of pricing a product for market entry. This method considers the direct out-of-pocket expenses of producing and selling products for export as a floor beneath which prices cannot be set without incurring a loss. For example, additional costs may occur because of product modification for the export market to accommodate different sizes, electrical systems, or labels. Costs may decrease, however, if the export products are stripped-down versions or made without increasing the fixed costs of domestic production. Thus, many costs that apply only to domestic production, such as domestic labeling, packaging, and advertising costs, are subtracted, as are costs such as research and development expenses if they would have been spent anyway for domestic production.

Other costs should be assessed for domestic and export products according to how much benefit each product receives from such expenditures. Additional costs often associated with export sales include the following:

- Fees for market research and credit checks
- Business travel expenses
- International postage and telephone rates
- Translation costs
- Commissions, training charges, and other costs involving foreign representatives

TABLE 13.1 SAMPLE COST-PLUS CALCULATION OF PRODUCT COST

Factory price	
Domestic freight	
Subtotal	
Export documentation	
Subtotal	
Ocean freight and insurance	
Subtotal	
Import duty (12 percent of landed cost)	
Subtotal	
Wholesaler markup (15 percent)	
Subtotal	
Importer or distributor markup (22 percent)	
Subtotal	
Retail markup (50 percent)	
Final consumer price total	

- Consultant and freight forwarder fees
- Product modification and special packaging costs

After the actual cost of the export product has been calculated, you should formulate an approximate consumer price for the foreign market.

Market Demand

For most consumer goods, per capita income is a good gauge of a market's ability to pay. Some products create such a strong demand (for example, Levi's denim jeans) that even low per capita income will not affect their selling price. Simplifying the product to reduce its selling price may be an answer for your company in markets with low per capita income. Your firm must also keep in mind that currency fluctuations may alter the affordability of its goods. Thus, pricing should try to accommodate wild changes in U.S. and foreign currencies. A relatively weak dollar makes the price of U.S. goods more competitive in many markets around the world, thereby enabling you to compete with domestic producers as well as with other foreign competitors whose production costs are suddenly reflected in their inflated domestic currencies. Your firm should also anticipate the kind of customers who will buy your product. If your firm's primary customers in a developing country are expatriates or are local people with high incomes, a higher price might be feasible even if the average per capita income is low.

Competition

In the domestic market, few companies are free to set prices without carefully evaluating their competitors' pricing policies. This situation is true in exporting and is further complicated by the need to evaluate the competition's prices in each potential export market (see Box 13.1).

If there are many competitors within the foreign market, you may have little choice but to match the market price or even underprice the product or service in order to establish a market share. If the product or service is new to a particular foreign market, however, it may actually be possible to set a higher price than in the domestic market.

BOX 13.1 PRICING INFORMATION TIP

Pricing information can be collected in several ways. One source is overseas distributors and agents of similar products of equivalent quality. Also, traveling to the country where your products will be sold provides an excellent opportunity to gather pricing information.

Pricing Summary

In summary, here are the key points to remember when determining your product's price:

• Determine the objective in the foreign market.

• Compute the actual cost of the export product.

• Compute the final consumer price.

• Evaluate market demand and competition.

• Consider modifying the product to reduce the export price.

• Include "non-market" costs, such as tariffs and customs fees.

• Exclude cost elements that provide no benefit to the export function, such as domestic advertising.

QUOTATIONS AND PRO FORMA INVOICES

Many export transactions, particularly initial export transactions, begin with the receipt of an inquiry from abroad that is followed by a request for a quotation. A pro forma invoice is a quotation prepared in the format of an invoice; it is the preferred method in the exporting business.

A quotation describes the product, states a price for it, sets the time of shipment, and specifies the terms of sale and terms of payment. Because the foreign buyer may not be familiar with the product, the description of the product in an overseas quotation usually must be more detailed than in a domestic quotation. (See Sample Form 13.1 for a sample pro forma invoice and Sample Form 13.2 for a worksheet for calculating the export quotation.) The description should include the following 15 points:

• Seller's and buyer's names and addresses

• Buyer's reference number and date of inquiry

• Listing of requested products and a brief description

• Price of each item (It is advisable to indicate whether items are new or used and to quote the price in U.S. dollars to reduce foreign exchange risk.)

• Appropriate total cubic volume and dimensions packed for export (in metric units where appropriate)

- Appropriate gross and net shipping weight (in metric units where appropriate)
- Trade discount (if applicable)
- Delivery point
- Terms of sale
- Terms of payment
- Insurance and shipping costs
- Validity period for quotation
- Total charges to be paid by customer
- Estimated shipping date from a U.S. port or airport
- Currency of sale

Pro forma invoices are not used for payment purposes. In addition to the 15 items previously mentioned, a pro forma invoice should include two statements—one that certifies the pro forma invoice is true and correct, and another that indicates the country of origin of the goods. The invoice should also be clearly marked "pro forma invoice."

Pro forma invoices are models that the buyer uses when applying for an import license, opening a letter of credit, or arranging for funds. In fact, it is a good practice to include a pro forma invoice with any international quotation, regardless of whether it has been requested. When final commercial invoices are being prepared before shipment, it is advisable to check with your local Export Assistance Center for any special invoicing provisions that may be required by the importing country.

If a specific price is agreed on or guaranteed by your company, the precise period during which the offer remains valid should be specified.

TERMS OF SALE

In any sales agreement, it is important to have a common understanding of the delivery terms because confusion over their meaning may result in a lost sale or a loss on a sale. Terms of sale define the obligations, risks, and costs of the buyer and seller involving the delivery of goods that make up the export transaction. The terms in international business transactions often sound similar to those used in domestic business, but they frequently have very different meanings. For this reason, the exporter must know and understand the terms before preparing a quotation or a pro forma invoice.

The most commonly applied terms of sale in the global marketplace are the international commercial terms, or Incoterms. A complete list of these important terms and their definitions is provided in *Incoterms 2000*, a booklet issued by the International Chamber of Commerce (ICC). To purchase the booklet, contact ICC Books, 1212 Avenue of the Americas, 18th Floor, New York, NY 10036; call (212) 703-5066; or go online at *www.iccbooksusa.com*.

Following are a few of the more frequently used terms in international trade:

• *CIF* stands for cost, insurance, and freight to a named overseas port. The seller quotes a price for the goods (including insurance), all transportation, and miscellaneous charges to the point of debarkation from the vessel. (The term is used only for ocean shipments.)

• *CFR* applies to cost and freight to a named overseas port. The seller quotes a price for the goods that includes the cost of transportation to the named point of debarkation from the vessel. The buyer covers the cost of insurance. (The term applies only for ocean shipments.)

• *CPT* (carriage paid to) and *CIP* (carriage and insurance paid to) apply to a named destination. These terms are used in place of CFR and CIF, respectively, for all modes of transportation, including intermodal.

• *EXW* (ex works) means "from a named point of origin" (e.g., ex factory, ex mill, ex warehouse); the price quoted applies only at the point of origin (i.e., the seller's premises). The seller agrees to place the goods at the buyer's disposal at the specified place within a fixed time period. All other obligations, risks, and costs beyond the named point of origin are the buyer's.

• *FAS,* or free alongside ship, refers to the seller's price quote for the goods, including the charge for delivery of the goods alongside a vessel at the named port of export. The seller handles the cost of wharfage, while the buyer is accountable for the costs of loading, ocean transportation, and insurance. It is the seller's responsibility to clear the goods for export. FAS, as the term implies, is used only for waterborne shipments.

• *FCA,* or free carrier, refers to a named place within the country of origin of the shipment. This term defines the seller's responsibility for handing over the goods to a named carrier at the named shipping point. According to *Incoterms 2000,* the named shipping point may be the seller's premises. In that case, it is the seller's responsibility to clear the goods for export from the United States. The term may be used for any mode of transport.

• *FOB,* or free on board, refers to a named port of export in the country of origin of the shipment. The seller quotes the buyer a price that covers all costs up to and including the loading of goods aboard a vessel. (FOB is used only for ocean shipments.) As with other "F" terms, it is the seller's responsibility to clear the goods for export.

Some of the more common terms used in chartering a vessel are as follows:

• *Free in* is a pricing term that indicates that the charterer of a vessel is responsible for the cost of loading goods onto the vessel.

• *Free in and out* is a pricing term that indicates that the charterer of the vessel is responsible for the cost of loading and unloading goods from the vessel.

• *Free out* is a pricing term that indicates that the charterer is responsible for the cost of unloading goods from the vessel.

It is important to understand and use sales terms correctly. A simple misunderstanding may prevent you from meeting contractual obligations or make you responsible for shipping costs that you sought to avoid.

When quoting a price, you should make it meaningful to the prospective buyer. For example, a price for industrial machinery quoted "EXW Saginaw, Michigan, not export packed" is meaningless to most prospective foreign buyers. The buyers might find it difficult to determine the total cost and, therefore, might hesitate to place an order. You should quote CIF or CIP prices whenever possible because such quotes show the foreign buyer the cost of getting the product to or near the desired country.

If possible, you should quote the price in U.S. dollars. This will eliminate the risk of exchange rate fluctuations and problems with currency conversion.

If you need assistance in figuring CIF or CIP prices, an international freight forwarder can help. You should furnish the freight forwarder with a description of the product to be exported and its weight and cubic measurement when packed. The freight forwarder can compute the CIF price, usually at no charge.

PROFORMA INVOICE/EXPORT ORDER

SHIPPER: Tech International 1000 J Street, N.W. Washington, DC 20005	Ph. 202-555-1212 Fax 202-555-1111

PRO FORMA INVOICE NO. Col.91-14	DATE July 12

CUSTOMER:

Gomez Y. Cartagena
Aptdo. Postal 77
Bogota, Colombia

COMMERCIAL INVOICE NO.	DATE

CUSTOMER REFERENCE LTR	DATE July 9

SHIP TO (if different than Customer):

TERMS OF SALE
CIP Buenaventura, Colombia

(INCOTERMS 2000)

NOTIFY (Intermediate Consignee):

SHIP VIA AIR	EST. SHIP DATE 60 DAYS FROM RECEIPT OF ORDER AND LETTER OF CREDIT

PART NUMBER	UNIT OF MEASURE	QUANTITY	DESCRIPTION	UNIT PRICE	TOTAL PRICE
2-50	EA	3	Separators in accordance with attached specifications	$14,750.00	$44,250.00
14-40	EA	3	First-stage Filter Assemblies per attached specifications	$ 1,200.00	$ 3,600.00
custom	EA	3	Drive units - 30 hp each (for operation on 3-phase 440 v., 50 cy. current) complete with remote controls	$ 4,235.00	$12,705.00
			TOTAL EX WORKS Washington, D.C. domestic paked...		$60,555.00
			Export processing, packaging, prepaid inland freight to Dulles international Airport & forwarder's handling charges		$ 3,115.00
			TOTAL FCA WASHINGTON DULLES AIRPORT Estimated air freight and insurance TOTAL Est. CIP Bueanventura, Colombia		$60,555.00 $ 2,960.00 $66,630.00
			Estimated gross weight 9,360 lbs. • Estimated cube 520 cu. meters Export packed 4.212 kg. • Export packed 15.6 cu. meters		

1. All prices quoted herein are US dollars.
2. Prices quoted herein for merchandise only are valid for 60 days from July 12.
3. Any changes in shipping costs or insurance rates are for account of the buyer.

ADDITIONAL CHARGES

FREIGHT	☐ Ocean ☒ Air	INCLUDED
CONSULAR/LEGALIZATION		
INSPECTION/CERTIFICATION		
SPECIAL PACKING		
INSURANCE		INCLUDED

☒ LETTER OF CREDIT   Bank _____
☐ DRAFT   Terms _____
☐ OPEN ACCOUNT   Terms _____
☐ OTHER _____

CURRENCY OF PAYMENT US DOLLARS

Form No. 15-330 Printed and Sold by *UNZ&CO* 201 Circle Drive N, Suite 104, Piscataway, NJ 08854 (800) 631-3098 www.unzco.com

Source: Unz & Co.

chapter
13

PRICING AND TERMS

EXPORT QUOTATION WORKSHEET

Date Prepared: _____ Ref./Pro Forma/Inv. No.: **6** _____

Product: **1** _____ Estimated Ship Date: _____

Customer: _____ Packed Dimensions: _____

Country Destination: **2** _____ Packed Weight: **7** _____

Terms of Payment: **3** _____ Packed Cube: _____

Terms of Sale: **4** _____ Mode of Transport: **8** _____

Port/Place of Our Delivery: **5** _____

_____

To be Shipped From: **9** _____

To be Shipped To: _____

Total Selling Price of Product: .... $ **10** _____

Special Export Packing .... $ **11** _____

     $ _____   Quoted By: _____

Inland Freight:.. $ **12** _____

     $ _____   Quoted By: _____

Inland Freight Includes:

    ___ Unloading   ___ Pier Delivery   ___ Terminal Handling

    _____ Other: _____

International Freight:.. $ **13** _____

     $ _____   Quoted By: _____

     $ _____   Quoted By: _____

Ocean Freight Includes:

    ___ Port Congestion   ___ Wharfage   ___ CAF   ___ BAF

    ___ Heavy Lift   ___ Container Rental   ___ Terminal

Air Freight Includes:

    ___ Fuel Adjustment   ___ Container Stuffing

    ___ Other:_____

Insurance:.. $ **14** _____

Rate per $100 of value: $ _____

Includes: ____ All Risk   ___ SR&CC   ___War Risk

Forwarding Fees:.. $ **15** _____

Consular / Legalization Fees:.. $ _____

Inspection Fees:.. $ _____

Banking Charges:... $ _____

Other Charges:

    .... $ _____

    .... $ _____

    .... $ _____

TOTAL EXPORT QUOTATION: .... $ **16** _____

Form No. 10-020 Printed and Sold by *UNZCO* 201 Circle Drive N, Suite 104, Piscataway, NJ 08854   (800) 631-3098 www.unzco.com ©Copyright Unz & Co., 2008

Source: Unz & Co.

INSTRUCTIONS FOR SAMPLE FORM 13.2, EXPORT QUOTATION WORKSHEET

The purpose of the Export Quotation Worksheet is for the seller to ensure that all elements of cost incurred in the fulfillment of the transaction are made known and, as appropriate, included in the total quotation offered to the prospective buyer. Too often costs are incurred by the seller that were not contemplated in advance, and such costs may then not be recoverable.

1. Product. Provide a brief description of the products that are the subject of the transaction.

2. Country destination. Enter the final country destination to which the seller will be consigning the goods.

3. Terms of payment. Indicate the proposed terms of payment for the goods with consideration given to any costs the seller might incur on the basis of the payment terms.

4. Terms of sale. Indicate the terms of sale (Incoterm) proposed. It is critical for the seller to understand the cost implications for the delivery of the goods on the basis of the proposed terms of sale and then calculate them to be included in the body of the worksheet.

5. Port/place of delivery. Provide the exact port or place where delivery to the buyer will be concluded.

6. Ref./pro forma/invoice number. Assign some unique reference to this transaction and, thus, the worksheet on which the quotation is based.

7. Packed dimensions, weight, and cube. Determine the approximate physical dimensions, gross weight, and total cube, as this information may be important when determining transportation costs.

8. Mode of transport. Describe the proposed mode of transport of the goods to the port or place where the buyer will then assume any further obligations, risks, and delivery costs for the goods to whatever the buyer's desired final destination may be.

9. Shipped from/shipped to. Provide detail as to exactly where the goods will originate their journey to the buyer and exactly where they will end their journey—at which point the buyer will then assume any further obligations, risks, and delivery costs for the goods to whatever the buyer's desired final destination may be.

10. Total selling price of product. Enter the total proposed selling price for only the product itself.

11. Special export packing. If special export packing or crating is requested by the buyer or required for the movement of the goods, note the cost to the seller of having this packing performed.

12. Inland freight. Depending on the proposed terms of sale, the seller may or may not arrange and pay for inland transport cost to get the goods to the port or place where they will begin their international transport.

13. International freight. Depending on the terms of sale, the seller may or may not arrange and pay for the international transport of the goods. Depending on the mode, surcharges and other ancillary fees or charges may apply and should be included in the total amount to be quoted.

14. Insurance. Depending on the terms of sale, the seller may or may not arrange and pay for cargo insurance to the benefit of the buyer. In the case of a CIF or CIP term of sale, this amount may be a separate line item on formal quote to the buyer. If the seller acquires cargo insurance for its own benefit, it may wish to recover this cost from the buyer through inclusion, ultimately, in the price of the goods.

15. Other fees and charges. Determine and indicate any other fees and charges that may be incurred in concluding the transaction.

16. Total export quotation. Calculate the total amount sought to be recovered from a prospective buyer for this transaction.

Home Instead Senior Care

"Knowing the quality of life is being enhanced worldwide by our services makes me go to bed feeling good at night."

— Yoshino Nakajima, vice president of international development, Home Instead Senior Care

THE COMPANY

Having to leave a home full of memories in exchange for a nursing home or an assisted living facility is a burden no one wants to face. Yet options for aging people worldwide have been few. Today, however, millions of people around the world are finding an affordable and meaningful alternative to assisted living. Home Instead Senior Care, a franchise service company based in Omaha, Nebraska, is a worldwide leader of non-medical care for senior citizens who choose to remain at home but require personal care, companionship, meal preparation, light housekeeping, medicine reminders, and help with errands and shopping.

THE CHALLENGE

Established in 1994, Home Instead Senior Care expanded to nearly 100 domestic franchise offices in just three years, making it one of the fastest-growing franchise companies in the United States. Having found success in the domestic market, the company began receiving inquiries about taking its franchise concept international.

With a career in the United States and her family in Japan, Yoshino Nakajima was in search of quality in home care for her aging parents. After reading an article about Home Instead Senior Care, Nakajima, then an international liaison for the franchise industry, connected with Paul Hogan, Home Instead Senior Care's founder, to discuss taking the franchise concept abroad. "I was very impressed with Home Instead Senior Care's brand promise of reliable, responsive, and trained caregivers who create an atmosphere of trust for clients and their families," Nakajima recalls. "With the world's aging population increasing, families like mine, worldwide, are in need of these meaningful services for their aging relatives."

According to Hogan, Nakajima's enthusiasm and experience was just what the company needed in its pursuit of international markets, and Nakajima was brought on board. Now vice president of international development for Home Instead Senior Care, Nakajima is a true believer in the company's mission. "Our concept is very meaningful, and it's not just about money, but making a difference

for the elderly," says Nakajima. "Doing business internationally presents many challenges, and for us, it's finding people with the same core values and culture."

THE SOLUTION

Nakajima first decided to target the Japanese market. Recalling her experiences with the U.S. Commercial Service as a consultant for a food franchise company, she chose to enlist the services of the Omaha U.S. Export Assistance Center and its worldwide network. "The selection of good partners, training, and the building relationships are the same key steps in the expansion of any franchise company internationally," Nakajima explains. "At the Omaha assistance center, I received market research, export counseling, and requested partner searches that put me on the right path to entering the Japanese market."

With help from the Commercial Service, Nakajima participated in a franchising trade mission to Japan, where the company's services were showcased at Japan's largest franchise show. While Home Instead Senior Care's participation in the show created a lot of interest, the company faced a unique challenge—creating a new word for companionship. "Our concept of companionship [for senior citizens] did not exist in Japan," Nakajima explains. "We had to focus on educating a community on the expanded meaning of companionship for the elderly and how our services could help families."

A press conference was held to introduce the new word *konpanyanshippu* to the Japanese community. Together with market research and trade show publicity generated by the Commercial Service, the company was able to initiate an effective market entry strategy.

"Japan is the world's second-largest economy, and its family-oriented culture and aging population showed strong potential for introducing our services," Nakajima says. "With the assistance of the Commercial Service, we signed a master franchising agreement with Japan's leading service-oriented provider that has generated 110 Japanese franchise offices."

Having succeeded in Japan, Home Instead Senior Care wanted to enter the Western European market. It soon faced new hurdles. "In Japan, the public was not concerned with the price so much as the type of service, whereas in Europe, price was a major concern," Nakajima remarks. "Instead of having to introduce the concept of companionship, we had to reclassify our services into three levels as a way for clients to save money."

In Portugal, two men approached Home Instead Senior Care about opening a franchise in Lisbon. They had been unable to find the right level of care for their ailing parents without having to pay for unneeded services, and they wanted to help other families with similar problems. The men signed an agreement with the company in 2003 to start their

own franchise and were helped through the licensing process by the Commercial Service's Lisbon office. This experience initiated the company's three-tiered marketing strategy for Europe.

Along with its accomplishments in Japan and Portugal, the company has signed master franchising agreements in Australia, Ireland, New Zealand, and the United Kingdom. In April 2006, the company signed additional agreements in Spain and Taiwan.

LESSONS LEARNED

Home Instead Senior Care found the Commercial Service an excellent resource for learning about a country's cultural issues and regulations. "We are now able to anticipate the challenges of new markets," Nakajima says. "We can depend on the Commercial Service to help us with overcoming licensing issues, finding the right partners, and additional challenges we face in future endeavors."

According to Nakajima, the company's international success has contributed to its growth, with the development of a new technology department in its international division that has created new jobs at the company's headquarters in Omaha. The new department saves the company time and helps ensure the quality of services.

"We are fulfilling our mission of providing meaningful care for independent elders worldwide," Nakajima says. "Knowing the quality of life is being enhanced worldwide by our services makes me go to bed feeling good at night."

ACTION

How can you expand your company's mission abroad?

- **Participate in the Commercial Service's trade missions.** "Trade missions are an excellent tool for finding intelligent, compassionate entrepreneurs to join the Home Instead Senior Care family," Nakajima notes. "The missions saved us valuable time and resources that we could put toward enhancing our mission of providing quality care for senior citizens."

- **Try the Commercial Service's Gold Key Service.** Home Instead Senior Care found the Gold Key Service particularly useful in its European marketing strategy. The Gold Key Service identifies potential partners whose profiles parallel the company's ideal qualifications and prearranges meetings abroad.

Home Instead Senior Care of Omaha, Nebraska, developed a franchising concept that aims to enhance the quality of life for older adults through the recruitment of highly motivated in-home caregivers.

METHODS OF PAYMENT

PRUDENT CREDIT PRACTICES

Experienced exporters extend credit cautiously. They evaluate new customers with care and continuously monitor older accounts. You may wisely decide to decline a customer's request for open-account credit if the risk is too great, and you may propose instead payment-on-delivery terms through a documentary sight draft or an irrevocable confirmed letter of credit—or even payment in advance. For a fully creditworthy customer, however, you may decide to allow a month or two for payment or perhaps even extend open-account terms.

Other good credit practices include being aware of any unfavorable changes in your customers' payment patterns, refraining from going beyond normal commercial terms, and consulting with your international banker on how to cope with unusual circumstances or in difficult markets. It is always advisable to check a buyer's credit (even if the safest payment methods are used). A U.S. Commercial Service International Company Profile (ICP) provides useful information for credit checks (see Chapter 6). For a fee, you may request an ICP on companies in many countries. The ICP contains financial background on the company and a discussion regarding its size, capitalization, years in business, and other pertinent information, such as the names of other U.S. companies that conduct business with the firm. You can then contact those U.S. companies to find out about their payment experience with the foreign firm.

Because being paid in full and on time is of the utmost concern to you, the level of risk you are willing to assume in extending credit is a major consideration. There are several

ways in which you can receive payment when selling your products abroad, depending on how trustworthy you consider the buyer to be. With domestic sales, if the buyer has good credit, sales are typically made on open account; otherwise, cash in advance is required. For export sales, those are not the only common methods of payment.

Listed in order from most secure for the exporter to least secure, the basic methods of payment are

- Cash in advance
- Documentary letter of credit
- Documentary collection or draft
- Open account
- Other payment mechanisms

CASH IN ADVANCE

Receiving payment by cash in advance of the shipment might seem ideal. In this situation, your company is relieved of collection problems and has immediate use of the money. A wire transfer is commonly used and has the advantage of being almost immediate. Payment by check may result in a collection delay of up to six weeks—perhaps defeating the original intention of receiving payment before shipment.

Many exporters accept credit cards in payment for consumer goods and other products that generally have a low dollar value and that are sold directly to the end user. Domestic and international rules governing credit card transactions sometimes differ, so U.S. merchants should contact their credit card processor for more specific information. International credit card transactions are typically handled by telephone or fax. Because those methods are subject to fraud, you should determine the validity of transactions and obtain the proper authorizations before sending goods or performing services.

For the buyer, advance payment tends to create cash flow problems and to increase risks. Furthermore, cash in advance is not as common in most of the world as it is in the United States. Buyers are often concerned that the goods may not be sent if payment is made in advance or that they will have no leverage with the seller if goods do not meet specifications. Exporters who insist on advance payment as their sole method of doing business may find themselves losing out to competitors who offer more flexible payment terms.

DOCUMENTARY LETTERS OF CREDIT
AND DOCUMENTARY COLLECTIONS OR DRAFTS

Documentary letters of credit or documentary collections or drafts are often used to protect the interests of both buyer and seller. These two methods require that payment be made on presentation of documents conveying the title and showing that specific steps have been taken. Letters of credit and drafts may be paid immediately or at a later date. Drafts that are paid on presentation are called *sight drafts*. Drafts that are to be paid at a later date, often after the buyer receives the goods, are called *time drafts* or *date drafts.* A transmittal letter is used, which contains complete and precise instructions on how the documents should be handled and how the payment is to be made (see Sample Form 14.1).

Because payment by these two methods is made on the basis of documents, all terms of payment should be clearly specified in order to avoid confusion and delay. For example, "net 30 days" should be specified as "30 days from acceptance." Likewise, the currency of payment should be specified as "US$30,000." International bankers can offer other suggestions.

Banks charge fees—mainly based on a percentage of the amount of payment—for handling letters of credit and smaller amounts for handling drafts. If fees charged by both the foreign and U.S. banks are to be applied to the buyer's account, this term should be explicitly stated in all quotations and in the letter of credit.

The exporter usually expects the buyer to pay the charges for the letter of credit, but some buyers may not agree to this added cost. In such cases, you must either absorb the costs of the letter of credit or risk losing that potential sale. Letters of credit for smaller amounts can be somewhat expensive because fees can be high relative to the sale.

Letters of Credit

A letter of credit adds a bank's promise to that of the foreign buyer to pay the exporter. A letter of credit issued by a foreign bank is sometimes confirmed by a U.S. bank. This confirmation means that the U.S. bank (the confirming bank) adds its promise to that of the foreign bank (the issuing bank) to pay the exporter. If a letter of credit is not confirmed, it is "advised" through a U.S. bank and is thus called an *advised letter of credit.* U.S. exporters may wish to have letters of credit issued by foreign banks confirmed through a U.S. bank if they are unfamiliar with the foreign bank or are concerned about the political or economic risk associated with the country in which the bank is located. An Export Assistance Center or international banker can assist exporters in evaluating the risks to determine what might be appropriate for specific export transactions.

A letter of credit may be *irrevocable,* which means that it cannot be changed unless both parties agree. Alternatively, it can be *revocable,* in which case either party may unilaterally make changes. A revocable letter of credit is inadvisable because it carries many risks for the exporter.

FACT:

Credit cards are a popular method of payment for exports.

INSIGHT:

Because international credit card transactions are typically handled by telephone or fax, fraud can be an issue. Determine the validity of transactions and obtain the proper authorizations before sending goods or performing services.

To expedite the receipt of funds, you can use wire transfers. You should consult with your international banker about bank charges for such services.

A TYPICAL LETTER OF CREDIT TRANSACTION

Here are the typical steps in issuing an irrevocable letter of credit that has been confirmed by a U.S. bank:

1. After the exporter and the buyer agree on the terms of a sale, the buyer arranges for its bank to open a letter of credit that specifies the documents needed for payment. The buyer determines which documents will be required.

2. The buyer's bank issues, or opens, its irrevocable letter of credit and includes all instructions to the seller relating to the shipment.

3. The buyer's bank sends its irrevocable letter of credit to a U.S. bank and requests confirmation. The exporter may request that a particular U.S. bank be the confirming bank, or the foreign bank may select a U.S. correspondent bank.

4. The U.S. bank prepares a letter of confirmation to forward to the exporter along with the irrevocable letter of credit.

5. The exporter carefully reviews all conditions in the letter of credit. The exporter's freight forwarder is contacted to make sure that the shipping date can be met. If the exporter cannot comply with one or more of the conditions, the customer is alerted at once because an amendment may be necessary.

6. The exporter arranges with the freight forwarder to deliver the goods to the appropriate port or airport.

7. When the goods are loaded aboard the exporting carrier, the freight forwarder completes the necessary documentation.

8. The exporter (or the freight forwarder) presents the documents, evidencing full compliance with the letter of credit terms, to the U.S. bank.

9. The bank reviews the documents. If they are in order, the documents are sent to the buyer's bank for review and then transmitted to the buyer.

10. The buyer (or the buyer's agent) uses the documents to claim the goods.

11. A sight or time draft accompanies the letter of credit. A sight draft is paid on presentation; a time draft is paid within a specified time period.

EXAMPLE OF A CONFIRMED IRREVOCABLE LETTER OF CREDIT

Sample Form 14.2 illustrates the various parts of a typical confirmed irrevocable letter of credit. In this example, the letter of credit was forwarded to the exporter, Walton Building Supply Company, by the confirming bank, Megabank Corporation, as a result of a letter of credit issued by the Third Hong Kong Bank, Hong Kong, for the account of the importer, HHB Hong Kong. The date of issue was March 8, 2006, and the exporter must have submitted the proper documents (e.g., a commercial invoice in one original and three copies) by June 23, 2006, for a sight draft to be honored.

TIPS ON USING LETTERS OF CREDIT

When preparing quotations for prospective customers, you should keep in mind that banks pay only the amount specified in the letter of credit—even if higher charges for shipping, insurance, or other factors are incurred and documented.

On receiving a letter of credit, you should carefully compare the letter's terms with the terms of the pro forma quotation. This step is extremely important because the terms must be precisely met or the letter of credit may be invalid and you may not be paid. If meeting the terms of the letter of credit is impossible or if any of the information is incorrect or even misspelled, you should contact the customer immediately and ask for an amendment to the letter of credit.

You must provide documentation showing that the goods were shipped by the date specified in the letter of credit or you may not be paid. You should check with your freight forwarders to make sure that no unusual conditions may arise that would delay shipment.

Documents must be presented by the date specified for the letter of credit to be paid. You should verify with your international banker that there will be sufficient time to present the letter of credit documents for payment.

You may request that the letter of credit specify that partial shipments and trans-shipment will be allowed. Specifying what will be allowed can prevent unforeseen problems at the last minute.

Documentary Collections or Drafts

A draft, sometimes called a *bill of exchange,* is analogous to a foreign buyer's check. Like checks used in domestic commerce, drafts carry the risk that they will not be honored. However, in international commerce, title does not transfer to the buyer until the buyer pays the draft.

FACT: Some letters of credit are revocable, which means that you or the buyer can unilaterally make changes. As a result, such letters of credit carry more risk than irrevocable letters of credit.

INSIGHT: Smart exporters insist on irrevocable letters of credit.

chapter
14

METHODS OF PAYMENT

SIGHT DRAFTS

A sight draft is used when the exporter wishes to retain title to the shipment until it reaches its destination and payment is made. Before the shipment can be released to the buyer, the original "order" for the ocean bill of lading (the document that evidences title) must be properly endorsed by the buyer and surrendered to the carrier. It is important to note that air waybills do not need to be presented for the buyer to claim the goods. Risk increases when a sight draft is used with an air shipment.

In actual practice, the ocean bill of lading is endorsed by the exporter and sent by the exporter's bank to the buyer's bank. It is accompanied by the sight draft, invoices, and other supporting documents that are specified by either the buyer or the buyer's country (e.g., packing lists, commercial invoices, and insurance certificates). The foreign bank notifies the buyer when it has received these documents. As soon as the draft is paid, the foreign bank turns over the bill of lading, thereby enabling the buyer to obtain the shipment.

There is still some risk when a sight draft is used to control transferring the title of a shipment. The buyer's ability or willingness to pay might change between the time the goods are shipped and the time the drafts are presented for payment. There is no bank promise to pay standing behind the buyer's obligation. Also, the policies of the importing country could change. If the buyer cannot or will not pay for and claim the goods, returning or disposing of the products becomes the problem of the exporter.

TIME DRAFTS AND DATE DRAFTS

A time draft is used when the exporter extends credit to the buyer. The draft states that payment is due by a specific time after the buyer accepts the time draft and receives the goods. By signing and writing "accepted" on the draft, the buyer is formally obligated to pay within the stated time. When this is done, the time draft is then called a *trade acceptance*. It can be kept by the exporter until maturity or sold to a bank at a discount for immediate payment.

A date draft differs slightly from a time draft in that it specifies a date on which payment is due, rather than a time period after the draft is accepted. When either a sight draft or time draft is used, a buyer can delay payment by delaying acceptance of the draft. A date draft can prevent this delay in payment, though it still must be accepted.

OPEN ACCOUNT

In a foreign transaction, an open account can be a convenient method of payment if the buyer is well established, has a long and favorable payment record, or has been thoroughly checked for creditworthiness. With an open account, the exporter simply bills the customer, who is expected to pay under agreed terms at a future date. Some of the largest firms abroad make purchases only on open account.

However, there are risks to open-account sales. The absence of documents and banking channels might make it difficult to pursue the legal enforcement of claims. The exporter might also have to pursue collection abroad, which can be difficult and costly. Another problem is that receivables may be harder to finance, because drafts or other evidence of indebtedness is unavailable. There are several ways to reduce credit risk, including export credit insurance and factoring.

Exporters contemplating a sale on open-account terms should thoroughly examine the political, economic, and commercial risks. They should also consult with their bankers if financing will be needed for the transaction before issuing a pro forma invoice to a buyer.

CONSIGNMENT SALES

International consignment sales follow the same basic procedures as in the United States. The goods are shipped to a foreign distributor, who sells them on behalf of the exporter. The exporter retains title to the goods until they are sold, at which point payment is sent to the exporter. The exporter has the greatest risk and least control over the goods with this method. Also, receiving payment may take a while.

It is smart to consider risk insurance with international consignment sales. The contract should clarify who is responsible for property risk insurance that will cover the merchandise until it is sold and payment is received. In addition, it may be necessary to conduct a credit check on the foreign distributor.

FOREIGN CURRENCY

A buyer and a seller who are in different countries rarely use the same currency. Payment is usually made in the buyer's or seller's currency or in a third mutually acceptable currency.

One of the risks associated with foreign trade is the uncertainty of future exchange rates. The relative value between the two currencies could change between the time the deal is concluded and the time payment is received. If you are not properly protected, a devaluation or depreciation of the foreign currency could cause you to lose money. For example, if the buyer has agreed to pay 500,000 for a shipment, and the euro is valued at $0.85, you would expect to receive $425,000. If the euro later decreased in value to $0.84, payment under the new rate would be only $420,000, meaning a loss of $5,000 for you. If the foreign currency increased in value, however, you would get a windfall in extra profits. Nonetheless, most exporters are not interested in speculating on foreign exchange fluctuations and prefer to avoid risks.

One of the simplest ways for you to avoid such risk is to quote prices and require payment in U.S. dollars. Then the burden of exchanging currencies and the risk are placed on the buyer. You should also be aware of any problems with currency convertibility. Not all currencies are freely or quickly converted into U.S. dollars. Fortunately, the U.S. dollar is widely accepted as an international trading currency, and U.S. firms can often secure payment in dollars.

If the buyer asks to make payment in a foreign currency, you should consult an international banker before negotiating the sales contract. Banks can offer advice on the foreign exchange risks that exist with a particular currency.

PAYMENT PROBLEMS

In international trade, problems involving bad debts are more easily avoided than rectified after they occur. Credit checks and the other methods that have been discussed in this chapter can limit the risks. Nonetheless, just as in a company's domestic business, exporters occasionally encounter problems with buyers who default on their payment. When these problems occur in international trade, obtaining payment can be both difficult and expensive. Even when the exporter has insurance to cover commercial credit risks, a default by a buyer still requires the time, effort, and cost of the exporter to collect a payment. The exporter must exercise normal business prudence in exporting and exhaust all reasonable means of obtaining payment before an insurance claim is honored. Even then, there is often a significant delay before the insurance payment is made.

FACT:

Even exporters who take precautions occasionally experience payment problems.

INSIGHT:

If you experience payment problems, try these three avenues:

1. Try to negotiate directly with the customer.
2. Work with your bank, legal counsel, and the U.S. Commercial Service—particularly if negotiations fail and the sum involved is large.
3. Try arbitration through the International Chamber of Commerce if other means fail. This route is often faster and less costly than legal action.

The simplest and least costly solution to a payment problem is to contact and negotiate with the customer. With patience, understanding, and flexibility, you may often resolve conflicts to the satisfaction of both sides. This point is especially true when a simple misunderstanding or technical problem is to blame and there is no question of bad faith. Even though you may be required to compromise on certain points—perhaps even on the price of the committed goods—your company may save a valuable customer and profit in the long run.

However, if negotiations fail and the sum involved is large enough to warrant the effort, your company should obtain the assistance and advice of its bank, legal counsel, and the U.S. Commercial Service, which can often resolve payment problems informally. When all else fails, arbitration is often faster and less costly than legal action. The International

Chamber of Commerce handles most international arbitration and is usually acceptable to foreign companies because it is not affiliated with any single country. For information, visit the Web site of the U.S. Council of the International Chamber of Commerce at *www.iccwbo.org.*

U.S. $ **(1)** _____   _____ **(2)** 20 ____

_____ **(3)** _____ of this *FIRST* of Exchange (Second unpaid)

Pay to the Order of

(4) _____ **(5)** _____   United States Dollars

for Value received and charge the same to account of

(6)

To _____

No. **(7)** _____   _____ **(8)**

Authorized Signature

(9)   _____ **(10)**

Date

(12)

Gentlemen: ☐ for collection,

We enclose Draft Number _____ **(11)** and documents below   ☐ for

                                                   ☐ for payment/negotiation under L/C

(13)

BILLS OF LADING	B/L COPY	COMM. INV.	INS. CTF.	CTF. ORIG.	CONS. INV.	PKNG. LIST	WGT. CTF.	OTHER DOCUMENTS

Please handle in accordance with instructions marked "X"

☐ Deliver all documents in one mailing. **(14)**

☐ Deliver documents in two mailings.

☐ Deliver documents against payment if sight draft, or acceptance if time draft. **(15)**

☐ All charges for account of drawee. **(16)**

☐ Do not waive charges.

☐ Protest for $\frac{\text{non-payment}}{\text{non-acceptance}}$ **(17)**

☐ Do not protest.

☐ Present on arrival of goods. **(18)**

☐ Advise $\frac{\text{non-payment}}{\text{non-acceptance}}$ by $\frac{\text{airmail}}{\text{cable}}$ giving reasons. **(19)**

☐ Advise $\frac{\text{payment}}{\text{acceptance}}$ by $\frac{\text{airmail}}{\text{cable}}$

IN CASE OF NEED refer to:

Name _____ **(20)** _____

Address _____

who is empowered by us:

a ☐ To act fully on our behalf, i.e., authorize reductions; extensions, free delivery, waiving of protest, etc.

b ☐ To assist in obtaining acceptance or payment of draft, as drawn, but not to alter its terms in any way.

OTHER INSTRUCTIONS:

(21)

Please refer all questions concerning this collection to:

☐ Shipper

☐ Freight Forwarder: **(22)**

_____   _____ **(23)**

Authorized Signature

Form No. 20-015 Printed and Sold by *UNZ&CO* 201 Circle Drive N, Suite 104, Piscataway, NJ 08854   (800) 631-3098   www.unzco.com

Source: Unz & Co.

1. U.S. dollars. Enter the entire amount to be collected; if not in U.S. dollars, specify the currency.

2. Date. Enter the date the draft is issued.

3. Terms of payment. Enter the terms of payment (also called the tenor of the draft); for example, at 45 days, at sight, or at 30 days bill of lading. "Second unpaid" refers to the duplicate copy of the draft (which reads "of this Second of Exchange, First unpaid"); once payment has been made against either copy, the other becomes void.

4. Pay to the order of. Enter the name of the party to be paid (seller or payee). This party may be the seller or the seller's bank and will be the party to whom the foreign buyer's bank will remit payment.

5. United States dollars. Enter the amount from Field 1 in words; if payment is not to be made in U.S. dollars, cross out "United States Dollars" and enter the correct currency.

6. Charge to account of. Enter the name and address of the paying party (buyer or drawee). For letter of credit payments, enter the name and address of the buyer's opening bank as well as the letter of credit number and issue date.

7. Number. Enter the identification or draft number, as assigned by the seller to reference the transaction.

8. Authorized signature. The signature of the authorized individual for the seller or the seller's agent (drawer) should be entered here.

9. Forwarding name and address. Enter the name and address of the party to whom the draft is being sent. Unless there is a letter of credit being negotiated in the United States, enter the name and address of a foreign bank.

10. Forwarding date. Enter the date the draft is being sent to the bank in Field 9.

11. Draft number. Enter the seller's draft number, as noted in Field 7.

12. Purpose of draft. Check the applicable box if the draft is part of letter of credit negotiation, a collection, or an acceptance.

13. List of documents. Enter the number and type of each original and duplicate document to be included with this transmittal letter. Any document attached will eventually be released to the buyer.

14. Deliver all documents. Check either "Deliver all documents in one mailing" or "Deliver documents in two mailings." Generally, documents are delivered in one mailing.

15. Deliver documents against payment or acceptance. Ensure that the type of draft attached (Field 3) is compatible with the "deliver against" instructions. Sight drafts should accompany "deliver against payment" instructions, and time drafts should accompany "deliver against acceptance" instructions.

16. Bank charges. The correspondent bank will not pay unless all charges are collected. Depending on your agreement with the buyer, indicate which party is responsible for both remitting and presenting the bank's charges. If you check "All charges for account of drawee," the buyer is responsible for these charges; if the buyer does not pay (or is not to pay) these charges, and if "Do not waive charges" has not been checked, the seller will be billed for expenses incurred.

17. Protest. Check "Protest" (specify "for non-payment" or for "non-acceptance," depending on the type of draft attached—see instructions for Field 15) if you wish the correspondent bank to process written,

notarized documentation in the event that the buyer refuses to pay or accept the draft. Additional bank expenses associated with a protest are usually charged to the seller.

18. Present on arrival. Check if you wish the draft to be presented on the arrival of the goods to the buyer.

19. Advise. Check the appropriate fields and cross out the non-applicable terms if you wish to be advised of payment or acceptance (or of non-payment or non-acceptance).

20. In case of need. Enter the representative of the seller in the country to which the draft and documents are going, if one exists; check the box that describes the representative's authority.

21. Other instructions. Enter any instructions to the remitting or correspondent bank, such as remittance instructions, clarification of protest procedures, and multiple-draft instructions.

22. Refer all questions. Enter the name of the contact in the seller's country, along with his or her address and telephone number. Specify whether this contact is employed by the shipper (seller) or the seller's agent (freight forwarder).

23. Authorization. Enter the person authorized to sign the transmittal letter (see Field 8), the date it was prepared, and the authorized person's signature.

INTERNATIONAL BANKING GROUP   **ORIGINAL**

Megabank Corporation

P.O. BOX 1000, ATLANTA GEORGIA 30302-1000
CABLE ADDRESS: MegaB
TELEX NO. 1234567
SWIFT NO. MBBABC 72

OUR ADVICE NUMBER: EA0000091
ADVICE DATE: 08MAR2006   ****AMOUNT****
ISSUE BANK REF: 3312/HBI/22341   USD****25,000.00
EXPIRY DATE: 23JUN2006

BENEFICIARY: APPLICANT:
THE WALTON SUPPLY CO.   HHB HONG KONG
2356 SOUTH N.W. STREET   34 INDUSTRIAL DRIVE
ATLANTA, GEORGIA 30345   CENTRAL, HONG KONG

WE HAVE BEEN REQUESTED TO ADVISE TO YOU THE FOLLOWING LETTER OF CREDIT AS ISSUED BY:

THIRD HONG KONG BANK
1 CENTRAL TOWER
HONG KONG

PLEASE BE GUIDED BY ITS TERMS AND CONDITIONS AND BY THE FOLLOWING:

CREDIT IS AVAILABLE BY NEGOTIATION OF YOUR DRAFT(S) IN DUPLICATE AT SIGHT FOR 100 PERCENT OF INVOICE VALUE DRAWN ON US ACCOMPANIED BY THE FOLLOWING DOCUMENTS:

1. SIGNED COMMERCIAL INVOICE IN 1 ORIGINAL AND 3 COPIES.

2. FULL SET 3/3 OCEAN BILLS OF LADING CONSIGNED TO THE ORDER OF THIRD HONG KONG BANK, HONG KONG NOTIFY APPLICANT AND MARKED FREIGHT COLLECT.

3. PACKING LIST IN 2 COPIES.

EVIDENCING SHIPMENT OF   : 5000 PINE LOGS—WHOLE—8 TO 12 FEET
                           FOB SAVANNAH, GEORGIA

SHIPMENT FROM : SAVANNAH, GEORGIA   TO: HONG KONG
LATEST SHIPPING DATE : 02JUN2006

PARTIAL SHIPMENTS NOT ALLOWED   TRANSSHIPMENT NOT ALLOWED

ALL BANKING CHARGES OUTSIDE HONG KONG ARE FOR BENEFICIARY'S ACCOUNT.
DOCUMENTS MUST BE PRESENTED WITHIN 21 DAYS FROM B/L DATE.

AT THE REQUEST OF OUR CORRESPONDENT, WE CONFIRM THIS CREDIT AND ALSO ENGAGE WITH YOU THAT ALL DRAFTS DRAWN UNDER AND IN COMPLIANCE WITH THE TERMS OF THIS CREDIT WILL BE DULY HONORED BY US.

PLEASE EXAMINE THIS INSTRUMENT CAREFULLY. IF YOU ARE UNABLE TO COMPLY WITH THE TERMS OR CONDITIONS, PLEASE COMMUNICATE WITH YOUR BUYER TO ARRANGE FOR AN AMENDENT.

Source: U.S. Department of Commerce.

This sample form illustrates the various parts of a typical confirmed irrevocable letter of credit. In this example, the letter of credit was forwarded to the exporter, Walton Supply Company, by the confirming bank, Megabank Corporation, as a result of a letter of credit issued by the Third Hong Kong Bank, Hong Kong, for the account of the importer, HHB Hong Kong. The date of issue was March 8, 2006, and the exporter must submit the proper documents (e.g., a commercial invoice in one original and three copies) by June 23, 2006, for a sight draft to be honored. For tips on using letters of credit, see page 181.

LuLu's Dessert

"When it comes to exporting, don't do everything by yourself."

—Maria de Lourdes Sobrino, founder, president, and chief executive officer, LuLu's Dessert

THE COMPANY

For Maria de Lourdes Sobrino, it all began in 1982 in a 700-square-foot storefront in Torrence, California, with a milk crate for a chair and her mother's Mexican-style recipe for gelatin. From humble beginnings and driven by her entrepreneurial spirit, Sobrino, known as LuLu to her friends and customers, began preparing tasty treats—and soon thereafter founded her own company, LuLu's Dessert.

Starting with snacks from her childhood, such as jalapeno-flavored carrots and roasted peanuts, Sobrino soon graduated to making jiggly fruit-flavored taste treats known in Spanish as *gelatina*. Unlike Jell-O®, which then was made only in powdered form, Sobrino's gelatin was ready to eat from the time a customer bought it—a concept that Jell-O® would not market for another 11 years.

With gelatins such as Fruit Fantasia, Orange Blast, Creamy Vanilla with Cinnamon, and Sugar Free-De-Light, LuLu's has something for everyone. With total sales projected to reach $10 million for 2005, LuLu's is pleasing the palates of customers in the United States and Mexico.

THE CHALLENGE

Sobrino began exporting to Mexico in 1992 and opened offices and a distribution center there, but despite her knowledge of the Mexican market, she faced great difficulty in selling her product because of her inexperience in the export process.

She often had only vague information on potential distributors of her product and did not know how to ensure that they were qualified and legitimate. She also did not have the most updated market research reports on Mexico.

After reading an article about Sobrino in a local newspaper, however, Tony Michalski, a trade specialist at the U.S. Commercial Service's Export Assistance Center in Newport Beach, California, contacted her to see how he could help her realize her exporting goals. Michalski and Sobrino soon began their partnership.

THE SOLUTION

With the help of Michalski, who provided services such as export counseling and market research, Sobrino began to make progress. She was put in touch with organizations such as the California Trade and Commerce Agency and the U.S. Agricultural Trade Office. As a result, LuLu's Dessert began to have greater success in foreign markets, especially Mexico.

Today, the company competes with local food manufacturers in Mexico, having contracts at grocery chains like Wal-Mart and Oxxo and an exclusive distributorship in the Mexican state of Baja California.

The success of LuLu's Dessert in foreign markets has been boosted considerably by the assistance of the Western U.S. Agricultural Trade Association (WUSATA), which has provided money to LuLu's Dessert and other companies for marketing outside of the United States. The funds gave Sobrino the opportunity to travel, to participate in trade shows, and to create brochures targeted to overseas markets while being reimbursed a large percentage by WUSATA.

Today, Sobrino has far-reaching goals for LuLu's Dessert. Currently, exporting accounts for 2 to 3 percent of the company's total revenues, but with a greater production capacity, LuLu's is on a course for explosive growth, especially internationally. Sobrino would like to expand her sales beyond Mexico and into other parts of Latin America. "We think that all the world deserves one of our treats," says Sobrino. "The Commercial Service saved our company time and money, and I highly recommend their services for firms looking to increase their export sales."

LESSON LEARNED

Sobrino says that the biggest lesson learned early on was not to try to do it alone when it comes to exporting. At the time Sobrino began exporting, she had no idea that government resources, like those of the Commercial Service and the Export–Import Bank, were available. "I spent 10 years trying to make international sales and continued to run into all kinds of problems—especially buyers who wouldn't pay or couldn't afford letters of credit."

Sobrino says that one time she even went to Chile to try to collect a debt from a customer but had no luck. By using Commercial Service and Export-Import Bank services that provide background checks on potential partners and letters of credit to guarantee payment, she has much more confidence in doing business with foreign partners.

Sobrino also says she could have benefited from the Commercial Service's customized market research reports much earlier in her export endeavors. She advises that companies be diligent about trademark protection, because in one European country, LuLu's trademark was stolen and used by another company.

Sobrino also found that customers abroad often prefer sweeter desserts than do people in the United States. "When it comes to exporting, don't do everything by yourself," she says. "When I go out to speak, I give businesses a good lesson in exporting."

ACTION

How can you get the assistance you need?

- **Use the resources of government agencies.** For financing assistance, contact the Export–Import Bank, which can provide seller as well as buyer financing at very competitive rates. For more information, visit *www.exim.gov.* The Small Business Administration (SBA) provides a full range of export assistance to small businesses, particularly those new to exporting. Counseling is provided at no cost. To learn more about the SBA, visit *www.sba.gov.*
- **Talk to the U.S. Commercial Service.** Make your nearest U.S. Export Assistance Center the first stop on your road to export success. The Commercial Service offers market entry strategies, export counseling, and much more.

- **Do your research.** Good market research can help you determine which markets are right for your product. For a complete listing of the market research the Commercial Service offers, visit *www.export.gov/mrktresearch.* Once you find the right market, the Commercial Service can also help you find international buyers in that market with services such as the International Partner Search and the Gold Key Matching Service.

Maria de Lourdes Sobrino, president and chief executive officer of LuLu's Dessert in Anaheim, California, established a significant market share in Mexico for her gelatin recipes. She is now pursuing opportunities throughout Latin America.

chapter 15

FINANCING EXPORT TRANSACTIONS

In This Chapter

- **Factors to consider in making financing decisions**

- **Private sources of financing**

- **Government sources of financing**

Export financing is often a key factor in a successful sale. Contract negotiation and closure are important, but ultimately your company must get paid. Exporters naturally want to get paid as quickly as possible, whereas importers usually prefer to delay payment until they have received or resold the goods. Because of the intense competition for export markets, being able to offer attractive payment terms is often necessary to make a sale. You should be aware of the many financing options open to you so that you choose the most acceptable one to both the buyer and your company. In many cases, government assistance in export financing for small and medium-sized businesses can increase your firm's options. The following factors are important to consider in making decisions about financing:

• **The need for financing to make the sale.** In some cases, favorable payment terms make a product more competitive. If the competition offers better terms and has a similar product, a sale can be lost. In other cases, the buyer may prefer buying from someone else but might buy your product because of shorter or more secure credit terms.

• **The length of time the product is being financed**. The term of the loan required determines how long you will have to wait before you receive payment from the buyer and influences your choice of how to finance the transaction.

• **The cost of different methods of financing.** Interest rates and fees vary, and an exporter may expect to assume some or all of the financing costs. Before submitting a pro forma invoice to the buyer, you must understand how those costs affect price and profit.

• **The risks associated with financing the transaction.** The riskier the transaction, the harder and more costly it will be to finance. The political and economic stability of the buyer's country can also be an issue. To provide financing for either accounts receivable or the production or purchase of the product for sale, the lender may require the most secure methods of payment—a letter of credit (possibly confirmed) or export credit insurance or a guarantee.

• **The need for preshipment financing and for postshipment working capital.** Production for an unusually large order or for a surge of orders may present unexpected and severe strains on your working capital. Even during normal periods, inadequate working capital may curb an exporter's growth. However, assistance is available through the public and private sectors. A number of those resources are discussed in this chapter.

For help in determining which financing options may be available or the most beneficial, you may consult the following sources:

• Your banker

• Your local Department of Commerce Export Assistance Center

• Your local Small Business Administration office

• The Export–Import Bank in Washington, D.C., and selected cities

• Your state export promotion or export finance office

EXTENDING CREDIT TO FOREIGN BUYERS

Foreign buyers often press exporters for longer payment periods. Although it is true that liberal financing is a means of enhancing export competitiveness, you need to carefully weigh the credit or financing that you extend to foreign customers. Moreover, the extension of credit by the seller to the buyer is more common outside the United States. U.S. sellers who are reluctant to extend credit may face the possibility of the loss of the sale to their competitors.

A useful guide for determining the appropriate credit period is the normal commercial terms in your industry for internationally traded products. Buyers generally expect to receive the benefits of such terms. For off-the-shelf items like consumer goods, chemicals and other raw materials, agricultural commodities, and spare parts and components, normal commercial terms (with few exceptions) range from 30 to 180 days. You may have to make allowances for longer shipment times than are found in domestic trade because foreign buyers are often unwilling to have the credit period start before receiving the goods. Custom-made or high-value capital equipment may warrant longer repayment periods. Once credit terms are extended to a buyer, they tend to be a precedent for future sales, so you should review with special care any credit terms extended to first-time buyers (see Box 15.1).

When exporting, your company should follow the same careful credit principles it follows for domestic customers. An important reason for controlling the credit period is the cost incurred through use of working capital or through interest and fees. If the buyer is not responsible for paying those costs, then you should factor them into the selling price. Your company should also recognize that longer credit periods may increase the risk of default.

Thus, you must exercise judgment in balancing competitiveness against cost and safety. Customers are frequently charged interest on credit periods of a year or longer but less frequently on short-term credit (up to 180 days). Most exporters absorb interest charges for short-term credit unless the customer pays after the due date.

Obtaining cash immediately is usually a high priority with exporters. Converting export receivables to cash at a discount with a bank is one way to do so. Another way is to expand working capital resources. A third approach, suitable when the purchase involves capital goods and the repayment period extends a year or longer, is to arrange for third-party financing. For example, a bank could make a loan directly to the buyer for the product, and you could be paid immediately from the loan proceeds while the bank waits for payment and earns interest. A fourth possibility, when financing is difficult to obtain, is to engage in countertrade. In a countertrade, you accept goods, services, or other instruments of trade in partial or whole payment for the product. Countertrade, therefore, provides the customer with an opportunity to generate earnings to pay for the purchase.

These options may require you to pay interest, fees, or other costs. Some options are more feasible for larger amounts. Your company should also determine whether it will incur financial liability should the buyer default.

WORKING WITH COMMERCIAL BANKS

The same commercial bank services used to finance domestic activities, including revolving lines of credit for working capital, are often sought to finance export sales until payment is received. Banks do not regularly extend financing solely on the basis of an individual order; they prefer to establish an ongoing business relationship.

A logical first step if you're seeking to finance short-term export sales is to approach the local commercial bank that your company already does business with. If the bank previously has extended credit to your company, it will be familiar with your financial standing,

---

BOX 15.1 FINANCING CONSIDERATIONS

Here are some important factors to consider about financing:

• The credit terms extended to first-time buyers are very important because they set a precedent for future sales.

• Longer credit periods may increase the risk of default.

• Your company may incur financial liability if the buyer defaults.

• The same careful credit principles you follow for domestic customers should guide you in your exporting business.

credit need, repayment record, and ability to perform. The bank may be willing to raise the overall limit on an existing working capital line of credit, to expand its scope to cover export transactions, or to approve a separate line specifically adapted to export-related transactions that involve arrangements such as discounting.

Alternatively, you may wish to approach a commercial bank with an international department. Such a bank will be familiar with export business and will also be in a position to provide international banking services related to documentary collections and letters of credit, including the discounting of drafts. An intermediate approach is to retain a relationship with your bank but seek a referral to a correspondent bank that has an international department.

You should visit the bank's international department to discuss export plans, available banking facilities, and applicable charges. You may wish to inquire about such matters as fees for amending or confirming a letter of credit, fees for processing drafts, and the bank's experience in working with U.S. government agencies that offer export financing assistance. Generally, the bank's representative handling your account will not be located in the international department. It is in your best interest to create and foster a close working relationship with the international department.

The responsibility for repaying a working capital loan ordinarily rests with you, the seller, even if the foreign buyer fails to pay. The bank takes this contingency into account in deciding on an export working capital line of credit. Both you and the bank will benefit, though, if you improve the quality of the export receivables by using letters of credit, credit insurance, or Export–Import Bank or Small Business Administration working capital guarantees.

When shipping capital goods, you may want the commercial bank to make medium-term loans directly to the foreign buyer to finance the sale. Such loans are available for well-established foreign buyers in more stable markets. But where there is an element of risk, the bank may require a standby letter of credit, a recourse to the exporter in case of default, or similar repayment reinforcement. You should be knowledgeable about loans from your own bank that are backed by Export–Import Bank guarantees and insurance—assuming that the commercial bank is willing to use them.

USING DISCOUNTING AND BANKER'S ACCEPTANCES

A time draft under an irrevocable letter of credit confirmed by a U.S. bank presents relatively little risk of default, so you may be willing to hold such a draft until it matures. Unless you have ample funds to use for other purposes, however, holding drafts will use up your working capital.

As another course of action, your bank may be willing to buy or lend against time drafts if you have a creditworthy foreign buyer who has accepted or agreed to pay at a specified future date. Such an arrangement allows you to convert the time draft into immediate cash. The amount that you receive will be less than the face value of the draft. The difference, called a *discount,* represents interest and fees that the bank charges for holding the draft until maturity. The bank may also require you to reimburse it if the draft is unpaid at the due date.

In a third option, known as a *banker's acceptance,* a commercial bank may undertake to accept the obligation of paying a draft for a fee. Banker's acceptances are usually in large denominations. Only a few well-known banks are accepted in the market as "prime name" banks for purposes of creating banker's acceptances.

USING EXPORT INTERMEDIARIES

In addition to acting as export representatives, many export intermediaries, such as export trading companies and export management companies, can help finance export sales. Export intermediaries may provide short-term financing, or they may simply purchase the goods to be exported directly from the manufacturer, thus eliminating any risks to the manufacturer that are associated with the export transaction as well as the need for financing.

USING GOVERNMENT ASSISTANCE PROGRAMS

Several federal, state, and local government agencies offer programs to assist exporters with their financing needs. Some are guarantee programs that require the participation of an approved lender; others provide loans or grants to the exporter or to a foreign government.

Government programs generally aim to improve exporters' access to credit rather than to subsidize the cost at below-market levels. With few exceptions, banks are allowed to charge market interest rates and fees, including those paid to the government agencies to cover the agencies' administrative costs and default risks. Commercial banks use government guarantee and insurance programs to reduce the risk associated with loans to exporters.

Export–Import Bank of the United States

The Export–Import Bank of the United States (Ex–Im Bank) is an independent U.S. government agency that facilitates the export of U.S. goods and services. As the federal govern-

FACT:
Owners of small businesses often believe that they can't afford to export.

INSIGHT:
Recognizing the special needs of small firms, several federal agencies have taken major steps to help small and medium-sized businesses access capital to support their export activities. The agencies include the Small Business Administration, the Export–Import Bank, and the Overseas Private Investment Corporation.

ment's export credit agency, Ex–Im Bank provides export credit insurance, loan guarantees to lenders, direct loans to exporters on market-related credit terms, and loans to foreign buyers.

Ex–Im Bank's insurance and loan guarantees are structured to encourage exporters and financial institutions to support U.S. exports by reducing the commercial risks (such as buyer insolvency and failure to pay) and political risks (such as war and currency inconvertibility) of international trade that could result in non-payment to U.S. exporters by foreign buyers of their goods and services. The financing made available under Ex–Im Bank's guarantees and insurance is on market terms, and most of the commercial and political risks are borne by Ex–Im Bank.

Ex–Im Bank's loan program is designed to neutralize interest rate subsidies offered by foreign governments. By responding with loan assistance, Ex–Im Bank enables U.S. financing to be competitive with that offered by foreign exporters.

PREEXPORT FINANCING

The working capital guarantee enables lenders to provide the financing that an exporter needs to purchase or produce a product for export, as well as to finance short-term accounts receivable. If the exporter defaults on a loan guaranteed under this program, Ex–Im Bank reimburses the lender for the guaranteed portion—generally, 90 percent of the loan— thereby reducing the lender's overall risk. For qualified loans to minority, woman-owned, or rural businesses, Ex–Im Bank can increase its guarantee coverage to 100 percent. The working capital guarantee can be used either to support ongoing export sales or to meet a temporary need for cash flow arising from a single export transaction.

The working capital guarantee offers generous advance rates, so that exporters can increase their borrowing capacity. Those rates apply in the following categories:

• Inventory—up to 75 percent advance rate (including work-in-process—that is, material that has been released to manufacturing, engineering, design, or other services)

• Foreign accounts receivable—up to 90 percent advance rate

Guaranteed working capital loans are secured by export-related accounts receivable and inventory (including work-in-process) tied to an export order. (For letters of credit issued under a guaranteed loan, Ex–Im Bank requires collateral for only 25 percent of the value of the letter of credit.)

POSTEXPORT FINANCING

Ex–Im Bank offers export credit insurance to offset the commercial and political risks that are sometimes associated with international trade. Under the majority of policies, the insurance protects an exporter's short-term credit extended for the sale of consumer goods, raw materials, commodities, spare parts, and other items for which payment is expected within 180 days. If the buyer fails to pay, Ex–Im Bank reimburses the exporter in accordance with the terms of the policy. The majority of payment terms are up to 180 days, with some transactions qualifying for terms up to 360 days. Ex–Im Bank insurance is the largest federal program supporting short-term export credit.

Ex–Im Bank insurance policies for exporters include the Small Business Policy, the Single-Buyer Policy, and the Multi-Buyer Policy. With prior written approval, an exporter can assign the rights to any proceeds from an Ex–Im Bank insurance policy to a lender as collateral for financing.

Ex–Im Bank's policies generally cover up to 100 percent of defaults caused by specified political risks, such as war and expropriation, and up to 98 percent of defaults arising from commercial risks, such as buyer default and insolvency. Exporters generally must meet U.S. content requirements and, under some policies, must insure all eligible foreign sales.

Several private companies also offer export credit insurance that covers political and commercial risks. Private insurance is available, often at competitive premium rates, to established exporters who have a proven history, although underwriting in particular markets may be limited.

Under a separate program, the bank buyer credit policy, Ex–Im Bank offers a guarantee to encourage banks and other lenders to make export loans to creditworthy foreign buyers of U.S. goods and services. Ex–Im Bank's guarantee supports either medium-term financing (1 to 5 years for repayment after delivery or equipment installation) or long-term financing (up to 10 years for repayment) for heavy equipment and capital projects, such as power plants, telecommunications systems, and transport facilities and equipment.

As an alternative to guarantees, Ex–Im Bank also offers medium- and long-term loans. Ex–Im Bank loans are made on the same terms and conditions as guarantees, with the important difference that the bank sets the interest rate in accordance with international agreements. In many cases, an Ex–Im Bank guarantee results in a cost that is lower than an Ex–Im Bank loan.

For more information on Ex–Im Bank's programs, visit *www.exim.gov* or write to the Business Development Group, Export–Import Bank of the United States, 811 Vermont Ave., NW, Washington, DC 20571, or telephone (202) 565-EXIM (202-565-3946). You may also contact your local Export Assistance Center (see Appendix B).

Small Business Administration

The Small Business Administration (SBA) also provides financial assistance to U.S. exporters. Through its partnership with national, regional, and community lenders, SBA provides loan guarantees for export working capital and acquisition of plant and equipment, as well as capital for enabling small businesses to commence or expand export activity.

SBA's Export Working Capital Program (EWCP) will guarantee up to $1.5 million or 90 percent of the loan amount, whichever is less. These loans provide working capital for export transactions and finance export receivables. They can also support standby letters of credit used as bid or performance bonds. The loans can be set up to support individual transactions or as revolving lines of credit. Interest rates are negotiated between the borrower and the lender and may be fixed or variable.

SBA and Ex–Im Bank joined their working capital programs to offer a unified approach to the government's support of export financing. The EWCP uses a one-page application form and streamlined documentation. Turnaround is usually in 10 days or less. A letter of prequalification is also available from SBA.

If a larger loan guarantee is needed, Ex–Im Bank has a similar loan program to handle loan amounts in the multimillion dollar range.

Under its International Trade Loan Program, SBA can guarantee up to $1.25 million in combined working capital loans and loans for facilities and equipment (including land and buildings; construction of new facilities; renovation, improvement, or expansion of existing facilities; and purchase or reconditioning of machinery, equipment, and fixtures). Applicants must either (a) certify that loan proceeds will enable them to significantly expand existing export markets or develop new ones or (b) show that they have been adversely affected by import competition. Interest rates are negotiated between the small business exporter and the lender.

Export Express is a program that expedites multipurpose loans for small businesses. The Small Business Administration delegates the authority to approved lenders to unilaterally approve SBA-guaranteed loans. The lenders can use their own forms and can usually approve applications within a week. Export Express loans have a cap of $250,000. Loans of up to $150,000 receive an 85 percent SBA guarantee, and loans over that amount receive a 75 percent SBA guarantee.

To be eligible, a business must have been in operation for at least one year and must show that it will enter into or increase its export sales as a result of the loan. SBA's other eligibility requirements also apply. Eligible use of proceeds includes financing of export development activities, transaction-specific financing for export orders, revolving export lines of credit, fixed asset loans, and financing of standby letters of credit used as bid and performance bonds.

The EWCP, the International Trade Loan Program, and Export Express all require the participation of an eligible commercial bank. Most bankers are familiar with SBA's guarantee programs, but you should ask to speak to the SBA division of the lender you approach.

In addition to these export-oriented programs, SBA offers a variety of other loan programs that may meet specific needs of small businesses. For example, SBA's Surety Bond Program may help small exporters obtain bid or performance bonds that are required on construction contracts and on many service and supply contracts. Bid and performance bonds may be required when a small U.S. company is bidding on a contract with a foreign government or with a foreign prime contractor.

For information on SBA's programs, contact the nearest Export Assistance Center or SBA field office, or call (800) U-ASK-SBA (800-827-5722). SBA's Web site is *www.sba.gov*.

Department of Agriculture

The Foreign Agricultural Service (FAS) of the U.S. Department of Agriculture (USDA) provides several programs to assist in the financing of exports of U.S. agricultural goods.

The USDA's Commodity Credit Corporation (CCC) administers export credit guarantees for commercial financing of U.S. agricultural exports. The guarantees encourage exports to buyers in countries where credit is necessary to maintain or increase U.S. sales but where financing may not be available without CCC guarantees.

The Export Credit Guarantee Program (GSM-102) covers credit terms up to three years. GSM-102 underwrites credit extended by the private banking sector in the United States (or, less commonly, by the U.S. exporter) to approved foreign banks using dollar-denominated, irrevocable letters of credit to pay for food and agricultural products sold to foreign buyers.

The Supplier Credit Guarantee Program (SCGP) is designed to make it easier for exporters to sell U.S. food products overseas by insuring short-term, open-account financing. Under the security of the SCGP, U.S. exporters become more competitive by extending longer credit terms or increasing the amount of credit available to foreign buyers without increasing financial risk. Foreign buyers benefit because they can increase their purchasing power and profit opportunities and can gain significant cash flow management advantages.

The Facility Guarantee Program (FGP) provides payment guarantees to facilitate the financing of manufactured goods and services exported from the United States to improve or establish agriculture-related facilities in emerging markets. By supporting such facilities, the FGP is designed to enhance sales of U.S. agricultural commodities and products to emerging markets, where the demand for such commodities and products may be constricted because of inadequate storage, processing, or handling capabilities for such products.

The FAS maintains a Web site to expedite and simplify applications to these financing programs. The General Sales Manager (GSM) Online System enables U.S. exporters and U.S. banks to submit required documentation electronically for the GSM-102, SCGP, and FGP. To apply online, visit *www.fas.usda.gov/excredits/gsmonline/intro.asp*.

Exporters who need further information should contact the Contract and Registration Branch of the FAS at (202) 720-3224 or by e-mail at *AskGSM@fas.usda.gov*. U.S. banks needing further information should contact the Bank Analysis Branch of FAS at (202) 690-1249 or by e-mail at *michelle.zissimos@usda.gov*.

Overseas Private Investment Corporation

The Overseas Private Investment Corporation (OPIC) is a federal agency that facilitates U.S. foreign direct investment in developing nations and emerging market economies. OPIC is an independent, financially self-supporting corporation that is fully owned by the U.S. government.

OPIC encourages U.S. investment projects overseas by offering political risk insurance, all-risk guarantees, and direct loans. OPIC political risk insurance protects U.S. investment ventures abroad against the risks of civil strife and other violence, expropriation, and inconvertibility of currency. In addition, OPIC can cover business income loss caused by political violence or expropriation.

OPIC can offer up to $400 million in total project support for any one project—up to $250 million in project financing and up to $250 million in political risk insurance. The amount of insurance and financing available to projects in the oil and gas sector with offshore, hard-currency revenues is $300 million per product and $400 million if the project receives a credit evaluation of investment grade or higher from major ratings agencies. However, the maximum support OPIC may offer an individual project is $400 million, either by combined or single OPIC products.

U.S. exporters often can benefit from the construction and equipping of new facilities financed by OPIC, although the recipients of OPIC transactions are U.S. investors. U.S. exporters and contractors operating abroad can benefit directly from an OPIC program covering wrongful calling of bid, performance, advance payment, or other guarantees. Under another program, OPIC ensures against expropriation of construction equipment temporarily located abroad, spare parts warehoused abroad, and some cross-border operating and capital loans.

OPIC also provides services to facilitate wider participation by smaller U.S. businesses in overseas investment. They include investment missions, a computerized data bank, and investor information services. OPIC has undertaken several initiatives to increase its support for U.S. small businesses in their efforts to invest in emerging markets overseas. The Small and Medium Enterprise Department and OPIC's Small Business Center were established specifically to address the needs of small and medium-sized American companies and to ease their entry into new markets. A small business insurance "wrap" is offered to companies undertaking projects through the Small Business Center. A partnership with SBA enhances OPIC's outreach to the small business community.

For more information on any of these programs, contact OPIC's InfoLine at (202) 336-8799 or FactsLine at (202) 336-8700. OPIC maintains a Web site at *www.opic.gov.*

OBTAINING FUNDING FROM MULTILATERAL DEVELOPMENT BANKS

Multilateral development banks (MDBs) are international financial institutions owned by member governments. Their individual and collective objective is to promote economic and social progress in their developing member countries. The MDBs consist of the African Development Bank, the Asian Development Bank, the European Bank for Reconstruction and Development, the Inter-American Development Bank, and the World Bank Group. They achieve their objective by providing loans, technical cooperation, grants, capital investment, and other types of assistance to governments, government agencies, and other entities in their developing member countries. The practical expression of MDB support usually takes the form of a project or study.

Increasingly, the MDBs are providing funding to private-sector entities for private projects in developing countries. A growing number of companies and project developers around the world are taking advantage of this funding, which is secured on the basis of the financial, economic, and social viability of the projects in question.

The MDBs have traditionally been heavily involved in infrastructure and poverty alleviation projects. All the banks support projects in the following areas: agriculture, energy, environment, finance, industry, transportation, telecommunications, health, education, urban development, tourism, microenterprises, and the public sector, as well as other types of economic reform. All the banks provide some funding for private ventures, too.

The MDBs also provide debt, equity, and guarantee financing to eligible private ventures in developing countries. These funds, offered on commercial terms, can be accessed directly by private project sponsors and do not require a government guarantee.

U.S. companies receive less business from the banks than do businesses from other developed countries because fewer U.S. companies compete for the banks' business. Substantial export opportunities are available to U.S. companies, and to increase U.S. business participation, the Department of Commerce maintains liaison offices at the MDBs. MDB contact information is available at *www.export.gov/advocacy.mdbs.*

EXPLORING STATE AND LOCAL EXPORT FINANCE PROGRAMS

Several cities and states have funded and operate export financing programs, including preshipment and postshipment working capital loans and guarantees, accounts receivable financing, and export insurance. To be eligible for these programs, an export sale must generally be made under a letter of credit or with credit insurance coverage. A certain percentage of state or local content may also be required. However, some programs may require only that certain facilities, such as a state or local port, be used.

To explore these and other options for financing, contact a U.S. Commercial Service Export Assistance Center (see Appendix B) at *www.export.gov/eac* or by telephone at (800) USA-TRADE (800-872-8723). You may also contact your state's economic development agency.

JQ American

"When it comes to creating trusting, enduring relationships—business is more effective than politics or diplomacy."

—Jamal Qureshi, chief executive officer, JQ American

THE COMPANY

With his first sale of medical equipment many years ago, Jamal Qureshi turned the dream of starting his own business into a long-term reality. Now, as chief executive officer of JQ American in Hayward, California, Qureshi is tapping the lucrative world market as an exporter of products and services in the energy, medical, pharmaceutical, and chemical industries. Qureshi, who immigrated to the United States years ago, recently came full circle and has just started doing business in the city where he was born.

About a year ago, while attending a high school reunion in his native city of Bhopal, India, Qureshi learned that the Bhopal Medical College Trust wanted to outfit its soon-to-be-built medical training hospital with equipment using some of the latest U.S. medical technologies. For Qureshi, helping the citizens of his old hometown would turn into the opportunity of a lifetime.

Selling internationally wasn't new to Qureshi. He already had a solid record of export successes. He sold to 16 countries—including a contract with the United Nations in Kosovo to outfit a hospital with medical supplies and sales of medical and laboratory equipment to Iraq and its Ministry of Health.

THE CHALLENGE

Looking at India, Qureshi knew that financing was key to making the deal happen. India, like many countries, does not have a tradition of credit cards or other forms of advance payment. Purchasers want terms—often 45 days—and sellers from competitor countries are ready to grant them. Qureshi, however, does not usually have a cash flow sufficient to meet the buyers' demand for expensive imaging and other devices. Would the schmoozing with high school pals and the chance to do some good (and some good business) in his old stomping grounds come to naught?

THE SOLUTION

Over several months, Qureshi, with help from the U.S. Commercial Service in Oakland, California, arranged key meetings through videoconference and phone calls with the Bank of Alameda (California), the U.S. Export–Import (Ex–Im) Bank, the State Bank of India, and the Bhopal Medical College Trust.

These efforts enabled Qureshi to obtain an Ex–Im Bank letter of interest and qualify for a subsequent commercial financing loan of $23 million through the Bank of Alameda and State Bank of India. Impressed with JQ American's reputation and its ability to meet the financial requirements of the project, Bhopal Medical College Trust considered JQ American its top choice for the supplier contract. After months of negotiation, Qureshi finalized the deal during a U.S. Commerce Department trade mission to India.

LESSONS LEARNED

Qureshi is aware that he personifies the American Dream, so much so that he made *American* part of his company name. Given that the markets JQ American works in often proclaim opposition to U.S. foreign policy and values in the form of consumer boycotts and worse, some people might consider the company's name the kiss of commercial death.

Qureshi doesn't buy it. "People around the world love our products and services," he says, directing a doubtful graphic designer to add more American flags to his new logo. "Even with embargoes, they want us. Iranians will shout, 'Down with America,' then buy our stuff through third parties."

Why do American companies have such an advantage? "Because we are world leaders in so many areas, but especially in setting high quality standards," Qureshi says. "In other countries, including China, quality varies from region to area and from company to company. My customers will pay more for the 'Made in America' label."

Qureshi's upbringing in a hardscrabble part of India gave him a certain comfort level for doing business in challenging parts of the world, but he says that the requisite skills can be learned by doing. "Get out in the world and get a feel for what people want and how they do business," he advises. "The opportunities for growth are tremendous, and the risks are very manageable, thanks to advances in logistics, banking, and market intelligence for the smaller U.S. company."

One lesson he learned in Kosovo and the Middle East is that it's important to have reliable locals perform after-sales service. In a new project in the Philippines, where he's equipping a medical tourism hospital, Qureshi plans to hire and train Filipinos to provide 24/7 maintenance for surgical and other sophisticated devices. "Hospitals are complex places that reflect local cultures," he explains. "By offering a turnkey solution with local maintenance, I was able to make a very favorable impression."

The U.S. Commercial Service has helped Qureshi find local equipment maintenance companies in markets around the world. Commercial Service specialists find and vet candidates and help Qureshi make the selection.

Working with U.S. government personnel has other advantages. Qureshi explains, "Showing up at a potential buyer's with U.S. officials in tow always makes a positive impression—so positive that I now conduct at least one business meeting with potential buyers who visit me in the U.S. at my local federal building."

The Commercial Service helped Qureshi line up financing and facilitate other deals in India during a recent trade mission there. Thanks to U.S. government resources such as the Ex–Im Bank, JQ American has lines of credit to finance new export sales and can get additional funds in turnaround times of five days or fewer.

By improving the lives of others through U.S. technology and innovation, Qureshi met a lifetime goal to make a positive difference in the world. "When it comes to creating trusting, enduring relationships—business is more effective than politics or diplomacy," he says.

ACTION

Are you ready to create enduring relationships abroad?

- **Learn to manage risk.** Visit Ex–Im Bank at *www.exim.gov* or the Small Business Administration at *www.sba.gov* for more information about risk insurance and export financing programs. You can obtain a free copy of the Department of Commerce publication "Trade Finance Guide: A Quick Reference for U.S. Exporters" by calling (800)-USA-TRADE (800-872-8723) or by visiting *www.ita. doc.gov/media/publications/abstract/ trade_finance_guide2007desc.html.* For additional advice on credit and risk management for exporters, visit FCIB, an association of executives in finance,

credit, and international business, at *www.fcibglobal.com.*

- **Attend trade missions.** Many state governments run their own trade missions, often led by governors. The Department of Commerce certifies industry-specific and multi-industry trade missions, and it operates its own missions. For information on upcoming missions, contact your state's office of international trade or economic development. For Department of Commerce missions, visit *www.export.gov* and *www.buyusa.gov.*

- **Follow leads.** For business leads other than those collected at your high school reunion, visit *www.export.gov/ tradeleads.*

Jamal Qureshi is chief executive officer of JQ American. The Hayward, California–based business, with an established record of selling medical and laboratory equipment in 16 countries, recently expanded to India.

chapter 16

BUSINESS TRAVEL ABROAD

In This Chapter

- **Documents you need to travel internationally**

- **Tips for travel and business meetings in your destination country**

- **Cultural factors to take into account**

FACT:
Gathering and generating the proper documentation for overseas business travel requires time and attention to detail.

INSIGHT:
Allow six to eight weeks to acquire all the documents.

It is important to visit overseas markets—before any transaction occurs. As discussed in Chapter 3, many foreign markets differ greatly from the domestic market, and by visiting another country you can familiarize yourself with cultural nuances that may affect the design, packaging, or advertising of your product. Traveling abroad can generate new customers. As in the United States, clients and customers overseas often prefer to conduct business in person before concluding a transaction.

A successful business trip typically requires substantial planning (see Box 16.1). This chapter focuses on the many steps you need to take before traveling abroad and offers recommendations that will make the trip more successful.

OBTAINING PROPER DOCUMENTATION

All overseas travelers are required to have proper documentation before leaving the United States. You must have a current U.S. passport, visas from certain host countries, and—in some instances—vaccination records. If you're bringing a product for demonstration or sample purposes, an ATA carnet may also be helpful. Businesses should allow six to eight weeks to acquire all the necessary documents.

Carnets

The ATA carnet is a standardized international customs document used to obtain duty-free temporary admission of certain goods. The abbreviation ATA is derived from the French words *admission temporaire* and the English words *temporary admission.* Countries that are signatories to the ATA Convention require the carnet. Under the ATA Convention, com-

BOX 16.1 PREPARING FOR BUSINESS MEETINGS AND TRAVEL ABROAD

Preparation will help make your trip smoother and more productive. Here are some tips:

• **Schedule meetings before leaving the United States.** You should determine if an interpreter is required and make all necessary arrangements before arriving. Business language is generally more technical than the conversational speech that many travelers are familiar with—and mistakes can be costly. The U.S. Commercial Service can assist in locating qualified translators.

• **Prepare new business cards in the proper languages.** In most countries, exchanging business cards at the first meeting is considered good business manners. As a matter of courtesy, it is best to carry business cards printed both in English and in the language of the country being visited.

• **Prepare for different weather conditions.** Seasonal weather conditions in the countries being visited are likely to be different from conditions in the United States.

• **Address health care issues.** Plan appropriately for prescription drugs, health insurance, vaccinations, diet, and other matters.

• **Find out about the country's electrical current.** A transformer, plug adapter, or both may be needed to demonstrate company products and to use personal electrical appliances.

• **Think about money.** U.S. banks can provide a list of automatic teller machines overseas, exchange rates, and traveler's checks.

• **Consider transportation.** You should be aware of the means of public and private transportation available in the country, have a plan in mind, and make any necessary arrangements before you arrive.

• **Prepare for differences in culture.** You should become familiar with basic cultural manifestations such as hand signals, street signs, and tipping.

mercial and professional travelers may temporarily take commercial samples; tools of the trade; advertising material; and cinematographic, audiovisual, medical, scientific, or other professional equipment into member countries without paying customs duties and taxes or posting a bond at the border of each country to be visited.

You should contact the U.S. Council for International Business to determine if the country you are visiting is a member of the ATA Convention. Carnets are generally valid for 12 months. To receive an application or to ask questions, contact the U.S. Council for International Business, 1212 Avenue of the Americas, New York, NY 10036; call (866) 786-5625; or visit *www.uscib.org*.

Passports

All travel outside the United States and its possessions requires a valid U.S. passport. Information is available from the nearest local passport office. A wealth of information is available online from the U.S. Department of State about U.S. passports, applications, and renewals. You can obtain a nationwide listing of government offices that have passport applications, or you can download a printable application from the State Department at *www.state.gov.*

Visas

Many countries require visas, but they cannot be obtained through the Passport Services Directorate. Visas are provided by a foreign country's embassy or consulate in the United States for a small fee. You must have a current U.S. passport to obtain a visa, and in many cases, a recent photo is required. You should allow several weeks to obtain visas, especially if you are traveling to developing nations. Some foreign countries require visas for business travel but not for tourist travel. When you request visas from a consulate or an embassy, you should notify the authorities that you will be conducting business. You should check visa requirements each time you travel to a country because regulations change periodically. Contact an Export Assistance Center to learn about documentation requirements for the countries where you will be traveling.

Vaccinations

Requirements for vaccinations differ by country. Although there may not be any restrictions on direct travel to and from the United States, there may be restrictions if you travel indirectly and stop over in another country before reaching your final destination. Vaccinations against typhus, typhoid, and other diseases are advisable even though they are not required. The Centers for Disease Control and Prevention (CDC) maintains a Web page to advise travelers of current conditions by country and region at *http://wwwn.cdc.gov/travel/default.aspx.*

Foreign Customs

Because foreign customs regulations vary by country, you are advised to learn in advance the regulations that apply to each country that you will be visiting. If allowances for cigarettes, liquor, currency, and certain other items are not taken into account, those items can be impounded at national borders.

PLANNING AN ITINERARY

Travel agents can arrange transportation and hotel reservations quickly and efficiently. They can also help plan the itinerary, obtain the best travel rates, explain which countries require visas, advise on hotel rates and locations, and provide other valuable services. Because hotels, airlines, and other carriers pay travel agents' fees, this assistance and expertise may be free.

A well-planned itinerary enables you to make the best use of your time abroad. Although it is expensive to travel and your time is valuable, an overloaded schedule can be counterproductive. Two or three definite appointments, confirmed well in advance and spaced comfortably throughout a day, are more productive and enjoyable than a crowded agenda that forces you to rush from one meeting to the next before business is really concluded. If possible, you should plan an extra day to rest to deal with jet lag before starting your scheduled business appointments. As you plan your trip, you should keep the following travel tips in mind:

• The travel plans should reflect your company's goals and priorities.

• You should obtain the names of possible contacts, arrange appointments, and check transportation schedules before the trip begins. The most important meetings should be confirmed before you leave the United States. The U.S. Commercial Service can offer assistance through programs such as the Gold Key Service. Refer to Chapter 6 for additional information.

• As a rule, you should keep the schedule flexible enough to allow for both unexpected problems (such as transportation delays) and unexpected opportunities. For instance, accepting an unscheduled luncheon invitation from a prospective client should not keep you from missing the next scheduled meeting.

• You should confirm the normal workdays and business hours in the countries being visited. In many Middle Eastern countries, for instance, the workweek typically runs from Saturday to Thursday. Lunchtimes of two to four hours are customary in many countries.

• You should also contact an Export Assistance Center to learn of any travel advisories issued by the U.S. Department of State for countries you plan to visit. Advisories alert travelers to potentially dangerous in-country situations. The U.S. Department of State also includes travel advisories on its Web site at *www.state.gov.*

OBTAINING ASSISTANCE FROM U.S. EMBASSIES AND CONSULATES

When planning a trip, you can discuss your needs and the services available at particular embassies with the staff of your local Export Assistance Center. You may also find it useful to read the appropriate Country Commercial Guide provided by the Department of Commerce.

Commercial and economic officers in U.S. embassies and consulates abroad assist U.S. exporters by providing in-depth briefings and arranging introductions to appropriate firms, individuals, or foreign government officials. Your local Export Assistance Center can help you access these services, or you can contact embassy and consulate personnel directly. Arrangements should be made as far ahead as possible. You may also find it useful to read the appropriate Country Commercial Guide provided by the Department of Commerce.

Also, a description of your firm and the extent of your international experience would be helpful to U.S. government officials abroad. Addresses of U.S. embassies and consulates throughout the world are available on the U.S. State Department Web site at *www.state.gov.*

CONSIDERING CULTURAL FACTORS

Businesspeople who hope to profit from their travel should learn about the history, culture, and customs of the countries they wish to visit. Flexibility and cultural adaptation should be the guiding principles for traveling abroad on business (see Box 16.2). Business manners and methods, religious customs, dietary practices, humor, and acceptable dress vary from country to country. You can prepare for your overseas visits by reading travel guides, which are located in the travel sections of most libraries and bookstores.

Some of the cultural differences that U.S. firms most often face involve business styles, attitudes toward business relationships and punctuality, negotiating styles, gift-giving customs, greetings, significance of gestures, meanings of colors and numbers, and customs regarding titles.

The cultural anthropology literature has given us many insights into how other countries do business and how to avoid cultural blunders. One example is that Thais consider it a serious offense for someone to touch them on the head. Useful to know? Maybe. But it's hard to imagine in the United States or anywhere else businesspeople meeting for the first time or even after several times and engaging in head touching or hair messing. So by all means read the literature and talk with people who know the culture. But don't be intimidated and don't be reluctant to meet people. And do keep these general rules in mind.

Understanding and heeding cultural differences are critical to success in international business. Lack of familiarity with the business practices, social customs, and etiquette of a country can weaken your company's position in the market, prevent you from accomplishing your objectives, and ultimately lead to the failure of your exporting effort.

Americans must pay close attention to different styles of doing business and the degree of importance placed on developing business relationships. In some countries, businesspeople have a very direct style, while in others they are more subtle and value personal relationships more than most U.S. businesspeople do. For example, in the Middle East, engaging in small talk before engaging in business is standard practice.

Attitudes toward punctuality vary greatly from one culture to another, and misunderstanding those attitudes may cause confusion. Romanians, Japanese, and Germans are very punctual, whereas people in many of the Latin countries have a more relaxed attitude toward time. The Japanese consider it rude to be late for a business meeting but acceptable—even fashionable—to be late for a social occasion. In Guatemala, though, one might arrive from 10 minutes early to 45 minutes late for a luncheon appointment.

FACT:
First impressions are important.

INSIGHT:
Americans must pay attention to different styles of doing business. In some countries, businesspeople have a very direct style, while in others they are more subtle and place more value on personal relationships.

BOX 16.2 TOP 10 BUSINESS CULTURE TIPS

1. Answer queries. Always politely and promptly answer e-mail, fax, and telephone inquiries from overseas. Provide price lists, quotes, and other information. Build your own marketing list from the contacts. The query you ignore today could be your next best source of future business.

2. Start with what you know. Consider doing business first with a business culture and system similar to that of the United States. Canada and the United Kingdom are good markets to start in.

3. Learn from your domestic customers. Apply cultural knowledge you gain from selling to Latino, Asian, and other consumers in the United States. Preferences, product usage, and business protocol won't translate perfectly, but helpful information can be harvested here in the United States and applied to market entry efforts abroad.

4. Be patient. Different cultures have different concepts of time. Few markets have a faster business pace than the United States; many are slower.

5. Take time to develop personal relationships. Especially do so with distributors or large-volume buyers. Remembering birthdays and other important events in the lives of your business associates and their families are good intercultural business practices. It is generally not difficult for Americans to be warm, welcoming, respectful, and thoughtful. Be yourself—or even a little more. If you can't, or the self you know doesn't fit this profile, consider sending someone else.

6. Learn the language. A few words of the native language of your buyers or business associates will go a long way. They will appreciate the effort. Words of welcome on your Web site, and maybe a currency converter, will further demonstrate your interest in doing business in ways that are mutually respectful.

7. Get an intern. As business develops with overseas customers, consider recruiting a college student intern who speaks the language and understands the business culture. Interns are especially valuable in doing business with customers in Japan, China, and Arabic-speaking countries.

8. Attend a U.S. trade show. Find one in your industry where foreign buyers are present. You can make good contacts—even sales—and test the waters before heading overseas.

9. Attend an international trade show in your industry. The U.S. embassy often staffs a U.S. pavilion where U.S. sellers and foreign buyers, often from many countries in a region, meet. A great way to understand a different business culture is to do business, not read about how others do it.

10. Get help. Before you head overseas on a business development trip, contact the U.S. embassy and the U.S. Commercial Service. They'll line up qualified buyers for you to meet, and they'll counsel you on business protocol, market intelligence, regulatory issues, and much more.

When cultural lines are being crossed, something as simple as a greeting can be misunderstood. Traditional greetings include shaking hands, hugging, kissing, and placing the hands in praying position. The "wrong" greeting can lead to an awkward encounter.

People around the world use body movements and gestures to convey specific messages. Misunderstandings over gestures are common occurrences in intercultural communication and can lead to business complications and social embarrassment.

Proper use of names and titles is often a source of confusion in international business relations. In many countries (including Denmark, France, and the United Kingdom), it is appropriate to use titles until use of first names is suggested. First names are seldom used when doing business in Germany. Visiting businesspeople should use the surname preceded by the title. Titles such as "Herr Direktor" are sometimes used to indicate prestige, status, and rank. Thais, however, address one another by first names and reserve last names for very formal occasions and written communications. In Belgium, it is important to address French-speaking business contacts as "Monsieur" or "Madame," whereas Flemish-speaking contacts should be addressed as "Mr." or "Mrs." To confuse the two is a great insult.

Understanding the customs concerning gift giving is also important. In some cultures, gifts are expected, and failure to present them is considered an insult. In other countries, though, offering a gift is considered offensive. Business executives also need to know when to present a gift (on the initial visit or afterward, for instance); where to present the gift (in public or private, for example); what type of gift to present; what color it should be; and how many gifts to present.

Gift giving is an important part of doing business in Japan, where gifts are usually exchanged at the first meeting. In sharp contrast, gifts are rarely exchanged in Germany and are usually not appropriate. Gift giving is not a usual custom in Belgium or the United Kingdom either, although in both countries, flowers are a suitable gift when you are invited to someone's home.

Customs concerning the exchange of business cards also vary. Although this point may seem of minor importance, card giving is a key part of business protocol. In Japan, for example, the Western practice of accepting a business card and pocketing it immediately is considered rude. The proper approach is to carefully look at the card after accepting it, observe the title and organization, acknowledge with a nod that the information has been digested, and perhaps make a relevant comment or ask a polite question.

Negotiating is a complex process even between parties from the same nation. It is even more complicated in international transactions because of the potential misunderstandings that stem from cultural differences. It is essential to understand the importance of rank in the other country and to know who the decision-makers are. It is important to be familiar with the business style of the foreign company, to understand the nature of agreements there, and to know the significance of gestures and negotiating etiquette.

Through research or training, you can have a working knowledge of the business culture, management attitudes, business methods, and consumer habits before you travel abroad. That knowledge is very likely to have a positive effect on your overseas travel. Your local Export Assistance Center can provide what you need to make a strong first impression.

CASE STUDY:
Candy Bouquet International

"If you do what you love, you will never work a day in your life."
—Margaret McEntire, founder, president, and chief executive officer, Candy Bouquet International

THE COMPANY

Chocolate vases, squares of vanilla fudge, and sugar-free lemon drops—what better way to grow a business than appealing to the world's sweet tooth? Margaret McEntire, founder, president, and chief executive officer of Candy Bouquet International, thought so. Her firm is now the largest candy franchise in the world. But it wasn't always that way. Candy Bouquet started as a one-room operation in 1989, but by 1995, McEntire was looking to expand her business overseas.

THE CHALLENGE

McEntire says her biggest challenges have been learning more about business practices in different cultures, gaining key market information, and learning about channels of trade. Educating foreign businesspeople about American franchises is another challenge, and so is describing what a candy bouquet is. The company has had to explain the concept of rolling a candy store and a florist together and making a product that is really all candy.

THE SOLUTION

In 1995, McEntire attended a trade show in Washington, D.C., where she met a trade specialist from the U.S. Commercial Service. That connection led to her participation in a Commercial Service mission to Eastern Europe and introduced her to doing business in foreign markets.

In the years that followed, Candy Bouquet expanded to dozens of foreign countries. The company's unique franchising system allows individuals to make a single purchase into the franchise and pay no continual overhead. The only requirement is that their supplies must come from the Candy Bouquet warehouse in Little Rock, Arkansas.

"One of the most helpful things I've found in doing foreign business is having a person we know in that country to help us out," says McEntire, referring to the Commercial Service's worldwide network of trade specialists. She credits much of her success to Dennis Millard, a trade specialist at the Little Rock Export Assistance Center. "When I know a foreign franchisee is coming, I call Dennis at our local U.S. Commercial Service office, and he provides me

with solid information on the business practices of that culture."

Millard has also helped her take advantage of many Commercial Service programs. Candy Bouquet participates annually in the International Franchise Trade Show and has taken part in trade missions around the world. In 1999, McEntire participated in the Women in Business Matchmaker Trade Mission to South America and the Women's Economic Summit of the Americas in Buenos Aires, Argentina. McEntire is also a frequent participant in Commercial Service global video teleconferencing. She is a regular presenter at the international trade events sponsored by the Little Rock Export Assistance Center and shares her experiences with other businesses that are new to exporting. McEntire also advertises in *Commercial News USA,* a product catalog produced by the Commercial Service and distributed to more than 400,000 overseas buyers.

With assistance from the Commercial Service, Candy Bouquet has expanded from a single-room operation to more than 700 franchises in more than 40 countries. McEntire says, "Nobody likes to pay taxes but [the Commercial Service] is the best use of my tax dollars."

LESSONS LEARNED

McEntire has several lessons to pass along to new exporters:

- **Adapt your product for other cultures.** In one instance, McEntire was trying to sell chocolate vases in Malaysia, but there were few takers: "We discovered that Malaysians … thought the chocolate pieces were too big. So we got the idea of ordering sample sizes from the manufacturer, and it did the trick."

- **Educate yourself about local practices.** On one occasion, McEntire shipped candy to Saudi Arabia in boxes that bore pictures of women's hands holding drinking glasses. Saudi Arabians don't drink, so their customs bureau returned the boxes. On another occasion, McEntire invited three potential Candy Bouquet franchise owners from Indonesia, Malaysia, and the United Arab Emirates (UAE) to visit her home for training. The gentleman from the UAE eventually wanted to pray. "Margaret," he asked, "which way is Mecca?" McEntire has learned to be prepared for any cultural contingency.

- **Realize that there will be setbacks.** One such setback occurred in Cairo, where women seldom start their own businesses. Much of the candy that her franchisees had ordered was burned on the airport tarmac. Eventually, many of the women were able to persuade their husbands to join in as business partners, making the venture more socially acceptable.

- **Protect your intellectual property.** In China, someone copied McEntire's brand name and then tried to order additional candy from her. Fortunately, other Candy Bouquet franchisees in China informed McEntire about what was going on. She is now pursuing legal action.

- **Enjoy your work.** "I love my job; it's fun to go around the world to help people eat candy and chocolate," McEntire says. "We are changing the face of the world with a brand-new industry, and it is very gratifying to see our franchises succeed and help the local economy. If you do what you love, you will never work a day in your life."

ACTION

Find out if franchising is your window to exporting:

- **Consider the advantages of franchising.** According to Sam Dhir of the U.S. Commercial Service, franchising offers several advantages for businesspeople interested in exporting. First, the franchisee is managing an established concept. It has already been market tested, so the franchise is a low-risk investment. Second, the franchisee is his or her own boss. And third, the franchisee receives the full support from the master franchiser in terms of training, advertising, and market support. For more information about franchising, visit the International Franchise Association Web site at *www.franchise.org*.

- **Be aware of the social customs of target markets.** Dhir recommends that potential franchisees look closely at the social customs in the country where they would like to do business. Contacting the Commercial Service office in that country is an excellent way to learn about cultural issues and ways of doing business. Visit *www. export.gov* for the nearest U.S. Export Assistance Center, and that office will contact the appropriate Commercial Service post in the country of interest.

Margaret McEntire, founder, president, and chief executive officer of Candy Bouquet International, started the business out of her garage in 1989. The Little Rock, Arkansas, firm now has candy and flower bouquet franchises in more than 40 countries.

SELLING OVERSEAS
AND AFTER-SALES SERVICE

Many successful exporters first started selling internationally by responding to an inquiry from a foreign firm. Thousands of U.S. firms receive such requests annually, but most firms do not become successful exporters. Generally, successful firms make it a priority to create systems to properly respond to inquiries, conduct research on foreign customers, differentiate between domestic and international sales, and build positive relationships with partners.

RESPONDING TO INQUIRIES

Most, but not all, foreign letters, faxes, or e-mails of inquiry are in English. Your firm may look to certain service providers (such as banks or freight forwarders) for assistance in translating a letter of inquiry in a foreign language. Colleges and universities are also excellent sources for translation services. Most large cities have commercial translators who are hired for a fee.

A foreign firm will typically request product specifications, information, and a price. Some inquiries will come directly from the end user, whereas other inquiries will come from distributors and agents who wish to sell the product in their market. A few foreign firms may already be familiar with your product and may wish to place an order immediately.

Regardless of the form such inquiries take, your firm should establish a policy to deal with them. Here are a few suggestions:

• Expect some inquiries to have grammatical or typographical errors because the writer may know English only as a second language.

• Reply promptly, completely, and clearly. The correspondent naturally wants to know something about your firm before a transaction takes place. The reply should introduce your firm

sufficiently and establish it as a reliable supplier. The reply should provide a short but adequate introduction to the firm, including bank references and other sources that confirm reliability. Your firm's policy on exports should be stated, including cost, terms, and delivery. Your firm may wish to respond with a pro forma invoice (see Chapter 13).

• Enclose information on your firm's goods or services.

• If the company needs to meet a deadline, send the information by e-mail or fax. Unlike telephone communications, these methods may be used effectively despite differences in time zones and languages.

• Keep a record of foreign inquiries. They may turn into definite prospects as your export business grows. If your firm has an intermediary handling exports, the intermediary may use the information.

LEARNING ABOUT POTENTIAL CLIENTS

There are many ways for a U.S. firm to research a foreign company before conducting any formal business. Your company can save time and money by using the following resources:

• **Business libraries.** Several private-sector publications list and qualify international firms. There are also many directories devoted to specific regions and countries.

• **International banks.** Bankers have access to vast amounts of information on foreign firms and are usually very willing to assist corporate customers.

• **Foreign embassies.** Foreign embassies are located in Washington, D.C., and some have consulates in other major cities. The commercial (business) sections of most foreign embassies have directories of firms located in their countries.

• **Sources of credit information.** Credit reports on foreign companies are available from many private-sector sources and from the U.S. Commercial Service. For help in identifying sources of credit reports, contact your nearest Export Assistance Center.

- **Commercial Service overseas offices**. Commercial Service officers can prepare International Company Profiles or help with background reports on foreign firms.

CONDUCTING BUSINESS INTERNATIONALLY

Companies should be aware of basic business practices that are essential to successful international selling. Because cultures vary, there is no single business code. The following basic practices transcend culture barriers, though, and will help your company conduct business overseas.

- **Keep promises**. The biggest complaint from foreign importers about U.S. suppliers is failure to ship as promised. A first order is particularly important because it shapes the customer's image of a firm as a dependable or an undependable supplier.

- **Be polite, courteous, and friendly**. It is important to avoid undue familiarity or slang, which may be misinterpreted. Some overseas firms feel that the usual brief U.S. business letter is lacking in courtesy.

- **Personally sign all letters**. Form letters are not satisfactory.

BUILDING A WORKING RELATIONSHIP

Once you have established a relationship with an overseas customer, representative, or distributor, it is important to work on building and maintaining that relationship. Common courtesy should dictate business activity. By following the points outlined in this chapter, your firm can present itself well. Beyond these points, you should keep in mind that a foreign contact should be treated and served as well as a domestic contact. For example, your company should keep customers and contacts notified of all changes, including changes in price, personnel, address, and phone numbers.

Because of distance, a contact can "age" quickly and cease to be useful unless communication is maintained. If your firm cannot afford frequent travel, you may use fax, e-mail, and telephone to keep the working relationship active and up to date.

PROVIDING AFTER-SALES SERVICE

Quality, price, and service are three factors critical to the success of any export sales effort. Quality and price are addressed in earlier chapters. Service, which is addressed here, should be an integral part of any company's export strategy from the start. Properly handled, service can be a foundation for growth. Ignored or left to chance, it can cause an export effort to fail.

Service is the prompt delivery of the product. It is courteous sales personnel. It is a user or service manual modified to meet your customer's needs. It is ready access to a service facility. It is knowledgeable, cost-effective maintenance, repair, or replacement. Service is location. Service is dealer support.

Service varies by the product type, the quality of the product, the price of the product, and the distribution channel used. For certain export products—such as food products, some consumer goods, and commercial disposables—service ends once distribution channels, quality criteria, and return policies have been identified.

However, the characteristics of consumer durables and some consumables demand that service be available after the purchase is completed. For such products, service is a feature expected by the consumer. In fact, foreign buyers of industrial goods typically place service at the forefront of the criteria they evaluate when making a decision about a purchase.

All foreign markets are sophisticated, and each has its own expectations of suppliers and vendors. U.S. manufacturers or distributors must therefore ensure that their service performance is comparable to that of the predominant competitors in the market. This level of performance is an important determinant in ensuring a competitive position, especially if the other factors of product quality, price, promotion, and delivery appeal to the buyer.

You may decide, as part of your exporting strategy, not to provide after-sales service. Your company may determine that its export objective is the single or multiple opportunistic entry into export markets. Although this approach may work in the short term, your subsequent product offerings will be less successful as buyers recall the failure to provide expected levels of service. As a result, market development and sales expenditures may result in one-time sales.

Reviewing Service Delivery Options

Service is an important factor in the initial export sale and ongoing success of products in foreign markets. Your firm has many options for the delivery of service to foreign buyers.

REQUIRING THE BUYER TO RETURN THE PRODUCT

A high-cost option—and the most inconvenient for the foreign retail, wholesale, commercial, or industrial buyer—is for the product to be returned to the manufacturing or distribution facility in the United States for service or repair. The buyer incurs a high cost and loses the use of the product for an extended period, while you must incur the export cost of the same product a second time to return it. Fortunately, there are practical, cost-effective alternatives to this approach.

USING A LOCAL PARTNER

For goods sold at retail outlets, a preferred service option is to identify and use local service facilities. Although this approach requires upfront expenses to identify and train the staff for local service outlets, the costs are more than repaid in the long run.

Exporting a product into commercial or industrial markets may dictate a different approach. For the many U.S. companies that sell through distributors, selection of a repre-

FACT:

Properly handled, service can be a foundation for growth. Ignored or left to chance, it can cause an export effort to fail.

INSIGHT:

You have many options for handling your after-sales service:

- Have the product returned to the United States for service or repair.
- Identify and use local service facilities.
- Provide on-site service.
- Create a branch or subsidiary to provide service in the country.
- Be prepared to accept return of merchandise if the foreign buyer refuses to accept it.

sentative to serve a region, a nation, or a market should be based not only on the distributing company's ability to sell effectively but also on its ability and willingness to service the product. Assessing that ability to provide service requires that you ask questions about existing service facilities; about the types, models, and age of existing service equipment; about training practices for service personnel; and about the firm's experience in servicing similar products.

If the selected export distribution channel is a joint venture or other partnership arrangement, the overseas partner may have a service or repair capability in the markets to be penetrated. Your firm's negotiations and agreements with its partner should include explicit provisions for repairs, maintenance, and warranty service. The cost of providing this service should be negotiated into the agreement.

If the product being exported is to be sold directly to end users, service and timely performance are critical to success. The nature of the product may require delivery of on-site service to the buyer within a very specific time period. You must be prepared to negotiate such issues. On-site service may be available from service organizations in the buyer's country, or your company may have to send personnel to the site to provide service. The sales contract should anticipate a reasonable level of on-site service and should include the associated costs. Existing performance and service history can serve as a guide for estimating service and warranty requirements on export sales. This practice is accepted by small and large exporters alike.

If your export activity in a particular region grows to a considerable level, it may become cost-effective for your company to establish its own branch or subsidiary operation in the foreign market. The branch or subsidiary may be a one-person operation or a more extensive facility staffed with sales, administrative, service, and other personnel, most of whom are local nationals. This high-cost option enables you to ensure sales and service quality, provided that personnel are trained in sales, products, and service on an ongoing basis. A benefit of this option is the control it gives you and the ability to serve multiple markets in a single region.

If you have neither partners nor joint venture arrangements in a foreign market, you must be prepared to accept return of merchandise that the foreign buyer refuses to take. This situation is not likely to occur in cash-in-advance or confirmed letter of credit transactions. However, in an open-account or documentary collection transaction, the buyer is in a position to refuse delivery of the goods and suffer no financial harm. If you cannot find another buyer in that market or if you elect not to abandon the goods, you will be faced with the fees and charges associated with returning the goods to the United States. Your freight forwarder can be of great assistance in this process should the need arise and can quote you a price to return the goods.

Considering Legal Options

Service is an important part of many types of representative agreements. For better or worse, the quality of service in a country or region affects your company's reputation there.

It is imperative that agreements with a representative be specific about the form of the repair or service facility, the number of people on the staff, inspection provisions, training programs, and payment of costs associated with maintaining a suitable facility. The depth or breadth of a warranty in a given country or region should be tied to the service facility that you have access to in that market. It is important to promise only what you can deliver.

Another part of the representative agreement may detail the training you will provide to your foreign representative. Such detail may include how often training will be provided, who must be trained, where training will be provided, and which party will absorb travel and per diem costs.

Taking Advantage of New Sales Opportunities and Improved Customer Relations

Foreign buyers of U.S.–manufactured products typically have limited contact with the manufacturer or its personnel. The foreign service facility is one of the major contact points between you and the buyer. To a great extent, your reputation is made by the overseas service facility.

Each foreign market offers a unique opportunity for your company. Care and attention to the development of in-country sales and distribution capabilities are paramount. Delivery of after-sales service is critical to the short- and long-term success of your company's efforts in any market.

Senior personnel from your company should commit to a program of regular travel to each foreign market to meet with representatives, clients, and others who are important to the success of your firm in that market. Among those people would be the commercial officer at the Commercial Service's post and representatives of the American Chamber of Commerce and the local chamber of commerce or business association.

The benefits of such a program are twofold. First, executive management learns more about the foreign marketplace and the foreign service facility's capabilities. Second, your customer will appreciate the attention and understand the importance of the foreign market in your company's long-term plans. As a result, such visits will help you build a continuing productive relationship with your overseas clients.

ProStuff LLC

"We have to take [our] technology to the rest of the world. And that's been one of the core principles in our success."

—Pierce Barker, founder and chief executive, ProStuff LLC

THE COMPANY

ProStuff LLC was founded in 2004 by Pierce Barker and a couple of his friends. As Barker tells the story of the business idea and how it germinated in Columbus, Ohio, it was "our inspiration meeting the opportunity."

Says Barker, "A customer came walking through the door one day and needed help with a piece of equipment that he had built, and from that we saw the opportunity to take this product—a starting gate for bicycle racing—on an international basis." Barker's expertise is in hydraulics, skills he learned from his dad. The starting gate is a pretty sophisticated piece of gear. Add pumps to fabricated sheet metal and some other devices, and the race is on.

The gate is especially popular with BMX, or bicycle motocross. BMX uses a small course of about 400 meters that includes jumps and tabletops.

THE CHALLENGE

Barker recognized early that the market in the United States wasn't as big as he thought. The company had to go global—fast. The biggest challenge for ProStuff was to generate international sales quickly and to produce a high-quality product. Small startup manufacturing companies (ProStuff has six employees) can't afford the cost of shipping equipment over great distances for repair. To be successful, ProStuff needed from the start to take a durable, reliable product to the world. But customers were not individual bikers; they were organizations that sponsor the races. Where were these organizations, and would they buy?

THE SOLUTION

Barker did his research and estimated that worldwide several million people are involved in the sport of BMX. If mountain biking is added, the market is much bigger. Contacting the individual riders was out of the question, so Barker decided to get ProStuff's starting gate adopted as the industry standard: "We found that BMX was going to be part of the 2008 Olympics, and I said, 'The best way to advertise our products is to go to the very top of the sport and work with those guys—become the international specification and let that filter down.' And that's exactly what we did."

Barker picked up the phone and called the Union Cycliste Internationale in Switzerland. He asked the person who answered, "Who do we talk to get our products specified and used in the Olympics?" The person in Switzerland replied, "That would be me." Says Barker about the call, "That's how it started."

Brand building at the Olympics was huge but insufficient to generate enough orders or to provide the financing needed to fill them. "I had no idea what to do when we first started," Barker says. "We were plowing new ground every day." Then he found Pat Hope, a commercial specialist at the U.S. Commercial Service. One of the first things Hope did was to introduce ProStuff to the Export–Import Bank of the United States. ProStuff applied and was accepted into the bank's loan guarantee program, which provides working capital to U.S. exporters at competitive rates. "With the bank's assistance and Pat's guidance, you can't stop us," Barker says. "We can go anywhere."

And they have. Since 2005, when ProStuff made its first export, the company has set up distribution on five continents and has sold products to customers in 41 countries.

"Just in the past 10 hours, I've been in contact with China, Latvia, Switzerland, Denmark, and Singapore," Barker says. "We actually received a contract from China this morning, and it's our contract. It's not their contract. They signed ours."

LESSONS LEARNED

First, Barker explains, you need an export plan, but make it short. ProStuff's is one page. It says, "Go do this."

Second, Barker claims, is incorporating the concept of "velocity" in your business. By this he means providing instantaneous response to customers' needs and requests. He says that it's not uncommon for him to get a phone call from a customer, and his team turns the request into a shipped order in less than 12 hours.

Third is a conscious business decision to produce the very best product in the world. Barker says that because of this unstinting focus on quality, ProStuff's business reputation over the past several years has become very strong.

Another lesson is to get out into world and not overlook any market. Barker clearly loves the sport and the young people who pursue it. You'll find him at tournaments giving advice, cheering on competitors, and, in what seems almost like an afterthought, promoting his company's products. He has found business in such unlikely places as Bolivia and Zimbabwe. "The political situations are really, really difficult [there]," Barker acknowledges. "[But] we have established successful distribution in both those countries. And where we couldn't get support because of political restrictions, we said, 'You

know what? We're going to figure out how to make it work.' And we've done it!"

Related to this is Barker's injunction not to be fearful. Recently, in South Africa, he was invited to meet a sports group. He was hesitant because of the political situation at the time but went anyway and got a lesson on what "fearless champions of freedom" many South Africans are. "If you don't go there and see for yourself, you'll never know."

Barker believes that a lot of products and manufactured items in the United States need to be taken to the world market in part because of the necessity of creating jobs here: "We're really good at technology, but we haven't been good at purveying it. And, philosophically, we have to take that technology to the rest of the world. And that's been one of the core principles in our success."

ACTION

How can you start exporting to the world?

- **Get an export plan.** There are many good templates for creating simple, useful export plans. In particular, see Chapter 2, "Developing an Export Strategy."

- **Contact your local Export Assistance Center.** See Appendix B, or call (800) USA-TRADE (800-872-8723).

- **Improve your manufacturing processes.** For advice and assistance, contact the National Manufacturing Partnership at (301) 975-5020, or visit *www.mfg.nist.gov*.

- **Learn about export financing.** A place to start is Chapter 15, "Financing Export Transactions."

Pierce Barker (left), founder and chief executive of ProStuff LLC, with Team ProGate rider Mariana Pajón (right) at the 2009 UCI BMX World Championships in Adelaide, Australia. His company, which started exporting in 2005, now has customers in 41 countries.

APPENDIX A: GLOSSARY

Air waybill: Bill of lading that covers both domestic and international flights transporting goods to a specified destination. It is a non-negotiable instrument of air transport that serves as a receipt for the shipper, indicating that the carrier has accepted the goods listed therein, and obligates the carrier to carry the consignment to the airport of destination according to specified conditions.

Antidiversion clause: To help ensure that U.S. exports go only to legally authorized destinations, the U.S. government requires a destination control statement on shipping documents. Under this requirement, the commercial invoice and bill of lading (or air waybill) for nearly all commercial shipments leaving the United States must display a statement notifying the carrier and all foreign parties that the U.S. material has been approved for export only to certain destinations and may not be diverted contrary to U.S. law.

Antidumping duty: Special duty imposed to offset the price effect of dumping that has been determined to be materially harmful to domestic producers. (See also *dumping*.)

Arbitration: Process of resolving a dispute or a grievance outside of the court system by presenting it to an impartial third party or panel for a decision that may or may not be binding.

Bill of lading: Contract between the owner of the goods and the carrier. For vessels, there are two types: a straight bill of lading, which is not negotiable, and a negotiable, or shipper's orders, bill of lading. The latter can be bought, sold, or traded while the goods are in transit.

Carnet: Standardized international customs document known as an ATA (*admission temporaire* or *temporary admission*) carnet that is used to obtain duty-free temporary admission of certain goods into the countries that are signatories to the ATA Convention. Under the ATA Convention, commercial and professional travelers may take commercial samples; tools of the trade; advertising material; or cinematographic, audiovisual, medical, scientific, or other professional equipment into member countries temporarily without paying customs duties and taxes or posting a bond at the border of each country to be visited.

Cash in advance (advance payment): Payment from a foreign customer to a U.S. exporter prior to actually receiving the exporter's products. It is the least risky form of payment from the exporter's perspective.

Certificate of origin: Signed statement required in certain nations attesting to the origin of the export item. Certificates of origin are usually validated by a semiofficial organization, such as a local chamber of commerce. A North American Free Trade Agreement (NAFTA) certificate of origin is required for products traded among the NAFTA countries (Canada, Mexico, and the United States) when duty preference is claimed for NAFTA qualified goods.

CFR: Cost and freight to a named overseas port.

CIF: Cost, insurance, and freight to a named overseas post. The seller quotes a price for the goods shipped by ocean (including insurance), all transportation costs, and miscellaneous charges to the point of debarkation from the vessel.

CIP: Carriage and insurance paid for delivery to a named destination.

Commercial invoice: Document prepared by the exporter or freight forwarder and required by the foreign buyer to prove ownership and to arrange for payment to the exporter. It should provide basic information about the transaction, including a description of goods, the address of the shipper and seller, and the delivery and payment terms. In most cases, the commercial invoice is used to assess customs duties.

Confirming house: Company, based in a foreign country, that acts as a foreign buyer's agent and places confirmed orders with U.S. exporters. The confirming house guarantees payment to the exporters.

Consignment: Delivery of merchandise to the buyer or distributor, whereby the latter agrees to sell it and only then pay the U.S. exporter. The seller retains ownership of the goods until they are sold but also carries all of the financial burden and risk.

Consular invoice: Document required in some countries that describes the shipment of goods and shows information such as the consignor, consignee, and value of the shipment. Certified by the consular official of the foreign country stationed in the United States, it is used by the country's customs officials to verify the value, quantity, and nature of the shipment.

Contract: Written or oral agreement that is legally enforceable.

Copyright: Protection granted to the authors and creators of literary, artistic, dramatic, and musical works, sound recordings, and certain other intellectual works. A computer program, for example, is considered a literary work in the United States and some other countries.

Countertrade: General expression meaning the sale or barter of goods on a reciprocal basis. There may also be multilateral transactions involved.

Countervailing duties: Additional duties imposed by an importing country to offset government subsidies in an exporting country when the subsidized imports cause material injury to domestic industry in the importing country.

CPT: Carriage paid to a named destination. This term is used in place of CFR and CIF for all modes of transportation, including intermodal.

Customs-bonded warehouse: Building or other secured area in which dutiable goods may be stored, may be manipulated, or may undergo manufacturing operations without payment of duty.

Customs declaration: Document that traditionally accompanies exported goods bearing such information as the nature of the goods, their value, the consignee, and their ultimate destination. Required for statistical purposes, it accompanies all controlled goods being exported under the appropriate permit.

Customs invoice: Document used to clear goods through customs in the importing country by providing evidence of the value of goods. In some cases, the commercial invoice may be used for this purpose.

Date draft: Document used when the exporter extends credit to the buyer. It specifies a date on which payment is due, rather than a time period as with the time draft.

Direct exporting: Sale by an exporter directly to an importer located in another country.

Distributor: Merchant in the foreign country who purchases goods from the U.S. exporter (often at a discount) and resells them for a profit. The foreign distributor generally provides support and service for the product, relieving the U.S. exporter of these responsibilities.

Dock receipt: Receipt issued by an ocean carrier to acknowledge receipt of a shipment at the carrier's dock or warehouse facilities.

Documentary letter of credit or documentary draft: Document used to protect the interests of both buyer and seller. A letter of credit requires that payment be made on the basis of the presentation of documents to a lender conveying the title and indicating that specific steps have been taken. Letters of credit and drafts may be paid immediately or at a later date. Drafts that are paid on presentation are called *sight drafts.* Drafts that are to be paid at a later date, often after the buyer receives the goods, are called *time drafts* or *date drafts.*

Dumping: Sale of an imported commodity at a price lower than the cost of production in the exporting country. Dumping is considered an actionable trade practice when it disrupts markets and injures producers of competitive products in the importing country. Article VI of the General Agreement on Tariffs and Trade (World Trade Organization) permits the imposition of special antidumping duties on goods equal to the difference between their export price and their normal value.

E-commerce: Buying and selling online over the Internet.

Export license: Government document that authorizes the export of specific goods in specific quantities to a particular destination. This document may be required for most or all exports to some countries or for other countries only under special circumstances.

Export management company (EMC): Company that performs the functions that would be typically performed by the export department or the international sales department of manufacturers and suppliers. EMCs develop personalized services promoting their clients' products to international buyers and distributors. They solicit and transact business in the names of the producers they represent or in their own name for a commission, salary, or retainer plus commission. EMCs usually specialize either by product or by foreign market. Because of their specialization, the best EMCs know their products and the markets they serve very well and usually have well-established networks of foreign distributors already in place. This immediate access to foreign markets is one of the principal reasons for using an EMC, because establishing a productive relationship with a foreign representative may be a costly and lengthy process.

Export packing list: List that itemizes the exported material in each package and indicates the type of package, such as a box, crate, drum, or carton. An export packing list is considerably more detailed and informative than a standard domestic packing list. It also shows the individual net, tare, and gross weights and measurements for each package (in both U.S. and metric systems).

Export processing zone (EPZ): Site in a foreign country established to encourage and facilitate international trade. EPZs include free trade zones, special economic zones, bonded warehouses, free ports, and customs zones. EPZs have evolved from initial assembly and simple processing activities to include high-tech and science parks, finance zones, logistics centers, and even tourist resorts.

Export quotas: Specific restrictions or ceilings imposed by an exporting country on the value or volume of certain exports designed, for example, to protect domestic producers and consumers from temporary shortages of the goods affected or to bolster their prices in world markets.

Export subsidies: Government payments or other financially quantifiable benefits provided to domestic producers or exporters contingent on the export of their goods and services.

Export trading company (ETC): Company that acts as an independent distributor, creating transactions by linking domestic producers and foreign buyers. As opposed to representing a given manufacturer in a foreign market, the ETC determines what U.S. products are desired in a given market and then works with U.S. producers to satisfy the demand. ETCs can perform a sourcing function, searching for U.S. suppliers to fill specific foreign requests for U.S. products.

FAS: Free alongside ship. This term refers to a seller's price for the goods, including the charge for delivery of the goods alongside at the named port of export. The seller handles the cost of wharfage, while the buyer is accountable for the costs of loading, ocean transportation, and insurance. It is the seller's responsibility to clear the goods for export.

FCA: Free carrier. FCA refers to a named place within the country of origin of the shipment. The terms define the seller's responsibility for handing over the goods to a named carrier at the named shipping point. According to *Incoterms 2000,* the named shipping point may be the seller's premises. In that case, it is the seller's responsibility to clear the goods for export from the United States. FCA may be used for any mode of transport.

FOB: An international commercial term (Incoterm) that means free on board and is used in international sales contracts. In an FOB contract, a buyer and a seller agree on a designated FOB point. The seller assumes the cost of having goods packaged and ready for shipment from the FOB point, whether it is the seller's own place of business or some intermediate point. The buyer assumes the costs and risks from the FOB point, including inland transportation costs and risks in the exporting country, as well as all subsequent transportation costs, including the costs of loading the merchandise on a vessel. If the contract stipulates "FOB vessel," the seller bears all transportation costs to the vessel named by the buyer, as well as the costs of loading the goods on that vessel. The same principle applies to the abbreviations FOR (free on rail) and FOT (free on truck).

Free in: Pricing term that indicates that the charterer of a vessel is responsible for the cost of loading goods onto the vessel.

Free in and out: Pricing term that indicates that the charterer of the vessel is responsible for the cost of loading and unloading goods from the vessel.

Free out: Pricing term that indicates that the charterer of the vessel is responsible for the cost of unloading goods from the vessel.

Foreign Corrupt Practices Act: Act making it unlawful for persons or firms subject to U.S. jurisdiction to offer, pay, or promise to pay money or anything of value to any foreign official for the purpose of obtaining or retaining business. It is also unlawful to make a payment to any person while knowing that all or a portion of the payment will be offered, given, or promised, directly or indirectly, to any foreign official for the purposes of assisting the firm in obtaining or retaining business. "Knowing" includes the concepts of "conscious disregard" and "willful blindness." The FCPA also covers foreign persons or firms that commit acts in furtherance of such bribery in the territory of the United States. U.S. persons or firms, or covered foreign persons or firms, should consult an attorney when confronted with FCPA issues.

Foreign-trade zones: Domestic U.S. sites that are considered outside U.S. customs territory and are available for activities that might otherwise be carried on overseas for customs reasons. For export operations, the zones provide accelerated export status for purposes of excise tax rebates. For reexport activities, no customs duties, federal excise taxes, or state or local ad valorem taxes are charged on foreign goods moved into zones unless and until the goods or products made from them are moved into customs territory. Thus, the use of zones can be profitable for operations involving foreign dutiable materials and components being assembled or produced in the United States for reexport.

Freight forwarder: Agent for moving cargo to an overseas destination. These agents are familiar with the import rules and regulations of foreign countries, the export regulations of the U.S. government, the methods of shipping, and the documents related to foreign trade.

Incoterms: *See terms of sale.*

Indirect exporting: Sale by the exporter to the buyer through a domestically located intermediary, such as an export management company or an export trading company.

Inspection certificate: Document required by some purchasers and countries to attest to the specifications of the goods shipped. The inspection is usually performed by a third party.

Insurance certificate: Document prepared by the exporter or freight forwarder to provide evidence that insurance against loss or damage has been obtained for the goods.

Intellectual property: Collective term used to refer to new ideas, inventions, designs, writings, films, and so on that are protected by a copyright, patent, or trademark.

Joint venture: Independent business formed cooperatively by two or more parent firms. This type of partnership is often used to avoid restrictions on foreign ownership and for longer-term arrangements that require joint product development, manufacturing, and marketing.

Letter of credit: Instrument issued by a bank on behalf of an importer that guarantees an exporter payment for goods or services, provided that the terms of the credit are met. A letter of credit issued by a foreign bank is sometimes confirmed by a U.S. bank. This confirmation means that the U.S. bank (the confirming bank) adds its promise to pay to that of the foreign bank (the issuing bank). A letter of credit may be either irrevocable, in which case it cannot be changed unless both parties agree, or revocable, in which case either party may unilaterally make changes. A revocable letter of credit is inadvisable as it carries many risks for the exporter.

Licensing: Arrangement in which a firm sells the rights to use its products or services but retains some control. Although not usually considered to be a form of partnership, licensing can lead to partnerships.

Market survey: Report that provides a narrative description and assessment of a particular market along with relevant statistics. The reports are often based on original research conducted in the countries studied and may include specific information on both buyers and competitors.

Packing list: *See export packing list.*

Patent: Right that entitles the patent holder, within the country that granted or recognizes the patent, to prevent all others, for a set period of time, from using, making, or selling the subject matter of the patent.

Piggyback marketing: Arrangement in which one manufacturer or service firm distributes a second firm's product or service. The most common piggybacking situation is when a U.S. company has a contract with an overseas buyer to provide a wide range of products or services. Often this first company does not produce all of the products it is under contract to provide, and it turns to other U.S. companies to provide the remaining products.

Primary market research: Collection of data directly from a foreign marketplace through interviews, surveys, and other direct contact with representatives and potential buyers. Primary market research has the advantage of being tailored to your company's needs and provides answers to specific questions, but the collection of such data is time consuming and expensive.

Pro forma invoice: Invoice prepared by the exporter before shipping the goods, informing the buyer of the goods to be sent, their value, and other key specifications.

Quotation: Offer by the exporter to sell the goods at a stated price and under certain conditions.

Remarketer: Export agent or merchant who purchases products directly from the manufacturer, packing and marking the products according to his or her own specifications. Remarketers then sell these products overseas through their contacts in their own names and assume all risks.

Sales representative: Representative who uses your company's product literature and samples to present the product to potential buyers. An overseas sales representative is the equivalent of a manufacturer's representative in the United States. The sales representative usually works on a commission basis, assumes no risk or responsibility, and is under contract for a definite period of time.

Secondary market research: Collection of data from various sources, such as trade statistics for a country or a product. Working with secondary sources is less expensive and helps your company focus its marketing efforts. Although secondary data sources are critical to market research, they do have limitations. The most recent statistics for some countries may be more than two years old, and the data may be too broad to be of much value to your company.

Shipper's export declaration (SED): Document used to control exports and act as a source document for official U.S. export statistics. SEDs, or their electronic equivalent, are required for shipments when the value of the commodities, classified under any single Schedule B number, is more than $2,500. SEDs must be prepared and submitted, regardless of value, for all shipments requiring an export license or destined for countries restricted by the Export Administration Regulations.

Sight draft: Document used when the exporter wishes to retain title to the shipment until it reaches its destination and payment is made. Before the shipment can be released to the buyer, the original "order" ocean bill of lading (the document that evidences title) must be properly endorsed by the buyer and surrendered to the carrier. It is important to note that air waybills do not need to be presented in order for the buyer to claim the goods. Thus, risk increases when a sight draft is being used with an air shipment.

Tariff: Tax imposed on a product when it is imported into a country. Some foreign countries apply tariffs to exports.

Technology licensing: Contractual arrangement in which the licenser's patents, trademarks, service marks, copyrights, trade secrets, or other intellectual property may be sold or made available to a licensee for compensation that is negotiated in advance between the parties. U.S. companies frequently license their technology to foreign companies that then use it to manufacture and sell products in a country or group of countries defined in the licensing agreement. A technology licensing agreement usually enables a firm to enter a foreign market quickly and poses fewer financial and legal risks than owning and operating a foreign manufacturing facility or participating in an overseas joint venture.

Terms of sale: Terms that define the obligations, risks, and costs of the buyer and seller involving the delivery of goods that comprise the export transaction. These terms are commonly known as *Incoterms*.

Time draft: Document used when the exporter extends credit to the buyer. The draft states that payment is due by a specific time after the buyer accepts the time draft and receives the goods. By signing and writing "accepted" on the draft, the buyer is formally obligated to pay within the stated time.

Trademark: Word, symbol, name, slogan, or combination thereof that identifies and distinguishes the source of sponsorship of goods and may serve as an index of quality of a particular product.

Trade statistics: Data that indicate total exports or imports by country and by product. They allow you to compare the size of the market for a product in various countries. By looking at statistics over several years, you can determine which markets are growing and which markets are shrinking.

Trading house: Company specializing in the exporting and importing of goods produced or provided by other companies.

Warehouse receipt: Receipt identifying the commodities deposited in a recognized warehouse. It is used to transfer accountability when the domestic carrier moves the export item to the port of embarkation and leaves it with the ship line for export.

APPENDIX B:
U.S. EXPORT ASSISTANCE CENTERS

U.S. Export Assistance Centers are located in more than 100 cities throughout the United States. They are supported by five federal agencies and serve as one-stop shops that provide small and medium-sized businesses with hands-on export marketing and trade finance support. For more information, visit the U.S. government's export portal at *www.export.gov* or call the Trade Information Center at (800) USA-TRADE (800-872-8723).

ALABAMA

Birmingham
950 22nd St. N., Rm. 707
Birmingham, AL 35203
Phone: (205) 731-1331
Fax: (205) 731-0076

ALASKA

Anchorage
431 W. 7th Ave., Ste. 108
Anchorage, AK 99501
Phone: (907) 271-6237
Fax: (907) 271-6242

ARIZONA

Phoenix
2828 N. Central Ave., Ste. 800
Phoenix, AZ 85004
Phone: (602) 640-2513
Fax: (602) 640-2518

Scottsdale
1475 N. Scottsdale Rd., Ste. 200
Scottsdale, AZ 85257
Phone: (480) 884-1658
Fax: (480) 884-1888

Tucson
33 N. Stone Ave., Ste. 830
Tucson, AZ 85701
Phone: (520) 622-2039
Fax: (520) 243-1910

ARKANSAS

Little Rock
425 W. Capitol Ave., Ste. 425
Little Rock, AR 72201
Phone: (501) 324-5794
Fax: (501) 324-7380

CALIFORNIA

Bakersfield (Kern County)
2100 Chester Ave., 1st Fl., Ste. 166
Bakersfield, CA 93301
Phone: (661) 637-0136
Fax: (661) 637-0156

Fresno
5245 N. Backer Ave., M/S PB5
Fresno, CA 93740
Phone: (559) 348-9859
Fax: (559) 348-1398

Indio/Cabazon
84-245 Indio Springs Pkwy.
Indio, CA 92203
Phone: (760) 772-3898
Fax: (760) 772-0337

Inland Empire (Ontario)
2940 Inland Empire Blvd., Ste. 121
Ontario, CA 91764
Phone: (909) 466-4134
Fax: (909) 466-4140

Los Angeles (Downtown)
444 S. Flower St., 34th Fl.
Los Angeles, CA 90071
Phone: (213) 894-4231
Fax: (213) 894-8789

Los Angeles (West)
11150 Olympic Blvd., Ste. 975
Los Angeles, CA 90064
Phone: (310) 235-7104
Fax: (310) 235-7220

Monterey
411 Pacific St., Ste. 316A
Monterey, CA 93940
Phone: (831) 641-9850
Fax: (831) 641-9849

Newport Beach
3300 Irvine Ave., Ste. 305
Newport Beach, CA 92660
Phone: (949) 660-1688
Fax: (949) 660-1338

Oakland
1301 Clay St., Ste. 630N
Oakland, CA 94612
Phone: (510) 273-7350
Fax: (510) 273-7352

Sacramento
1410 Ethan Way
Sacramento, CA 95825
Phone: (916) 566-7170
Fax: (916) 566-7123

San Diego
9449 Balboa Ave., Ste. 111
San Diego, CA 92122
Phone: (858) 467-7032
Fax: (858) 467-7043

San Francisco
50 Fremont St., Ste. 2450
San Francisco, CA 94105
Phone: (415) 705-2300
Fax: (415) 705-2299

San Jose (Silicon Valley)
55 S. Market St., Ste. 1040
San Jose, CA 95113
Phone: (408) 535-2757
Fax: (408) 535-2758

San Rafael (North Bay)
50 Acacia Ave.
San Rafael, CA 94901
Phone: (415) 485-6200
Fax: (415) 485-6219

Ventura County
333 Ponoma St.
Port Hueneme, CA 93041
Phone: (805) 488-4844
Fax: (805) 488-7801

COLORADO

Denver
World Trade Center
1625 Broadway, Ste. 680
Denver, CO 80202
Phone: (303) 844-6001
Fax: (303) 844-5651

CONNECTICUT

Middletown
213 Court St., Ste. 903
Middletown, CT 06457
Phone: (860) 638-6950
Fax: (860) 638-6970

DELAWARE

Served by the Philadelphia, PA,
U.S. Export Assistance Center

DISTRICT OF COLUMBIA

Served by the Arlington, VA,
U.S. Export Assistance Center

FLORIDA

Clearwater
13805 58th St. N., Ste. 1-200
Clearwater, FL 33760
Phone: (727) 893-3738
Fax: (727) 893-3839

Ft. Lauderdale
200 E. Las Olas Blvd., Ste. 1600
Ft. Lauderdale, FL 33301
Phone: (954) 356-6640
Fax: (954) 356-6644

Jacksonville
3 Independent Dr.
Jacksonville, FL 32202
Phone: (904) 232-1270
Fax: (904) 232-1271

Miami
5835 Blue Lagoon Dr., Ste. 203
Miami, FL 33126
Phone: (305) 526-7425
Fax: (305) 526-7434

Orlando
315 E. Robinson St., Ste. 100
Orlando, FL 32801
Phone: (407) 648-6170
Fax: (407) 487-1909

Tallahassee
Atrium Building
325 John Knox Rd., Ste. 201
Tallahassee, FL 32303
Phone: (850) 942-9635
Fax: (850) 922-9595

GEORGIA

Atlanta
75 5th St. N.W., Ste. 1055
Atlanta, GA 30308
Phone: (404) 897-6090
Fax: (404) 897-6085

Savannah
111 E. Liberty St., Ste. 202
Savannah, GA 31401
Phone: (912) 652-4204
Fax: (912) 652-4675

HAWAII AND THE PACIFIC ISLANDS

Honolulu
521 Ala Moana Blvd., Rm. 214
Honolulu, HI 96813
Phone: (808) 522-8040
Fax: (808) 522-8045

IDAHO

Boise
700 W. State St., 2nd Fl.
Boise, ID 83720
Phone: (208) 364-7791
Fax: (208) 334-2783

ILLINOIS

Chicago
200 W. Adams St., Ste. 2450
Chicago, IL 60606
Phone: (312) 353-8040
Fax: (312) 353-8120

Libertyville
28055 Ashley Cir., Ste. 212
Libertyville, IL 60048
Phone: (847) 327-9082
Fax: (847) 247-0423

Peoria
Bradley University
Jobst Hall, Rm. 141
922 N. Glenwood Ave.
Peoria, IL 61606
Phone: (309) 671-7815
Fax: (309) 671-7818

Rockford
EIGERlab
605 Fulton Ave., Ste. E103
Rockford, IL 61103
Phone: (815) 316-2380
Fax: (888) 628-2571

INDIANA

Indianapolis
11405 N. Pennsylvania St., Ste. 106
Carmel, IN 46032
Phone: (317) 582-2300
Fax: (317) 582-2301

IOWA

Des Moines
210 Walnut St., Rm. 749
Des Moines, IA 50309
Phone: (515) 288-8614
Fax: (515) 288-1437

KANSAS

Wichita
150 N. Main St., Ste. 200
Wichita, KS 67202
Phone: (316) 263-4067
Fax: (316) 263-8306

KENTUCKY

Lexington
World Trade Center
333 W. Vine St., Ste. 1600
Lexington, KY 40507
Phone: (859) 225-7001
Fax: (859) 201-1139

Louisville
601 W. Broadway, Rm. 634B
Louisville, KY 40202
Phone: (502) 582-5066
Fax: (502) 582-6573

LOUISIANA

New Orleans
2 Canal St., Ste. 2710
New Orleans, LA 70130
Phone: (504) 589-6546
Fax: (504) 589-2337

Shreveport
Louisiana State University–Shreveport
Business Education Building 119H
One University Pl.
Shreveport, LA 71115
Phone: (318) 676-3064
Fax: (318) 676-3063

MAINE

Portland
Maine International Trade Center
511 Congress St.
Portland, ME 04101
Phone: (207) 541-7430
Fax: (207) 541-7420

MARYLAND

Baltimore
300 W. Pratt St., Ste. 300
Baltimore, MD 21201
Phone: (410) 962-4539
Fax: (410) 962-4529

MASSACHUSETTS

Boston
JFK Federal Building
55 New Sudbury St., Ste. 1826A
Boston, MA 02203
Phone: (617) 565-4304
Fax: (617) 565-4313

MICHIGAN

Detroit
8109 E. Jefferson Ave., Ste. 110
Detroit, MI 48214
Phone: (313) 226-3650
Fax: (313) 226-3657

Grand Rapids
401 W. Fulton St., Ste. 349C
Grand Rapids, MI 49504
Phone: (616) 458-3564
Fax: (616) 458-3872

Pontiac
250 Elizabeth Lake Rd., Ste. 1300 W.
Pontiac, MI 48341
Phone: (248) 975-9600
Fax: (248) 975-9606

Ypsilanti
Eastern Michigan University
300 W. Michigan Ave., Ste. 306G
Ypsilanti, MI 48197
Phone: (734) 487-0259
Fax: (734) 485-2396

MINNESOTA

Minneapolis
100 N. 6th St., Ste. 210-C
Minneapolis, MI 55403
Phone: (612) 348-1638
Fax: (612) 348-1650

MISSISSIPPI

Jackson
175 E. Capitol St., Ste. 255
Jackson, MS 39201
Phone: (601) 965-4130
Fax: (601) 965-4132

MISSOURI

Kansas City
2509 Commerce Tower
911 Main St.
Kansas City, MO 64105
Phone: (816) 421-1876
Fax: (816) 471-7839

St. Louis
8235 Forsyth Blvd., Ste. 520
St. Louis, MO 63105
Phone: (314) 425-3302
Fax: (314) 425-3381

MONTANA

Missoula
University of Montana
Gallagher Business Building, Ste. 257
Missoula, MT 59812
Phone: (406) 542-6656
Fax: (406) 542-6659

NEBRASKA

Omaha
13006 W. Center Rd.
Omaha, NE 68144
Phone: (402) 597-0193
Fax: (402) 595-1194

NEVADA

Las Vegas
400 S. 4th St., Ste. 250
Las Vegas, NV 89101
Phone: (702) 388-6694
Fax: (702) 388-6469

Reno
1 E. 1st St., 16th Fl.
Reno, NV 89501
Phone: (775) 784-5203
Fax: (775) 784-5343

NEW HAMPSHIRE

Durham
University of New Hampshire
InterOperability Laboratory
121 Technology Dr., Ste. 2
Durham, NH 03824
Phone: (603) 953-0212
Fax: (603) 953-0213

NEW JERSEY

Newark
744 Broad St., Ste. 1505
Newark, NJ 07102
Phone: (973) 645-4682
Fax: (973) 645-4783

Trenton
20 W. State St.
P.O. Box 820
Trenton, NJ 08625
Phone: (609) 989-2100
Fax: (609) 989-2395

NEW MEXICO

Santa Fe
New Mexico Dept. of Economic
  Development
1100 St. Francis Dr.
(use for courier service)
P.O. Box 20003
Santa Fe, NM 87504
Phone: (505) 231-0075
Fax: (505) 827-0211

NEW YORK

Buffalo
130 S. Elmwood Ave., Ste. 530
Buffalo, NY 14202
Phone: (716) 551-4191
Fax: (716) 551-5290

Harlem
163 W. 125th St., Ste. 901
New York, NY 10027
Phone: (212) 860-6200
Fax: (212) 860-6203

Long Island
Serviced by the New York U.S. Export
  Assistance Center
33 Whitehall St., 22nd Fl.
New York, NY 10004
Phone: (212) 809-2675
Fax: (212) 809-2687

New York
33 Whitehall St., 22nd Fl.
New York, NY 10004
Phone: (212) 809-2675
Fax: (212) 809-2687

Rochester
400 Andrews St., Ste. 710
Rochester, NY 14604
Phone: (585) 263-6480
Fax: (585) 325-6505

Westchester
707 Westchester Ave., Ste. 209
White Plains, NY 10604
Phone: (914) 682-6712
Fax: (914) 682-6698

NORTH CAROLINA

Charlotte
521 E. Morehead St., Ste. 435
Charlotte, NC 28202
Phone: (704) 333-4886
Fax: (704) 332-2681

Greensboro
342 N. Elm St.
Greensboro, NC 27401
Phone: (336) 333-5345
Fax: (336) 333-5158

Raleigh
10900 World Trade Blvd., Ste. 110
Raleigh, NC 27617
Phone: (919) 281-2750
Fax: (919) 281-2754

NORTH DAKOTA

Fargo
51 Broadway, Ste. 505
Fargo, ND 58102
Phone: (701) 239-5080
Fax: (701) 237-9734

OHIO

Akron
Kent State University
Northeast Ohio Trade and Economic
  Consortium
Administrative Services Building
Kent, OH 44243
Phone: (330) 678-0695
Fax: (330) 678-0646

Cincinnati
36 E. 7th St., Ste. 2650
Cincinnati, OH 45202
Phone: (513) 684-2944
Fax: (513) 684-3227

Cleveland
600 Superior Ave. E., Ste. 700
Cleveland, OH 44114
Phone: (216) 522-4750
Fax: (216) 522-2235

Columbus
401 N. Front St., Ste. 200
Columbus, OH 43215
Phone: (614) 365-9510
Fax: (614) 365-9598

Toledo
420 Madison Ave., Ste. 510
Toledo, OH 43604
Phone: (419) 241-0683
Fax: (419) 241-0684

OKLAHOMA

Oklahoma City
301 N.W. 63rd St., Ste. 330
Oklahoma City, OK 73116
Phone: (405) 608-5302
Fax: (405) 608-4211

Tulsa
700 N. Greenwood Ave., Ste. 1400
Tulsa, OK 74106
Phone: (918) 581-7650
Fax: (918) 581-6263

OREGON

Portland
One World Trade Center
121 S.W. Salmon St., Ste. 242
Portland, OR 97204
Phone: (503) 326-3001
Fax: (503) 326-6351

PENNSYLVANIA

Harrisburg
Millersville University
Office of International Affairs
2 S. George St., Cumberland House
P.O. Box 40
Millersville, PA 17551
Phone: (717) 872-4386
Fax: (717) 871-2132

Philadelphia
601 Walnut St., Ste. 580 W.
Philadelphia, PA 19106
Phone: (215) 597-6101
Fax: (215) 597-6123

Pittsburgh
425 6th Ave., Ste. 2950
Pittsburgh, PA 15219-1854
Phone: (412) 644-2800
Fax: (412) 644-2803

PUERTO RICO

San Juan (Guaynabo)
Centro Internacional de Mercadeo
Torre II, Ste. 702
Guaynabo, PR 00968
Phone: (787) 775-1992
Fax: (787) 781-7178

RHODE ISLAND

Providence
315 Iron Horse Way, Ste. 101
Providence, RI 02908
Phone: (401) 528-5104
Fax: (401) 528-5067

SOUTH CAROLINA

Charleston
1362 McMillan Ave., Ste. 100
N. Charleston, SC 29405
Phone: (843) 746-3404
Fax: (843) 529-0305

Columbia
University of South Carolina
Darla Moore School of Business
1705 College St., Ste. 605
Columbia, SC 29208
Phone: (803) 777-2571
Fax: (803) 777-2615

Greenville (Upstate)
Greenville Technical College
Buck Mickel Center
216 S. Pleasantburg Dr., Ste. 243
Greenville, SC 29607
Phone: (864) 250-8429
Fax: (864) 250-6729

SOUTH DAKOTA

Sioux Falls
Augustana College
2001 S. Summit Ave., Madsen Center,
   Rm. 122
Sioux Falls, SD 57197
Phone: (605) 330-4264
Fax: (605) 330-4266

TENNESSEE

Knoxville
17 Market Sq., Ste. 201
Knoxville, TN 37902
Phone: (865) 545-4637
Fax: (865) 545-4435

Memphis
22 N. Front St., Ste. 200
Memphis, TN 38103
Phone: (901) 544-0930
Fax: (901) 543-3510

Nashville
Tennessee Tower
312 8th Ave. N., 10th Fl.
Nashville, TN 37423
Phone: (615) 736-2223
Fax: (615) 736-2226

TEXAS

Austin
221 E. 11th St., 4th Fl.
Austin, TX 78701
Mailing: P.O. Box 12428
Austin, TX 78711
Phone: (512) 916-5939
Fax: (512) 916-5940

El Paso
9570 Pan American Dr.
El Paso, TX 79927
Phone: (915) 929-6971
Fax: (915) 858-8827

Ft. Worth
Business Assistance Center
Guinn School Complex
1150 S. Freeway, Ste. 118
Ft. Worth, TX 76102
Phone: (817) 212-2644
Fax: (817) 741-5516

Houston
1919 Smith St., Ste. 1026
Houston, TX 77002
Phone: (713) 209-3104
Fax: (713) 209-3135

North Texas
1450 Hughes Rd., Ste. 220
Grapevine, TX 76051
Phone: (817) 310-3744
Fax: (817) 310-3757

San Antonio
203 S. St. Mary's St., Ste. 360
San Antonio, TX 78205
Phone: (210) 228-9878
Fax: (210) 228-9874

South Texas
6401 S. 36th St., Ste. 4
McAllen, TX 78503
Phone: (956) 661-0238
Fax: (956) 661-0239

West Texas
1400 N. FM 1788, Rm. 1303
Midland, TX 79707
Phone: (432) 552-2490
Fax: (432) 552-3490

UTAH

Salt Lake City
9690 S. 300 W., Ste. 300
Sandy, UT 84070
Phone: (801) 255-1871
Fax: (801) 255-3147

VERMONT

Montpelier
National Life Building, 6th Fl.
Montpelier, VT 05620
Phone: (802) 828-4508
Fax: (802) 828-3258

VIRGINIA

Arlington (Northern Virginia)
1100 N. Glebe Rd., Ste. 1500
Arlington, VA 22201
Phone: (703) 235-0331
Fax: (703) 524-2649

Richmond
400 N. 8th St., Ste. 412
P.O. Box 10026
Richmond, VA 23240
Phone: (804) 771-2246
Fax: (804) 771-2390

WASHINGTON

Seattle
2601 4th Ave., Ste. 320
Seattle, WA 98121
Phone: (206) 553-5615
Fax: (206) 553-7253

Spokane
Spokane Regional Chamber of Commerce
801 W. Riverside, Ste. 100
Spokane, WA 99201
Phone: (509) 353-2625
Fax: (509) 353-2449

WEST VIRGINIA

Charleston
1116 Smith St., Ste. 302
Charleston, WV 25301
Phone: (304) 347-5123
Fax: (304) 347-5408

Wheeling
Wheeling Jesuit University
316 Washington Ave., Ignatius Hall,
    Rm. G07E
Wheeling, WV 26003
Phone: (304) 243-5493
Fax: (304) 243-5494

WISCONSIN

Milwaukee
1025 N. Broadway
Milwaukee, WI 53202
Phone: (414) 297-3473
Fax: (414) 297-3470

WYOMING

Serviced by the Denver, CO, U.S. Export
    Assistance Center
World Trade Center
1625 Broadway, Ste. 680
Denver, CO 80202
Phone: (303) 844-6001
Fax: (303) 844-5651

INDEX